KONG HAN NGO CHO KUN

KONG HAN NGO CHO KUN:
FORMS WEAPONS FIGHTING

師 **HENRY LO**
盧思明 (LU, ZU-MING)

傅 **DANIEL KUN**
鄞萬人 (YIN, WANREN)

www.TambuliMedia.com
Spring House, PA USA

DISCLAIMER

The author and publisher of this book DISCLAIM ANY RESPONSIBILITY over any injury as a result of the techniques taught in this book. Readers are advised to consult a physician about their physical condition before undergoing any strenuous training or dangerous physical activity. This is a martial arts book and details dangerous techniques that can cause serious physical injury and even death. Practice and training require a fit and healthy student and a qualified instructor.

All Rights Reserved.
Copyright 2015 Daniel Kun

First Published on March 30, 2016

ISBN-13: 978-1-943155-16-3
ISBN-10: 194315516X
Library of Congress Control Number: 2015959351

Developmental Editor: Arnaldo Ty Núñez
Copy Editor: Jody Amato
Cover and Interior: Summer Bonne

FOREWORD BY DR. MARK WILEY

In the 1980s I read articles in *Inside Kung-Fu* on Five Ancestor Fist by Alex Co. To me this art was dynamic, its principles deep, and its curriculum comprehensive; I just had to learn it. I finally had the chance to meet and learn from Master Co in the early 1990s during my travels to Manila to research Filipino martial arts. Years later I became his disciple and the president of the International Beng Hong Athletic Association, the governing body for the Philippine-Chinese Beng Kiam Athletic Club, the oldest kung-fu club in the Philippines.

During my continuous travels to the Philippines I was introduced in 1995 to the Philippine Kong Han Athletic Club, and its headmaster Henry Lo. Kong Han is a brother club to Beng Kiam that is just a few years younger, but equally as famous. Sigong Tan, Kiong Beng (the founder of Beng Kiam) and Sigong Lo, Yan-Chiu (the founder of Hong Han) were well acquainted and friendly, as the clubs and their masters remain to this day.

One thing I noticed, however, was that while many forms shared by the clubs had the same name, their choreography was different. Their weapons sets were different, too. I soon discovered that there were 10 disciples of the founder, Chua, Giok-Beng, who each had their specialties and brought the art to different parts of Asia, most notably to SE Asian countries like the Philippines, Malaysia and Singapore. Ngo Cho Kun is made up of concepts and techniques from five distinct arts, so it only makes sense that a master may focus on one over the others. As I researched the art and met teachers from the various lines I discovered quite a difference in method. This makes Ngo Cho all the more intriguing.

I am honored and excited to publish this comprehensive book, *Kong Han Ngo Cho Kun*, by Sigong Henry Lo and Sifu Daniel Kun. It covers a lot of ground, including Kong Han's curriculum up to O-Duan (Black Belt). It also offers a history of Southern Fist and links this to the creation of Five Ancestor Fist. While I do not see the same correlation between the Five Elders of Shaolin and the five arts that make up Ngo Cho, I commend the authors for their research efforts and detailed explanations.

I find it baffling how the art of Five Ancestor Fist is so popular in South China and SE Asia, but remains relatively unknown in the West. Grandmaster Co and I have worked hard to promote it in the media through books, including *Five Ancestor Fist Kung-Fu* (Tuttle 2000), *The Bible of Ngo Cho Kun* (Tambuli 2013); articles in magazines such as *Kung-Fu Tai Chi, Inside Kung-Fu, Martial Arts Illustrated* (both US and UK versions), and *Seni Bela Diri* (in Malaysia); as well as via websites and blog posts, seminars and classes. Teachers of other Ngo Cho lines have done their part, too. Yet here we are decades later and Ngo Cho Kun is still a rare art in the West. It is our hope that this present work will make strides forward in introducing the West to Ngo Cho Kun, the Fukien art of Five Ancestor Fist Kung-fu.

Dr. Mark Wiley
Publisher, Tambuli Media
President, International Beng Hong Athletic Association
March 25, 2016

Dodong, Alphonzo, Topher Rickettes, Henry Lo, Alex Co, Mark Wiley and Simon T. Lailey at Kong Han Athletic Club, circa 1996

FOREWORD BY GRANDMASTER ALEX CO

I congratulate Sigong Henry Lo and Sifu Daniel Kun for coming out with this nice book, *Kong Han Ngo Cho Kun*. The information in this book comes from the lineage of Sigong Lo, Yan-Chiu, one of the famous kung-fu teachers in Quánzhōu, China.

In the Philippines there exist two old Ngo Cho clubs, Beng Kiam and Kong Han. Although the forms and techniques differ a little, both clubs uphold the same principles as we come from the same lineage of Chua Giok Beng. Today, Henry Lo and I are good friends. We share our lunch together as often as our schedules permit. Kong Han is still very active promoting Ngó Chó around the world. Dr. Lo, King-Hui promoted the creation of the International Southern Shàolín Wǔzǔquán Federation in China.

I offer my congratulations to my friends. This book is a most welcome addition to the sparse reference materials on the Fukien art of Ngó Chó Kûn. I know it will especially help spread the art of Five Ancestor Fist in the Western world.

Alexander Lim Co
Beng Kiam Athletic Club
March 22, 2016

THE CREED OF KONG HAN

by the founder, Dr. Lo, Yan Chu

Benelovent, Righteous, Courteous, Wise, True

True—Be truthful with your friends, neighbors, yourself, and family.

Wise—Know how to differentiate between what is right and wrong.

Courteous—Be respectful toward your elders, parents, and nation.

Righteous—Be just and fair, and have good moral values.

Benevolent—Be charitable, merciful, and ready to help others.

TABLE OF CONTENTS

Special Dedication to Grandmaster Dr. Lo, King-Hui 1

Introduction 3

SECTION ONE: SEED

Chapter 1 – The Heritage of Southern Fist 7

Chapter 2 – The Roots of Grand Ancestor-Five Ancestor Fist 11

Chapter 3 – Kong Han's Legacy Begins 15

Chapter 4 – The Kong Han Athletic Club 21

Chapter 5 – Second Generation—Lo, King-Hui 27

Chapter 6 – Third Generation—Lo, Zu-Ming 33

SECTION TWO: ROOTS

Chapter 7 – Guiding Principles 43

Chapter 8 – Ki Gong 61

Chapter 9 – The Methods 65

Chapter 10 – Rising Fist 73

Chapter 11 – Guarding Skill 77

SECTION THREE: BRANCHES

Chapter 12 – Three Battle Way 83

Chapter 13 – Three Battle Partner Drill.. 101

Chapter 14 – Three Battle Way Techniques 129

Chapter 15 – Twenty Punches Di Sip Kun 139

Chapter 16 – Twenty Punches Partner Drill Di Sip Kun Dui Lian 165

Chapter 17 – Di Sip Kun Techniques.. 193

Chapter 18 – Four Gate Striking Corner Fist Si Mun Da Kak Lo.. 199

Chapter 19 – Four Gate Striking Corner Fist Partner Drill Si Mun Da Gak Dui Lian...... 223

Chapter 20 – Four Gate Striking Corner Fist Techniques Si Mun Da Gak Techniques 257

Chapter 21 – Big Knife Skill Dai Dou Zut 267

Chapter 22 – Big Knife Partner Drill Dai Dou Dui Lian... 295

Chapter 23 – Five Foot Staff Skill Ngo Ciak Gua 329

Chapter 24 – Five Foot Staff Partner Drill Ngo Ciak Gua Dui Lian 353

Chapter 25 – Five Foot Staff Techniques Ngo Ciak Gua Techniques 385

Chapter 26 – Ngo Cho Kun Mu Sut Lui Dai (léitái) Arena Sports Fighting.................... 393

Conclusion 411

APPENDIXES

Appendix 1 – Green Lion... 413

Appendix 2 – The Elders.. 415

Appendix 3 – Forms and Weapons 423

Appendix 4 – Level and Ranking... 427

Appendix 5 – Terminology by Chapter... 431

About the Authors... 451

Acknowledgment and Reference Material 467

Dàshīfu Lo, King Hui
(1921-1995)

SPECIAL DEDICATION TO GRANDMASTER DR. LO, KING-HUI (盧慶輝)

This book is dedicated in the loving memory of the late Dr. Lo, King-Hui (1921-1995), the eldest son of and successor to Dr. Lo, Yan-Chiu, and the founder of the Philippine Kong Han Athletic Association. Dr. Lo, King-Hui nurtured and upheld his father's dream of spreading the art of Ngó Chó Kûn and the virtues of assisting others in times of need.

Dr. Lo, King-Hui upheld the standards set by his father and ancestors before him, which elevated him as one of leading authorities in the art of Ngó Chó Kûn. Dr. Lo has unselfishly taught many students, sharing his knowledge with all that were keen to learn. In 1987, Dr. Lo tirelessly worked with other Ngó Chó Kûn lineages from Quánzhōu, Xiàmén, Fúzhōu, Zhāngzhōu, Indonesia, Malaysia, Táiwān, Hong Kong, and Singapore to create an organization where all Ngó Chó Kûn groups and sects can gather in unity, mutual respect, cooperation, and equality for the advancement and promotion of the art.

Dàshīfu Lo, King Hui's booklet published by Quanzhou South Shaolin Temple in 2011

Finally, in 1990 his dream was realized, when all of the major sects of Ngó Chó Kûn (written in Mandarin as Wǔzǔquán)—and with the assistance of the Chinese government—established the International Southern Shàolín Wǔzǔquán Federation, which is headquartered in the art's ancestral port city of Quánzhōu, Fújiàn, China.

At the twentieth anniversary celebration of the establishment of the International Southern Shàolín Wǔzǔquán Federation, held on February 10, 2011 in the city of Quánzhōu, the late Dr. Lo, King-Hui was posthumously awarded the rank of 10th Duan, the highest award the organization can grant to an individual for years of dedication in preserving and promoting the art of Ngó Chó Kûn. To commemorate this, the International Southern Shàolín Wǔzǔquán Federation published Dr. Lo's book, *The Introduction to the Essentials of Five Ancestor Fist*, to preserve his teaching and the legacy of his father, with special acknowledgement from Abbot, Shi Changding.

> *This "Introduction to the Essentials" is a summary of the insight Dr. Lo, King-Hui has gained through a lifetime of practicing Five Ancestor Fist. He is well versed and provides unique insight regarding the origins, nature, form principles, and unique characteristics of Five Ancestor Fist. It is worthy of being titled a classic and has academic significance for research on Five Ancestor Fist, an intangible cultural asset.*
>
> *Mr. Zhou and Dr. Lo were close associates and successively held the position of the Chairperson of the International Five Ancestor Fist Association. They held in-depth exchanges and had a profound friendship. That is why he has compiled this work, which engages both the body and mind in a detailed yet elegant account that has clearly captured the essence of Dr. Lo, King-Hui's wisdom.*
>
> *Since devoting myself to the school of Five Ancestor Fist, I have referred to it again and again, obtaining significant gains. Furthermore, it is with immense joy that, in light of my deep appreciation of the significant aid that Kong Han and the Five Ancestor Fist associations around the world have provided for the reestablishment of the South Shaolin temple, a new edition has been issued in the spirit of generosity and celebration, as only one edition was printed at the time of the establishment of the Quánzhōu Five Ancestor Fist Academy, to be shared with the pupils of this school in commemoration.*

—Shi Changding
Abbot, Quanzhou Shaolin Temple
September 1, 2011

INTRODUCTION

From the dawn of time, the country of China—or as it once was referred to, the Middle Kingdom—has been the vanguard in the development of countless combative traditions designed to protect the populace, be it with one's own body or the use of weapons. These traditions have become the essence of many provinces in China. For example, the province of Shāndōng is well known for its martial art traditions. Numerous styles have emerged from its fertile soil, like the arts of Huáquán (Flowery Fist), Méihuāquán (Plum Blossom Fist), and various sects of Tánglángquán (Praying Mantis Fist). However, another province has also been fruitful in the development of combat disciplines.

South China's Fújiàn province has been extremely fruitful in developing disciplines with a new and unique characteristic—the specialization of close-quarter combat, or what is classically referred to as "short boxing." The broader area is well known by various sects of Báihèquán (White Crane Fist), and Yǒngchūnquán (Sing Spring Fist), which is better known by its Cantonese (Gwóngdūng Wah) pronunciation: Wihng Chèun Kyùhn (Wing Chun Kuen). However, another discipline absorbed the nutrients of various disciplines to become a formidable art: Wǔzǔquán (Five Ancestor Fist).

The discipline of Wǔzǔquán is perhaps better known by its Mǐnnányǔ pronunciation: Ngó Chó Kûn (which is used in the book moving forward). Its origins began in the harbor city of Quánzhōu in a time of hardship from nature and the tyranny of an oppressive government. In response, the art was envisioned to confront these conflicts. Its intent went beyond physical conflict, but to develop a sound personality, emotionally and physically, which upholds Confucius' ethics of self-cultivation, echoing of moral examples, and so on.

Ngó Chó Kûn's roots stem from five unique arts that focus on certain attributes. The art's exponents took these attributes to create an exceptional art that possesses various elements that an individual may need to survive a confrontation. These elements became the pillars of Ngó Chó Kûn, the fundamentals of which are presented in this book. You will be introduced to the core methods that make this discipline so effective: its physiology, principles, and routines. All of these components assist in developing the style's explosive energy and formidable body, which is ideal for close-range encounters or in the ring.

This book also includes discussion on using weapons, in particular the sword and the staff, which are two of the earliest weapons utilized by mankind. Even though society has changed, these two particular weapons still offer benefits other than combative implications. They provide the ability to coordinate one's body, and they also can be employed as a form of free-weight training to keep one's body toned.

In addition to these attributes, this book is the testament of a family's legacy: hardship and hope for a better tomorrow, which still resonates today. We are introduced to the Lo family, who confronted injustice in their native land and then confronted the horror of World War II in their new homeland. They finally saw their family treasure take root around the world, in the process spreading the virtue of style that was developed in the harbor city of Quánzhōu, in the late Qīng dynasty, to enrich one's body and soul.

A Note on Romanization
Within this book different pronunciations and romanization are utilized. It is not our intent to confuse the readers. However, Chinese culture is very rich and diverse, and standard spellings of words are in flux. Therefore, for the name of historical figures, cities, and provinces, we use the Mandarin pronunciation and the Pinyin romanization due to their official status. However, throughout the text we use Southern Min or Mǐnnán (闽南语) and Fújiànhuà, which is commonly referred to as Hokkien pronunciation. We have included a terminology appendix to assist readers with the Chinese traditional and simplified ideograms and romanization of Táiyǔ, Mǐnnán and Pinyin.

A Note of Gratitude
This book would not have been possible if not for the help of several individuals. To my publisher, Dr. Mark Wiley, for accepting my manuscript for publication and distribution to readers worldwide, I offer great appreciation and thanks for his time and effort. To the editor, Mr. Arnoldo Ty Núñez, whose scholarly knowledge of writing, the history of Chinese martial arts, and his professionalism in editing my manuscript to my satisfaction . . . thank you very much.

Special acknowledgment goes to Grandmaster Alexander Co, for opening the doors of Ngó Chó Kûn to the world with his first English-Chinese book, *The Way of Ngó Chó Kûn*, published in 1987. It is a very informative book and has greatly enhanced my knowledge of the art.

種
SECTION ONE: SEED

CHAPTER 1

THE HERITAGE OF SOUTHERN FIST

The roots of Ngó Chó Kûn, or Five Ancestors, stem from the art of the Grand Ancestor Fist (Tàizǔquán, also spelled Tai Cho Kun), which was initiated with the foundation of the Míng dynasty in 1368 by a onetime novice monk, Zhū, Yuánzhāng—who in 1352 joined an insurgent group that opposed the Mongolian reign over China. Over time he rose through the ranks to become a great commander, and led a successful rebellion against the Yuán dynasty (1271-1368), which was a Mongolian dynasty, not Chinese or Hàn. After gaining the throne Zhū, Yuánzhāng ascended to the title of Hóngwǔdì or the Great Military Emperor. During this dynasty, numerous styles of Chinese martial arts flourished in South China, the regions below the Yángzǐ River, especially in the Fújiàn Province.

Zhū, Yuánzhāng

One of earliest documented martial art styles in China is the aforementioned Tàizǔquán, which originated in the Sòng dynasty (960-1279) and is credited to Zhào, Kuāngyìn, who is the first emperor of the Sòng dynasty. The style was an amalgamation of all the best-known fighting styles of the time and was distinguished by its leg techniques and its directness in combat.

The Sòng dynasty came to an end after being conquered by the Nǚzhēn, or the Jurchens, a nomadic tribe of North Mǎnzhōu or Manchuria that founded the Dàjīn or Jīn dynasty (1115-1234). The art of Tàizǔquán was practiced secretly and eventually emerged in South China at the dawn of Míng dynasty.

Tàizǔquán

Nǚzhēn

Tàizǔquán reemerged with new fighting principles that expanded beyond the use of leg techniques to focus upon close-quarter fighting, which was a reflection of living in cramped cities. Now the style required an intense focus on conditioning to engage in close-quarter fighting, which also meant that practitioners needed to possess the explosive energy to generate devastating strikes at this range. This revised style was now referred to in Mandarin as Mínghóngquán—the Míng from Míng dynasty, Grand Fist. However, the tradition of the original Sòng dynasty, Tàizǔquán, continued to be practiced in Northern China, but was referred to as Tàizǔchángquán, or Grand Ancestor Long Fist.

Mínghóngquán flourished strongly within the province of Fújiàn, especially when the Hàn or Chinese were once again conquered by a nomadic tribe from the north; this time by descendants of the Jurchens, the Mǎnzú or Manchu.

In 1644, the Manchurians invaded and conquered China, in the process dethroning the Míng dynasty and establishing the Qīng dynasty (1644-1912). The training in Mínghóngquán intensified, especially within the province of Fújiàn; however, it was rechristened as Míngtàizǔquán to honor the fallen Hàn dynasty that was vanquished by northern invaders. However, some Míng loyalists from Northern China retreated to Southern China and some took refuge in various temples throughout China.

Shàolín Monastery

These temples were a sanctuary and training ground for Míng loyalists to skirmish against the Manchu in an attempt to restore the Hàn back into power. They developed a motto to rally the populace: "Fǎnqīngfùmíng" in the Mandarin dialect or "Oppose the Qīng, restore the Míng."

Due to these guerrilla forces, the Manchu set siege on various temples, in particular the Shàolín Monastery in Hénán Province. Five monks were said to survive the massacre; theses monks possessed the knowledge of various fighting arts, including Tàizǔquán, Shàolínquán, and others. These five monks went forth, teaching their respective arts to the loyalists. One particular art, which would emerge to signify their teaching, was Grand Ancestor Boxing.

Zhèng, Chénggōng

However, there was still some resistance from the monarchy. A Míng official, Admiral Zhèng, Chénggōng or Guóxìngyé (Koxinga) continued to fight the invading Manchurians. For instance, at the closing of the Míng dynasty, Admiral Zhèng defeated the forces of the Dutch East India Company on the island of Táiwān in 1662; after that Admiral Zhèng set his eyes on overthrowing the Manchu themselves.

Hóngmén

He was successful in holding back the Manchurian army, which was advancing toward the port cities of Quánzhōu and Xiàmén and his base of operation, the island of Táiwān. However, he shortly died of malaria at the age of thirty-seven. Upon his death, the Míng force dejectedly surrendered to the Manchu; however, the struggle did not end there. Secret societies like the Tiāndìhuì or Hóngmén were formed to combat the tyranny the Manchu imposed upon the Hàn.

Dr. Sūn, Yìxiān

Míngtàizǔquán became a symbol of resistance against the Manchu, with the hope of restoring a Hàn dynasty once more. However, it took close to three centuries for the Hóngmén societies to accomplish this undertaking. In 1911, Dr. Sūn, Yìxiān (1866-1925) was triumphant in restoring the Hàn as the rightful rulers of China.

CHAPTER 2

THE ROOTS OF GRAND ANCESTOR-FIVE ANCESTOR FIST

By the 1700s, the art of Tàizǔquán was prevalent within the cities of Zhāngzhōu, Quánzhōu, and Xiàmén. Wú, Xīn (1691-1758) or Ngo, Sim in the regional dialect of Mǐnnányǔ, who resided in the city of Quánzhōu, was a highly respected master of Tàizǔquán.

It is believed that he acquired his knowledge of Grand Ancestor Fist from a former family member of the Míng court who was able to escape the scrutiny of Manchu by entering the Buddhist order. Ngo, Sim was fortunate in meeting this revered monk at the Dōngchán Temple, located in Quánzhōu City; here he was introduced to the art of Grand Ancestor Fist, which he would devote his time to learning and mastering.

By the late 1880s, two other great masters of Grand Ancestor Fist emerged: Chua, Giok-Beng and Li, Zun-Lin. Each one taught a personalized version of Five Ancestor Fist, which was based upon the fighting method of five distinct disciplines. For example, Chua, Giok-Beng's version were a fusion of:

- Grand Ancestor Fist: Thài Chớ Kûn (太祖拳)
- Monkey Fist: Kâu Kûn (猴拳)
- Arhat Boxing: Lô-Hàn Kûn (羅漢拳)
- White Crane Fist: Pėh Hȯh Kûn (白鶴拳)
- Bodhidharma Fist: Tát-Mô (Dámó) Kûn (達摩拳)

Chua, Giok-Beng

Chua's version was referred to by some as Ngó Chó Kûn Ôa Iûⁿ Phài, or Five Ancestor He Yang School. Today, many of his lineage holders simply refer to it as Ngó Chó Kûn.

Li, Zun-Lin's version was known as Éng Chhun Pėh Hȯh Kûn or Yǒngchūn (as in the Yongchun County in Quánzhōu) Five Ancestor Fist; it consisted of:

- Ming [dynasty] Grand Ancestor Fist: Bêng Thài Chó Kûn (明太祖拳)
- Monkey Fist: Kâu Kûn (猴拳)
- Forever Spring White Crane Boxing: Éng Chhun Pėh Hȯh Kûn (永春白鶴拳)
- Arhat Boxing: Lô-Hàn Kûn (羅漢拳)
- Bodhidharma Fist: Tȧt-Mô (Dámó) Kûn (達摩拳)

Thus, the chronicling of Five Ancestor or Ngó Chó Kûn was started by a group of Thài Chó Kûn masters in the late 1760s, which took more than a hundred years. These findings were the foundation of Chua's Ôa Iûⁿ Phài Ngó Chó Kûn and Li's Éng Chhun Ngó Chó Kûn. Therefore, all of these branches of Ngó Chó Kûn possess the same roots and principles, making them interrelated and interchangeable.

The style of Ôa Iûⁿ Phài Ngó Chó Kûn had a strong presence in the cities of Quánzhōu and Pútián, which was due to Chua, Giok-Beng residing in these cities. Éng Chhun Ngó Chó Kûn flourished in the city of Yǒngchūn (Éng Chhun), which was the native city of Li, Zun-Lin.

It is known that Chua and Li were classmates, who compared theories and their personal research among themselves. These exchanges were instrumental in formulating their respective styles of Five Ancestor Fist.

Great Ancestors Boxing

THE FUSION

The Kong Han Martial Art Association was founded by Dr. Lo, Yan-Chiu, whose lineage and history are based on the long heritage of Tai Zo Ngó Chó Kûn. Therefore, today's Five Ancestor Fist is synthesis of:

Thài Chó Kûn (太祖拳) or **Bêng Hông Kûn** (明洪拳): Great Ancestors Boxing or Ming Great Boxing is characterized by its explosive energy and directness in close-quarter fighting. This is totally distinctive to its northern counterpart, which is more deceptive, relying on long distances to execute techniques.

Kâu Kûn (猴拳): Money Boxing is revered for its strong and puzzling footwork that allows the practitioner great mobility and nimbleness. It is distinguished by its side-stepping patterns; rapid foot shifting, which allows practitioners to dodge out of incoming attack; and its specialization on ground fighting. Also, it gives homage to Sūn, Wùkōng, better known as the Money King, the protagonist of the Chinese classic novel, *Journey to the West*.

Monkey Boxing

Lô-Hàn Kûn (羅漢拳): The roots of Arhat Boxing stem back to the legendary Shàolín Temple; it is distinguished for its ever-changing hand patterns, forceful stepping, and solid body structure. It combines long- and short-distance strategies when approaching an assailant, making it a direct style.

Pėh Hȯh Kûn (白鶴拳): White Crane Boxing, like its namesake, is astute and direct in its attacks. It specializes in close-range fighting and targeting vital points throughout the body. This particular version of Pėh Hȯh Kûn was developed in the city of Yǒngchūn.

Arhat Boxing

White Crane Boxing

Tàt-Mô Kûn (達摩拳): Dámó Boxing is actually a style of Qìgōng (气功) or Ki Gong, designed to energize the body. It consists of various breathing patterns and specific body movements to stimulate the body, in this case to reinforce the body's ability to absorb impact, and greatly enhances the practitioner's health.

In the next chapters we will look at the history and development of the Kong Han version of this dynamic style.

Dámó Boxing

CHAPTER 3

KONG HAN'S LEGACY BEGINS

Dr. Lo, Yan-Chu was born in 1878 in the city of Quánzhōu, Fújiàn Province, China. He was the youngest of three brothers. His father, Lo, Yung-Sheng, was a farmer by profession, but in time expanded his entrepreneurship to include a tobacco shop, candle shop, and an inn in the port city of Quánzhōu. Business was thriving for the Lo family until the latter part of the 1890s, when the province experienced natural disasters and political unrest that affected greatly the economy. This led to an increase in lawlessness and, unfortunately, the Lo family was a casualty of these harsh times.

At the age of thirteen, Lo, Yan-Chu's father passed away, which meant that Yan-Chu had to stop attending school and assist his family. During those trying times his mother pondered the future of her family, especially her youngest son, Yan-Chu.

Dr. Lo, Yan-Chu (1878-1944); founder of the Kong Han Athletic Club

Yan-Chu was an athletic youngster and also displayed the inclination of a righteous person, which led his mother to imagine him as a martial artist in the vein of the legendary folk hero, Fong, Sai-Yuk. However, society's perception of martial arts or that of martial artists was not positive; it was simply frowned upon when compared to academic pursuits, which were highly regarded within a Confucius society.

However, one night, his mother dreamt of a powerful man wielding a Green-Dragon Halberd. Upon waking the next day, she proceeded to the local Guānyǔ temple to pray for guidance. During her devotion, she received the divination she was seeking, which convinced her to allow her son Yan-Chu to pursue the path of a martial artist, a decision that would bear fruit in time.

Guānyǔ Temple

PATH TO FIVE ANCESTOR FIST

At the age of fourteen, Lo, Yan-Chu was introduced to Zong, Dam, a well-regarded exponent of the martial art style referred to as Grand Ancestor Boxing (Thài Chó Kûn); a popular regional style whose roots stemmed from the legendary Nánshàolínsì or Southern Young Forest Temple. Yan-Chu was a natural, a quick learner and an utmost dedicated student, but sadly five years into his training his teacher passed away. Due to his aptitude, Yan-Chu was appointed the instructor of the school and with great loyalty and respect toward his late teacher he remitted all of the student's fees to his late teacher's wife. He was conscious that he needed more guidance, so he sought out the noted Gong, Bou-Ziam, a well-known teacher of a style referred to as Grand Ancestor-Five Ancestor Fist or Thài Chó Kûn Ngó Chó Kûn. Yan-Chu was already an exponent of the Grand Ancestor Fist; however, this was the first time he would be introduced to the art of Five Ancestor Fist.

Gong Bou Ziam 公婆詹 a well-known master of Tai Cho Kun kung fu will take Lo Yan Chiu as his student, Grandmaster Gong was also a close acquaintance with Lim Kui Lu, Chua Giok Beng, Tan Kiong Beng and other masters of kung fu in that region. Tan Kiong Beng and Lo Yan Chiu will become very close friends together they will explore Tai Cho Kun. Later, Tan Kiong Beng will follow Chua Giok Beng's Ho Yang Pai while Lo Yan Chiu continues to retain and preserve his Tai Cho Ngo Cho Kun lineage under Gong Bou Ziam.

Lim, Kui-Lu

Lo Yan Chiu was also extremely fortunate to have been exposed to his teacher's acquaintances including the founder of Ho Yan Pai. Via these associations, he was introduced to other highly esteem martial arts elders from Quánzhōu City. These meetings influenced and assisted in his growth as a martial artist.

As mentioned before, Lo, Yan-Chu opened his first school at the age of nineteen in 1897, which was situated in the Wéitóu Village. Aside from his continuing study of Five Ancestor Fist, Yan-Chu decided to study Traditional Chinese Medicine (TCM) to enhance his martial arts knowledge and to assist the needy. As a Diat Da Dai or "falling, striking doctor," Lo was required to be knowledgeable in the areas of herbs, orthopedics, bone setting, and basic surgery. This newly acquire knowledge granted him the ability to provide medical services to the poor, which was one of his major concerns. Yan-Chu also assisted his family with farming and their newly acquired fishing business.

VOYAGE TO KNOWLEDGE

Lo, Yan-Chu's righteousness was well known within the city, reminiscent of the legendary acts of General Guānyǔ. For example, Yan-Chu took up causes for the poor and for those who were oppressed by the tyranny of the time, which meant that from time to time physical confrontations were the only option to rectify the wrong. For instance, on one occasion, while heading back home to the Quánzhōu City on the ferryboat, he was attacked by pirates. Without

Guānyǔ

Kong Han's Legacy Begins

hesitation, Yan-Chu confronted the pirates before they could do any serious harm to the other passengers. Yan-Chu, armed only with a steel container, launched himself into the pirates with no regard for his own safety. He fought ferociously and succeeded in defeating the pirates. As a gesture of gratitude, the British boat captain offered Yan-Chu some money, but instead of accepting the money for himself, Yan-Chu distributed the reward to his fellow companions on the ferry.

In 1899, at the age of twenty-one, Lo, Yan-Chu decided to travel overseas to expand his medical knowledge, which also presented him the opportunity to be exposed to other styles of martial arts that were not practiced within his native home. He was always eager to further his knowledge of martial arts; therefore, this was a great opportunity to do so.

His first destination was to be Burma and then to Southeast Asia, which consisted of Penang, Malaysia, Surabaya, Java, and finally Hong Kong. In all of his travels, he continued to share his knowledge of the Five Ancestor Fist with eager students or fellow martial artists, while broadening his medical knowledge and assisting the needy.

In 1907, he set sail to Singapore to further his studies in medicine, as well to teach the art of the Five Ancestor Fist. A year later, he also traveled to Vietnam on a medical mission.

In nine years of traveling, Lo was exposed to numerous things during his voyages. By coming into contact with other cultures and traditions, he was able to enrich his medical knowledge and greatly enhance his martial arts prowess, which resulted in his recognition as a leading authority in kung-fu and establish him as a doctor of traditional Chinese medicine.

Shortly after returning home from his voyage, Dr. Lo wedded Miss Chang, Fan-Niang in 1909. With his new family to worry about, and after witnessing firsthand the sufferings and unhappiness of so many individuals that it weighed on his heart, Lo sought solace within the teaching of Daoism to comprehend the world before him—and in the process strengthen his morality.

He began with the study of meditation, which eventually led him to become a member of a Daoist sect based in the Éméi Mountain in the Sìchuān Province. Dr. Lo's good reputation followed him wherever he went. In time, he became the head of a Daoist sect within Quánzhōu City.

THE FEARLESS TIGER

In 1910, two years before the end of the Manchu (Qīng) dynasty, Dr. Lo, Yan-Chu experienced several hostile confrontations with abusive Manchurian soldiers. One particular confrontation consisted of his martial arts brother being falsely accused of committing a crime and sentenced to be executed by Manchu officials. The Manchu officials based their judgment and sentencing on bribes that they received from the opposing parties, not on factual evidences presented within the trials. This was the last straw for Dr. Lu, and he took it upon himself to free his friend. He led a group of fellow martial artists to assist him.

As his friend was being escorted to the execution grounds, Dr. Lo and his followers confronted the soldiers at an intersection in the city. The soldiers were armed with guns and quickly opened fire, at which time Dr. Lo utilized his knowledge of dart throwing to counterattack. However, being conscious of the close-quarter environment, he was also armed with a short iron flogger, which he used in one hand, while in the other hand he possessed a nine-section steel whip.

Dr. Lo and his group fought the Manchus ferociously and gallantly. The encounter quickly turned into fierce close-quarter fighting. They succeeded in reducing the numbers of the soldiers and eventually forced the remaining Manchus into a corner, which allowed Dr. Lo to successfully free his martial arts brother. They quickly escaped into the narrow streets of the city before the Manchurian reinforcements arrived. Due to his extraordinary bravery and fighting prowess, Dr. Lo gained the moniker Hu Mu Chiu, or Tiger Chiu.

However, this righteous incident resulted in Dr. Lo being labeled as a subversive by authorities. A bounty was placed on his head; fortunately, he escaped to another village before the Manchurian officers were able apprehended him.

Months later, and upon the insistence from his friends and relatives, Dr. Lo left for Rangoon, Burma. In Burma, he joined the revolutionary movement to overthrow the Manchu dynasty. Finally, in October 1911, the Manchu dynasty ended. Dr. Lo was able to return to Quánzhōu a year later and was welcomed back as a hero. During his stay in Burma, he continued his medical practice and spreading the art of Five Ancestor Fist to the locals.

Dr. Lo, Yan-Chu's reputation as a skilled martial artist and of upright moral standing was ideal for leadership positions within the village assisting in mediations. He assumed that position and at the same time the position of chief instructor of the Quánzhōu Guóshù Club, which was the largest martial arts school in the city.

During the struggle of establishing the new Republic, Dr. Lo served as a combat instructor and medical doctor for the 183rd division of the 19th Route Army; also, he took part in the northern expedition of the Nationalist Army, whose objective was to defeat the local warlords and assist in uniting China under the leadership of the Republic of China. On these campaigns, he encountered many situations that brought into play his skills as a martial artist, his leadership ability, and proficiency as a physician.

From 1912 to 1935, Dr. Lo witnessed the hardship and suffering in China and the struggle to rebuild and unite the country as one nation. These experiences galvanized his sense of patriotism such that, in 1937, he renamed his school in Manila the Kong Han Mu Guan, to demonstrate his sense of love for country, ancestry, and tradition.

The word "Kong" means bright or gleaming, while "Han" is the ancient term for Chinese; Mu references martial and Guan means school. Therefore, the phrase is meant to recognize the struggle and hardship of the Han people against foreign invaders that precipitated in the development of the southern fighting style.

Dr. Lo, Yan-Chiu's ideas were simple and direct. He posted them at the entrance of his school so all the students would learn to be Lin, Ngi, Le, Di, Sin, which means to be benevolent, righteous, courteous, wise, and faithful.

After all, in the end, training in Five Ancestor Fist is not for selfish gain, but to aid others in need, to be a model citizen, and proactive in building your nation.

CHAPTER 4

THE KONG HAN ATHLETIC CLUB

In 1937, the Imperial Japan Army invaded China, marking the beginning of the Sino-Japanese War. Japanese forces occupied the city of Xiàmén, Fújiàn Province and soon the entire province fell to the Japanese. Because of Dr. Lo, Yan-Chu's association with the Chinese military, his students feared for his life.

Imperial Japanese Army invading China

They struggled to convince him that he needed to be safe in these trying times. They succeeded and quickly made arrangements for his departure to Manila, Philippines. At that time, the Philippines was a commonwealth of the United States of America, and the United

States was not yet at war with Japan; therefore, it was considered an ideal haven for Dr. Lo.

Dr. Lo, Yan-Chu arrived in Manila in 1938 and quickly set up a medical clinic to earn a living. His good reputation as a martial arts master and his exploits did not escape him in the new city; many local Chinese showed him great respect and asked him to teach martial arts to his fellow Chinese; by chance, many originated from the same city or province as him.

With the overwhelming support of an enthusiastic Chinese community, and upon taking the advice of his elder Tan, Kiong-Beng, who had been already well established in the Philippines, Dr. Lo opened an informal martial arts school, which was located at No. 329 Lilan-Ilang Street in Binondo, Manila's Chinatown.

Tan, Kiong-Beng

The response was positive and the actual turnout of students so unexpectedly high and favorable that Dr. Lo was forced to relocate to a new location at No. 631 Tomas Mapua Street, Sta. Cruz, Manila, and officially established the Philippine Kong Han Mu Guan, better known as Kong Han Athletic Club, where he taught the art of Grand Ancestor-Five Ancestor Fist or Tai Cho Ngó Chó Kûn to the Chinese community. Dr. Lo also chose an animal figure to be placed on the school's code of arms: the tiger, which was Dr. Lo's moniker, Hu Bu Chiu or Tiger Chu.

Dr. Lo, Yan-Chu set high standards for his school; however, possessing good morals was the prerequisite to being accepted as a student. Also, two members of the club had to vouch for a new candidate and act as sponsors to the admission committee, which established his or her eligibility to enter the school. If candidates were under age, their parents were required to be present during the interview. After acceptance into the club, students were informed that there was one grave rule that would lead to instantaneous expulsion: an act of violence within the school or outside of the school.

Support from the local community was awesome and soon many individuals from Dr. Lo, Yan-Chu's native village also migrated to Manila. Some were actually former students, who quickly started training under their old teacher again.

The Kong Han School was very active within the community;

Plaza Moraga

for example, in 1940 Dr. Lo sent a delegation to participate in an event celebrating the establishment of the Cantonese Athletic Association. This was one of the first public exhibitions of the Five Ancestor Fist, which left a lasting impression on the audiences.

By 1941, the prestige of Kong Han had reached the northern provincial city of Dagupan; upon hearing of this, the local Chinese-Filipino community formally requested an instructor to introduce and teach the art of Five Ancestor Fist in their community. Dr. Lo responded shortly and sent his eldest son Lo, King-Hui to handle this important task, and eventually a new school was established. This was the first branch of Kong Han outside of Manila; it was named Kong Hua Athletic Club.

In the beginning, the school consisted of ten students; however, it quickly multiplied to more than a hundred. The Manila school was also experiencing rapid growth, which led Dr. Lo to open another branch on Jaboneros Street in Binondo.

The responsibility of running this school fell on the shoulders of one of Dr. Lo's senior students, Hsu, Chiu-Yao, who was officially appointed the chief instructor of this branch. However, on the morning of December 7, 1941 the United States entered World War II, changing the course of the Philippines and its people.

FACING UP TO THE ENEMY

By 1942, the entire Philippine nation fell to the Imperial Japanese war machine; however, Dr. Lo continued to operate his schools. In fact, almost like a sign of resistance, a third branch was opened in Sampaloc, Manila with another of Dr. Lo's senior students taking on the task. This time it was Hsieh, Chun-Hsing who assumed the position of chief instructor.

Because of his great influence on the local Chinese-Filipino community, Dr. Lo's reputation did not escape the attention of the Japanese authorities. The Japanese tried to convince Dr. Lo to work for their campaign. They also wanted him to instruct their infantry in the art of the Five Ancestor Fist, but Dr. Lo refused to do so, which led to his arrest. Under their custody, he experienced all kinds of intimidation, but Dr. Lo would not change his mind and waiver from his principals.

The Japanese authorities admired Dr. Lo's courage and took into account his old age and eventually released him. However, he was under constant surveillance as they suspected he was training and assisting the resistance. They were not wrong in their assumption, because many Kong Han members were indeed part of the resistance against the Japanese. The Japanese would strike at them in and around Manila. In time, students started to fear potential reprisal against their teacher due to their actions, and begged him to leave Manila and go into hiding.

In the beginning, Dr. Lo moved to one of his student's residences; however, the Japanese agents were on his track. Reluctantly, Dr. Lo was forced to flee to the northern region of the Philippines. He settled in Manaog, a municipality located in the province of Pangasinan in the western area of the island of Luzon. His students and locals were able to care for him until the end of the war.

By 1944, the Japanese were starting to lose the war against the United States as the American forces advanced toward the city of Manila. Bombs were dropped by the liberating forces, and Kong Han's main school was one of the many structures destroyed by the bombings. At the end of the year, Japanese forces were driven out of Manila. Shortly after the liberation of the Philippines, Dr. Lo, Yan-Chu passed away of heart failure at age of sixty-six.

REVIVAL OF KONG HAN

The incredible journey that Dr. Lo, Yan-Chu started as a child was meant to continue beyond his death. Dr. Lo's torch was passed on to his eldest son, Lo, King-Hui. After Dr. Lo's burial, King-Hui was able to return to Manila, reuniting with the surviving members of his father's school. By March 1945 they were able to rebuild the Kong Han Athletic Club, once more preserving and spreading the legacy of their teacher, Dr. Lo, Yan-Chu.

With the assistance of the community, the rebuilding of Kong Han was successful and membership numbers surpassed the pre-war numbers—to the point where they reached in excess of seven hundred students.

Sadly, with the newly reestablished Kong Han, internal struggle occurred between Dr. Lo's senior students. The inheritor of the school was Lo, King-Hui, being Dr. Lo's eldest son. Nevertheless, he was pressured to relinquish his position as the head of the school. Reluctantly, King-Hui had no other alternative but to give into the demands of the new committee set up to administrate Kong Han's affairs.

Even this drastic change did not halt the power struggle among the seniors, which eventually had an adverse effect on the school. There was too much indecisiveness, which meant bickering, stagnation, and division among its leaders. This got to the point where it was suggested to rename the school, something that would have been considered greatly disrespectful to the memory of the founder Dr. Lo, Yan-Chu.

Finally, in the summer of 1954, the seniors of Kong Han realized their mistakes and decided to revive the old ways. The method that made Kong Han what it was, sadly was crumbling before their eyes. Lo, King-Hui was officially recognized as the headmaster of Kong Han Athletic Club once more. The newly reorganized school relocated to Misericordia Street, Manila. Enrollment immediately picked up, which returned the school's prominence within the Filipino-Chinese community once again.

Dr. Lo, Yan-Chu and Kong Han War Heroes Memorial Pavilion at the Chinese Cemetery in the Philippines

In 1955, a war memorial was erected at the Chinese cemetery in honor of Dr. Lo, Yan-Chu and the seventeen school members who died during World War II fighting the Japanese. That same year, a grand martial arts exhibition was organized at the downtown Manila YMCA gymnasium to celebrate the seventeenth anniversary of Dr. Lo's vision: Kong Han.

In 1960, Kong Han set up its fourth branch, located on Soler Street, which was headed by Master Lo, King-Hui's youngest brother Lo, King-Chiok. The school was given the name Heng Han Athletic Club. In time, other branches were established in the cities of Quezon and Cebu. Kong Han was at its peak; making it the most active Chinese martial arts school in the Philippines.

Newspaper clippings of Kong Han Athletic Club demonstrating in Taiwan in 1967

In 1965, Kong Han accepted an invitation to perform at the Asian Martial Arts Festival and Karate Championship sponsored by the Philippine Journalist Association. Then in 1967, Kong Han was invited to participate in a martial arts tour of Táiwān; the tour commenced in Táiběi, and was followed by the southern region of Táinán. The Kong Han delegation showcased the prowess of the Five Ancestor Fist to an eager audience.

The following year, 1968, Kong Han accepted an invitation to compete in the Chinese Martial Arts Exhibition Competition in Táiběi, Táiwān. The team performed superbly, placing first and second in numerous divisions and finally winning the overall championship. Then in 1969, they received a special invitation from the government of Singapore to attend the jubilant celebration of the 150th foundation of the Republic of Singapore, which coincided with the First Southeast Asian Sparring Competition. Against overwhelming matches and visiting, the Kong Han's representative, Tseng, Kuo-Ming, achieved the bronze medal in the heavyweight sparring division.

In 1970 and 1971, Kong Han again accepted an invitation from Táiwān to compete in the Overseas Chinese Martial Arts Championship in Táiběi, and again the Kong Han participant performed very well, winning several first and second place in hand form, weapon forms, and contact sparring division. These achievements illustrated that Lo, King-Hui was upholding the legacy his father planted in the soil of the Philippines back in 1938.

CHAPTER 5

SECOND GENERATION—LO, KING-HUI

Dàshīfu Lo, King Hui
(1921-1995)

Lo, King-Hui was born on January 19, 1921. He began his martial arts training at the early age of seven, under the guidance of his father Dr. Lo, Yan-Chu. By the age of thirteen, his parents sent him to Xiānggǎng, to further his education. Financial difficulties made it hard for him to continue with his studies abroad and he was reluctantly forced to return home. Then in 1939 he was able to join his father, who had a flourishing medical and martial arts practice serving the growing Chinese-Filipino community.

King-Hui's training resumed under the watchful eyes of his father, who also introduced King-Hui to traditional Chinese medicine. In the evenings, he attended classes to further his academic education. By 1940, he was an intricate part of his father's medical clinic and martial arts school. King-Hui excelled in his studies; he was a natural like his father. But most of all, he trained vigorously to uphold his father's standards and in the process became a leading exponent of the Five Ancestor Fist.

A NEW ERA

After the untimely death of his father at the closing of War World II, Lo, King-Hui assumed the responsibility of his father's medical clinic and the position of headmaster of Kong Han. King-Hui was fortunate to have the assistance of his younger brother Lo, King-Chiok, who originally was the head instructor of the Heng Han Athletic Club, and helped him spread their father's dream of teaching the true essence of the Five Ancestors Fist to those eager and earnest to learn this precious art.

Dr. Lo, King-Hui was instrumental in ushering Five Ancestors Fist in a new era and in the process, furthered Kong Han's reputation as a formidable martial arts school. This was accomplished by participating in local and international martial arts competitions and conferences. These events granted him the ability to demonstrate his beloved art and his father's legacy to a larger audience unfamiliar with this dynamic art.

Newspaper clipping of Dr. Lo, King (1962) instruction of the 7th Foot Staff

In addition to waving proudly the banner of the Five Ancestor Fist abroad, Dr. Lo, King-Hui's reputation as a practitioner of traditional Chinese medicine was increasing, especially as he started to produce commercially a muscle and bone ointment. Like his father, he was active in teaching the art of Five Ancestor Fist and running his medical clinic, which provided gratis treatments to the students and other members of Kong Han injured training in class or while competing in competition.

Tseng, Kuo-Ming participating in a full-contact match in 1969, which earned him a bronze medal

When it came to teaching, Dr. Lo, King-Hui spent hours teaching and coaching his students. Each time correcting every student's form and especially emphasizing the techniques within the forms. This was done on a one-on-one basis, which was rare, but he knew that this was the only way he could uphold his father's standards. Personally, Dr. Lo enjoyed when his students asked questions concerning their training, be it a principle of the style or significant techniques hidden within the forms. Above all, he was extremely patient with those students who did not possess the natural ability to excel in their training. He wanted them to be the best students they could possibly be. For that reason, he treated

Po, Suan-Uy (Samuel) participating in weapon sparring match in 1978

all of his students equally and was eager to share his knowledge with those students who were sincere in their learning.

Daniel Kun, on his way in winning the Grand Champion for Junior Lightweight Division (Undefeated in 9 matches)

Dr. Lo, King-Hui was a traditionalist and a loyal Five Ancestor Fist exponent. He strongly believed in its effectiveness as a fighting art, which meant he could not betray the legacy set

Dr. Lo, King-Hui with students in 1973

by those who came before him. For example, his loyalty to his beloved art was put to test during the mid-1980s with the introduction of Contemporary Wǔshù in the Philippines. Dr. Lo was knowledgeable of various styles of martial arts and aware of the developments in mainland China; he knew that Wǔshù was a contemporary form of Chinese martial arts, which was designed to be a demonstrative art and sport. Wǔshù typically consisted of flowery movements with no combative merit, which was distinctly different from Five Ancestor Fist, a combative art.

1978, Kong Han 41st Anniversary Celebration, which was marked with a performance at King's theater Ongpin Street Chinatown, Manila City

Very few of his students understood the true significance behind Five Ancestor Fist compared to Contemporary Wǔshù. Typically, they were glamorized with the elegance of the movements, which indeed were visual, but they did not realize that the movements were hollow. One no longer possessed the ability to defend oneself or one's nation, which was a crucial element of the school's canon set by Dr. Lo, Yan-Chu himself back in 1937.

Many Kong Han senior members pressured Dr. Lo, King-Hui to include Contemporary Wǔshù in the school's curriculum. This was something that Dr. Lo would not allow; he knew that Kong Han's martial arts identity must be preserved and furthermore, his father's legacy could not be corrupted.

Sadly, this led to disputes among the senior members to the point that some of them left Kong Han to form the Wǔshù Federation of the Philippines. In the process, Kong Han lost many members to this newly formed federation; however, this did not discourage Dr.

Lo, King-Hui and his mission to spread and teach the art of Five Ancestor Fist. In fact, this poignant moment in the school's history motivated him to expand Five Ancestor Fist even more.

For instance, in 1985 Dr. Lo embarked on a gigantic task: a mission to bring all of the Five Ancestor Fist sects together. To accomplish this, he sent invitations to all the known sects in Indonesia, Malaysia, Singapore, Táiwān, Japan, China, and the Philippines. The responses to his invitation were positive and a conference was held at in the city of Quánzhōu, the birthplace of the style.

Finally, in 1990 his dream was fulfilled with the inauguration of the International South Shàolín Wǔzǔquán Union. Not only did Dr. Lo, King-Hui succeed in uniting all the Five Ancestor Fist families, but also the newly reconstructed South Shàolín Temple in Quánzhōu City officially adapted Five Ancestor Fist as the official martial art and physical fitness program of the temple.

South Shàolín Temple in Quánzhōu City

Dr. Lo, King-Hui's student base expanded beyond the confines of the Philippines, returning back to its birthplace. In 1990, Dr. Lo was elected as the first chairperson of the International South Shàolín Wǔzǔquán Federation. Originally, the federation started with fourteen member nations; it has expanded to include twenty-two nations today.

At present, the federation is still very active with annual conferences and numerous events encouraging unity within the families and promoting the splendor of Five Ancestor Fist to others. The primary objective of the federation is to promote and preserve the true essence

Dr. Lo, King-Hui demonstrating his beloved art

of Five Ancestor Fist and actively working with other martial arts groups that have a historical link with Five Ancestor Fist.

After ushering in a new era for Kong Han and the art of Five Ancestor Fist, Dr. Lo, King-Hui passed away in 1995 at the age of seventy-five. Shortly before his passing, the International South Shàolín Wǔzǔquán Federation inducted him as an honorary chairperson for life. At the end of the day Dr. Lo, King-Hui lived up to his father's expectations, making certain that his legacy continued to be a beacon for others to follow in spreading the legacy of Kong Hon and the virtues of Five Ancestor Fist to another generation.

CHAPTER 6

THIRD GENERATION—LO, ZU-MING

During Dr. Lo, King-Hui's tenure as the head of Kong Han, he was able to train several outstanding students, among them his eldest son Lo, Zu-Ming, better known by his English first name, Henry. Henry Lo inherited not only the legacy of the Lo family, but also the Kong Han Athletic Association, when he assumed the position of headmaster after the death of his father.

Grandmaster Lo, Zu-Ming, better known as Henry Lo, was born in 1961 and started his official training of Five Ancestor Boxing at the age of eleven. Like his grandfather and father before him, he was a diligent student who possessed natural ability. To this day Grandmaster Lo, Zu-Ming continues to operate the Kong Han Athletic Association and instruct others in the beloved art of his family.

Lo, Zu-Ming (Henry)

In 1996, Grandmaster Lo and the Kong Han School were invited to a tournament hosted in Zhèngzhōu City, Hénán Province, China. Lo formed a team of his top students to represent the school. These students entered the forms division and the newly created full-contact sparring division, referred to as sànshǒu.

To everyone's shock, Henry Lo entered the lightweight sànshǒu division, which consisted of men much younger than himself. He did this to prove the effectiveness of Five Ancestor Boxing on the lèitái, or platform stage. Henry Lo placed second in his weight division, earning him and the school a silver medal.

Henry Lo participating various matches, which finally earned him a silver medal at the 1996 Zhèngzhōu, China International Sǎnshǒu tournament.

Henry Lo receiving his honors at the 1996 Zhèngzhōu, China International Sǎnshǒu tournament.

Henry Lo demonstrating the Five Ancestors Tiger Folk form

Since 1996, the Kong Han Athletic Association has remained active in participating and competing in numerous international wǔshù events. For example, each year Henry Lo leads a Kong Han delegation to the city of Quánzhōu to attend its annual conference of the International South Shàolín Wǔzǔquán Union. In 2003, Grandmaster Lo was chosen to be the team captain of the Philippine Wǔshù team to compete in the First Traditional Wǔshù competition. Once more he stepped out onto floor to represent his school and his beloved art, and earned a gold medal in the traditional hand forms division.

The year 2010 was a notable one for the International South Shàolín Wǔzǔquán Union, as it was celebrating the twentieth anniversary of the foundation of the federation. Grandmaster Lo and twelve other distinguished masters were awarded 10th Duan ranking, which is the highest ranking that can be awarded by the federation to an individual—truly a great honor.

Kong Han's participation went beyond the competition floor and onto the streets of their own communities, which was an essential principle set forth by their founder, Dr. Lo, Yan-Chu. Kong Han also upheld its founder's legacy by assisting the less fortunate.

Henry Lo has been instrumental in guiding the expansion of Kong Han within the Philippines and beyond. In 2000, Kong Han opened branches in the city of Iloilo under the direction of Rene Lao, and another branch in the city of Caloocan under the leadership of Vicky Co. In 2002, Daniel Kun established a branch in Vancouver, British Columbia, Canada. Then in 2010, Jeffrey Yang established a branch in Canton, Ohio, US. In 2011,

The Kong Han Athletic Association team/delegation; consisting of practitioners/competitors from the United States and Canada, which was headed by Henry Lo and Daniel Kun at the Quánzhōu Southern Shàolín Temple in 2010.

Ademilson dos Reis established the Fei Lung Kong Han Kung Fu Academy in Sao Paolo, Brazil.

With the onset of the twenty-first century, society has been moving forward into the digital age, affecting us socially and economically, which has affected greatly the martial arts community. Many martial arts schools have adapted to the changes. However, Grandmaster Lo continues to preserve and uphold the standards set forth by his grandfather and father, but also looks toward the future. The legacy of Dr. Lo, Yan-Chu's Kong Han Athletic Club and the art of Five Ancestor Fist has become a cultural institution within the Filipino-Chinese community and now has taken root in other soils under the guidance of Henry Lo.

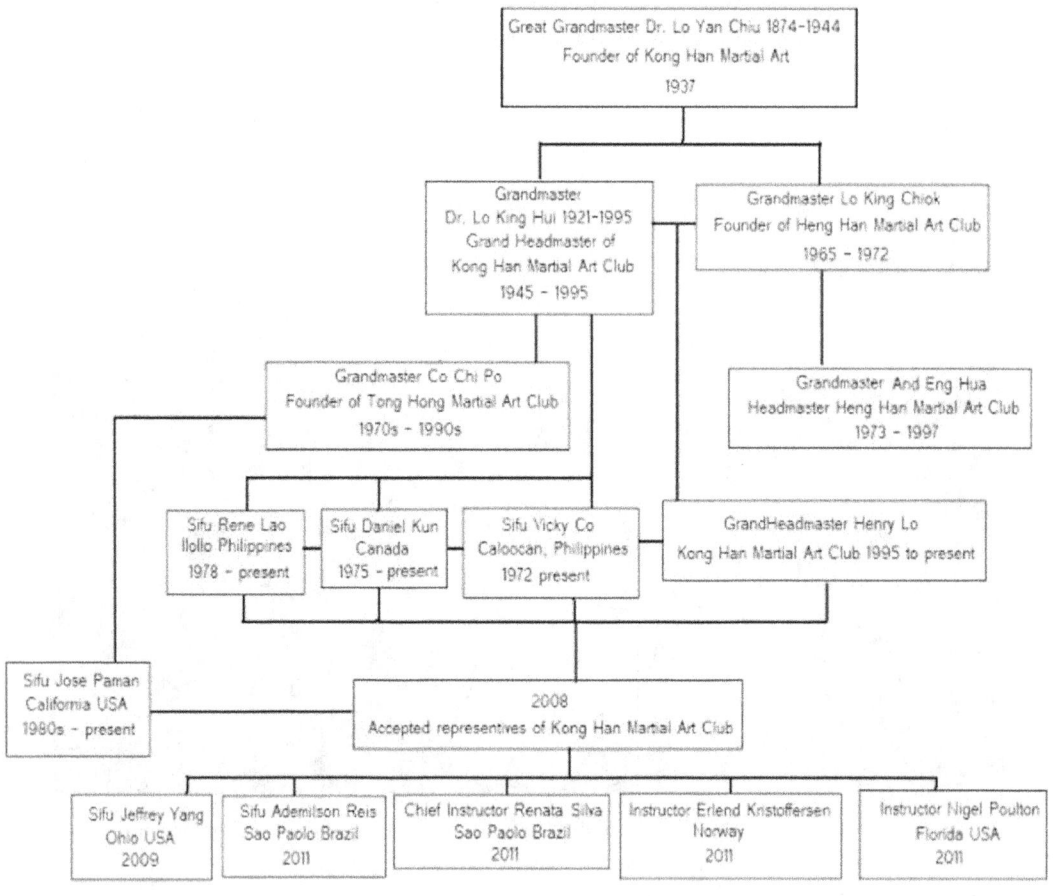

Kong Han Athletic Association Family Tree of Representatives

Henry Lo and the Kong Han Athletic Association preparing to march at the First International Southern Shàolín Wǔzǔquán (Ngo Cho Kun) competition in 2005.

The Kong Han Athletic Association team/delegation at the 20th Anniversary Celebration of the International Southern Shàolín Wǔzǔquán (Ngo Cho Kun) Federation.

Henry Lo and Daniel Kun with the Canadian delegation.

The Kong Han Athletic Association team/delegation at the 2011 International Southern Shàolín Wǔzǔquán competition.

Kong Han's Sǎnshǒu delegates from the Philippines, United States, Canada, Indonesia, and Quánzhōu at the 2011 International Southern Shàolín Wǔzǔquán competition.

Kong Han 73rd Anniversary

Quánzhōu Southern Shàolín Temple, 2012

Henry Lo leading the Kong Han team/delegation at the 2013 International Southern Shàolín Wǔzǔquán Federation competition, which was held in Quánzhōu, China.

2012 International Southern Shàolín Wǔzǔquán Federation convention.

SECTION TWO: ROOTS

CHAPTER 7

GUIDING PRINCIPLES

THE FIVE ATTACKS

Five Ancestor Fist's fighting principles are grounded in a direct approach that is based on utilizing the whole body for close-quarter fighting. This principle is referred to as the Five Attacks, or Ngo Giak. The Five Attacks refer to:

1. **Striking:** *Da*—or striking—implies hitting an opponent with an open or closed hand.

Planting Strike

2. **Kicking**: *Tiak*—or kicking—implies any strikes done with the legs or feet.

Going-Up Leg

3. **Seizing**: *La*—or seizing—is the skill of restraining an opponent by manipulating his own limbs and joints against himself.

Elbow Press

4. **Throwing**: *Sut*—or throwing—is the skill of taking an opponent down to the ground by using one's body as a fulcrum, e.g., shoulder, hip, leg, etc.

Sticking Body Throw

5. **Bumping**: *Dong*—or bumping—is the skill of using one's body, e.g., shoulder, back, etc., to strike an opponent's body.

Elbow Bump

THE TWO ELEMENTS

The core of Five Ancestor Fist powers consists of using two elements:

Strength: *Zi*—or strength—relates to the notion of utilizing isolated power in one particular limb, e.g., arms or legs.

Zi

Ging

Energy: *Ging*—or energy—refers to using the whole body to generate power by utilizing a particular energy that is referred to as Ki (氣) or vital energy. [Photo: 7.7]

These two elements are developed by practicing a series of forms *(lo)*, referred to as Chien Lo, or Battle Forms. These forms are the fiber of Five Ancestor Fist; without them the system does not exist. Within Kong Han there are three crucial Battle Forms:

Sam Chien (三戰): Translated as "Three Battles," Sam Chien emphasizes the development of one's body structure and, most importantly, the proper breathing pattern associated with tensing certain areas of the body. This helps with coordination of the body, mind, and spirit, and also taps into Ki or vital energy.

Tien Ti Lin Chien (天地靈戰): Translated as "Heaven, Earth, Man Battle," Tien Ti Lin Chien continues with the emphasis on body structure and the development of Ki begun

Sam Chien

Tien Ti Lin Chien

in Three Battles. However, wherein Three Battles concentrates on the development of the body (i.e., man), this particular routine more fully develops the Ki or vital energy that comes from the earth and heaven, with which it creates a cosmic trinity (i.e., heaven, earth, man). [Photo: 7.9]

Sam Chien Sip Li Kun (三戰二十拳): Translated as "Three Battles Cross Pattern," Sam Chien Sip Li Kun continues to stress what was emphasized in the prior forms and introduces new elements; for example, the theory of the Ten Character pattern, or Sip Li, which is a popular pattern within southern Chinese styles of martial arts. Whereas Three Battle consists of going up and down a linear line, here the practitioner goes in a cross pattern, which covers the four corners. This pattern and theory was envisioned to be useful when fighting more than one assailant.

Sam Chien Di-Sip Kun

Guiding Principles

FIVE PARTS POWERS

These Chien Lo introduce practitioners to a theory referred to as Ngo Ki Lat (Five Limb Strength; Five Parts Powers). Ki development is crucial in binding all these components into one effective unit. The Ngo Ki Lat include:

Leg: *Tui*—or the legs—is used to provide sturdiness and stability. The objective is to root oneself into the ground, thus establishing one's center, which allows us to use the ground to generate our energy.

Hip: *Dun Bo*—or the buttocks and hips—are where the energy, which is originally drawn up from the ground, gets amplified.

Shoulder: *Pok*—or the shoulder area—is where the energy is cocked and stored, ready to be released.

Arm: *Ciu*—or the arms, which consist of the elbow, forearm, hand, and fingers—is the part of the body that typically releases the energy that we have been cocking back in the shoulder. Therefore, the arms are the releasing point of this explosive energy, whose objective is to penetrate deeply into its target. This explosive energy can also be used to execute seizing or throwing techniques.

Vital Energy: *Ki*—in Ki Gong is one's vital energy or bioelectric energy that flows throughout the body—improves one's health, but it also can be utilized as a devastating power source within an actual physical encounter.

Five Parts Powers simultaneously uses the legs, hips, shoulders, arms, and vital energy when executing a technique. For instance, the legs must remain rooted to the ground to provide stability, which is needed to generate energy. The hip is like a turbine, which spins this energy to increase it. This energy travels up to the shoulder, which stores it for release through the arms and hands. Due to the shifting of the hips, the shoulders round off, which allows the transference of energy to the arms to be released. Hence, the arms receive the energy from the shoulders and then release it to hit the target with an explosive impact. Ki assists in focusing and generating this explosive energy, which can be devastating. Visually the Five Parts Powers seems like that body is jerking or whipping, akin to a tiger generating energy to pounce its prey or in the case of a crane, evading an attack.

KI - VITAL ENERGY

The underlying current within the theory of internal arts is a notion still being studied by scientists and doctors: Ki. The logogram for Ki depicts the notion of steam rising from a pot of rice. Within Asian cultures, Ki is perceived as a cosmic energy, which can be deemed as bioelectrical energy within scientific terms. Thus, Ki exists in all organic matter, including humans. The objective here is to provide a basic introduction of Ki due to its importance within one's training in Five Ancestor Boxing.

Within this particular concept lies the theory of Ging Lok, or the meridian system, which carries the Ki or vital energy throughout the body. The practitioner needs to be relaxed (or Song) to allow the Ki to flow through the Ging Lok, which can visualized as energy moving from the arches of the feet to the top of the head. By doing this, practitioners are able to manifest Ki into their techniques and thought process.

Key Note: One's breath should be deep and long. Avoid holding the breath, or the Ki will rise and float away, which leads to unsteady footwork and a sluggish posture. This would also affect one's mind and energy.

Without Ki there is no true energy because Ki is like an unending river flow; hence, the term "energy water." Five Ancestor is a fighting style based on the theory of issuing energy, or Huat Ging, and it has been stated that the Five Ancestor strikes are among the hardest in the world and it is due to the use of Huat Ging—Ki at work.

THE FOUR METHODS

Aside from the Five Parts Powers, there are the Four Methods, or Si Huat. The notion of bridges implies a few things; for example, the distance between an exponent and his opponent. It also refers to theories of body movements used in actual combat, which are interwoven with the use of techniques. And bridges allow the transfer of energy, which are:

Swallowing: *Tun*—or swallowing—refers to the ability to absorb energy.

Swallowing

Spitting

Sinking

Floating

Spitting: *To*—or spitting—is manifested by executing techniques with decisiveness, explosiveness, and with precise accuracy.

Sinking: *Sim*—or sinking—is downward energy established via strong and sturdy footwork.

Floating: *Pu*—or—floating is the ability to unbalance one's opponent.

The Four Methods are a crucial element in mastering the intricacy of Five Ancestor Fist, which correlates to the theories of Ki, or vital energy. For example, when one's hands are retracted, the body naturally becomes concave while breathing through one's nostrils. Therefore, the oxygen passes throughout the joints of the body, while slightly holding one's breath and remaining relaxed.

This allows the Ki to sink into the abdomen and correlates to the notion of swallowing. Therefore, swallowing can be perceived as inhaling because we are absorbing energy. The opposite of this action is to spit, or exhale. Now the energy moves up to the shoulders and releases through the hands. After completing these two motions, the body returns to an upright position.

The next two movements are sinking and floating. Sinking refers to holding one's energy in the joints, while maintaining balance between two acupressure points. The first point, located at the top the head, is referred to as bǎihuì, and the second point, called huiyin, is located between the anus and the genitals. Therefore, the body needs to remain centered and stable while tightening the anus (e.g., sink). Then the Ki is able to flow smoothly up the back, guaranteeing that the technique will be solid.

As before, there is the opposite, which is floating. This corresponds to a long stream of energy being released. In the process the chest is emptied out, with the arms extended forward to absorb the essential energy from the heavens and the earth, which is then transferred into the center area of the body (referred to as Dan Dian or the Cinnabar Field). This is the area of the body that develops, stores, and circulates Ki.

Therefore, a practitioner should be conscious of the extension and retraction of the arms, which is the concept of swallowing and sinking at play, followed with floating and sinking. When applying techniques, you are floating and the opponent is sinking; when the opponent is floating, you are sinking. Therefore, when the opponent is swallowing, you are spitting.

A crucial notion here is to build bridges, then shorten the distance between the opponents. By building bridges, one is able to flow with the opponent's force and then break or defuse it by neutralizing it.

INTERNAL

We have been introduced to the theory of bridging. However, beyond the obvious (i.e., distancing), there is something intricate occurring here that is classified as internal, or Lai. This refers to notions that are not obvious to the naked eye because the exponent is employing inner mechanisms that consist of particular breathing patterns in sync with certain body movements.

Just physical body movements are referred to as external, or Ngua. They are direct and easy to learn, but not as powerful when compared to an individual who is utilizing internal components to enhance those external movements. Therefore, a practitioner also needs to be conscious that there is an interchange of substantial and insubstantial, referred to as Im and Iong, and better known in Mandarin as Yīn-Yáng. This is manifested by expanding and contracting the chest in sync with the hands.

This notion can be perceived as being empty or full; reclining or extending; or supple and firm, which are crucial for short-range fighting. The exponent needs to be able to draw his opponent in to absorb his energy or use it against him and then release it upon him. It can also be perceived as being supple or soft before executing a technique, and finally being firm or hard when executing it.

ENERGY

Kong Han's Five Ancestor Fist's core root is Grand Ancestor Fist; therefore, it embodies the essences of the dragon and tiger, which are manifested within the movements, but at the same time possess the appearance of an emperor. This means the strikes are powerful, but also relaxed. Metaphorically, it is powerful and gentle, like the Yángzǐ River.

Five Ancestor Fist is the balance of harshness and gentleness, or what is referred to as the theory of Tai Giak, which is the balance of Im and Iong, or positive and negative. Therefore, the underlying theory is to apply a strike with force, but initiate it from a relaxed state of being.

Therefore, the Five Ancestor Fist ideology regarding energy can be summarized with three words:

- **Density**: *Me*—or density—refers to the mass of the substance, in this case a person.
- **Intensity**: *Giu*—or intensity—can be viewed from three points of view: 1) a degree or extent of something, b) the depth of one's feeling, and c) the force per unit of area.
- **Tension**: *Gin*—or tension—refers to the amount of applied pressure.

Energy can be perceived like the Tàishān Mountain, dense and solid. It can also be fast, like a tiger springing from the woods. But it can also possess gentleness, like pulling back the string of a bow, at the same time illustrating the notion of tension while aiming the arrow.

When intent and energy are united, strength is born. Thus, internal energy is derived from using the mind to stimulate the Ki throughout the Conception Vessel (Rènmài) and Governing Vessel (Dūmài). As such, the key to exerting this power first lies at one's Dan Dian, a point two inches below the navel where one's Ki is generated. The buttocks are tightened and the stomach remains relaxed, allowing the energy to flow within and to exert it externally. However, prior to issuing it, the waist acts as an axis or bed stone and the shoulders act like a bearing or runner stone, which stimulates a sudden burst of energy.

At the beginning of issuing energy, a practitioner tightens his gluteus (butt) muscles, while in the Three Battle Stance or Sam Chien Be. The knees are at shoulder width and the Dan Dian is tucked while breathing naturally. The mouth is closed and the teeth are clenched, while exerting the energy and focusing on the Ki, which is traveling through the Conception Vessel and Governing Vessel. While breathing, the chest should be slightly concave and the lumbar (lower back) must be allowed to expand and contract. By opening and closing, the energy will flow throughout the upper torso and then emit from the limbs.

After exerting energy, the body returns to an upright, relaxed posture. Inhale to gather energy once more, regenerating Ki within the Dan Dian. Therefore, energy manifestation can be viewed as sturdiness embedded in softness, or softness embedded in sturdiness.

Key Note: Upper-body muscle contraction must be avoided at all costs because it does not utilize Ki, but physical strength, and is a contradiction of Five Ancestor Boxing's principles.

In terms of victory and defeat in battle, it's always the one with the greater power that defeats the one with less power. The one who's faster defeats the one who's slower. Therefore, relaxed limbs are of critical importance.

LIGHT ON THE FEET

There are other unique body attributes found within Five Ancestor Fist, such as the concept of light body movement, referred to as Kin Dang. The practitioner develops the ability to leap and drop at different heights or simply possesses light footwork, also referred to as Pak Kok or escaping swiftly. This is an excellent attribute to possess in close-quarter fighting.

CORE FIST FORMS

The Battle Forms set the foundation and are then followed by core routines, which are designed to develop speed, mobility, dexterity, timing, and hand-and-eye coordination. Such core routines are:

Se Mun Pa Kak (四門打角): Four Doors, Striking Corner, as the name implies, teaches the theory of Four Doors or four angles, which consist of going forward, backward, and to the sides. This is due to the influence of Monkey Boxing, which is an agile style. However, the explosive energy of Grand Ancestor style is preeminent, as well the whipping energy of White Crane. At the same time, one will notice that the hands and feet are coordinated, which is a trademark of Arhat Boxing style. Finally, the breathing and isometric theories from the Da-Mao style are included.

Song Sui Kun (双綏拳): Double Pacifying Fist is a more advanced form, and possesses the strong influence of Grand Ancestor, Monkey, Arhat, and White Crane Boxing.

Zong Hap Kun (綜合拳): Linking Fist is a new addition to Five Ancestor Fist, which was organized at the International South Shàolín Wǔzǔquán Union and developed by a community of Five Ancestor masters from around the world, who contributed to developing this unique form that represent all the sects of the art.

However, Five Ancestor Fist is a synthesis of five highly respected fighting disciplines; therefore, it has an abundance of forms and has preserved the essence of each one of those disciplines. The forms are divided into two categories:

- **Kun To** (套拳), **Tou Lo** (套路), or **Ciu Hing** (手型): all refer to hand forms.
- **Hai Sut** (械術): Weapon skills, which refers to weapon forms.

There are roughly seventy-two forms in total within the discipline of Five Ancestor Fist. Typically, three-quarters of the forms are lengthy and the other one-quarter isn't. This does not imply that the shorter ones are easier due to their length, because they consist of intricate body mechanics that actually make them more difficult than the longer forms.

A unique attribute of Five Ancestor Boxing is the notion of Partner Drill or Dui Lian, which are actually two-man fighting forms. These routines are designed to apply the bridge technique concepts. The objective is to teach the practitioner timing, focus, confidence, and muscle memory, which will come into play when partaking in actual free-sparring.

WEAPONS

Weapons are crucial components within a tactical or combative art because they develop energy, strength, eye-and-hand coordination, and focus. They also enhance timing, which is crucial in responding to an incoming attack. Therefore, weapons are considered an extension of the body, offering counterbalance training and accuracy.

Traditionally, weapons were a common part of society, especially before the development of modern-day firearms. Early Five Ancestor Fist exponents were typically members of their local militia and some were Biao Giak, or armed escorts, for officials and local businessmen.

Today, weapons are practiced for cardiovascular condition and strength training, and for the sake of preservation. Therefore, Five Ancestor Fist uses weapons divided into the categories of long, short, double, flexible, and so on:

- **Dan Dou** (單刃): Single Knife
- **Dai Dou** (大刀): Big Knife
- **Giam** (劍): Sword

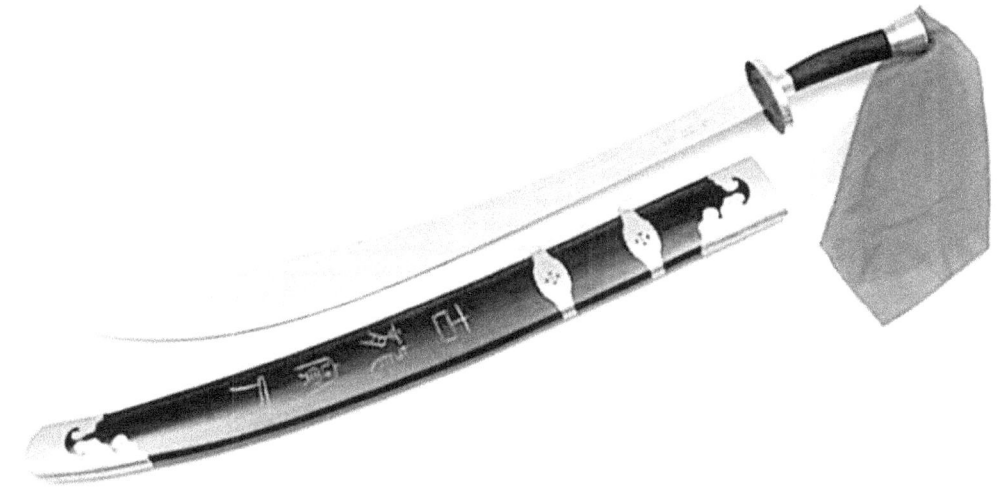

Dan Dou

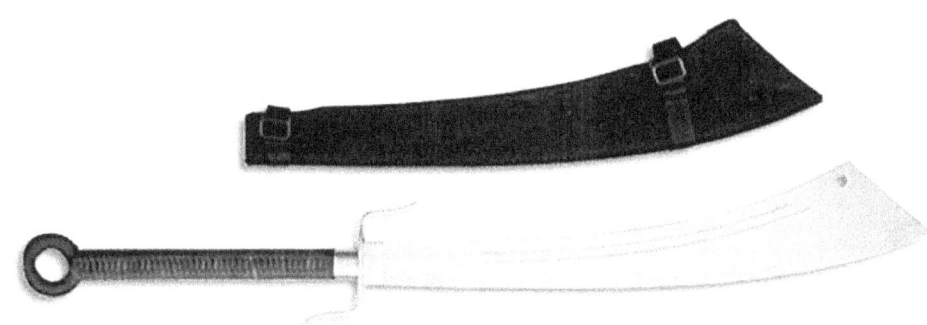

Dai Dou

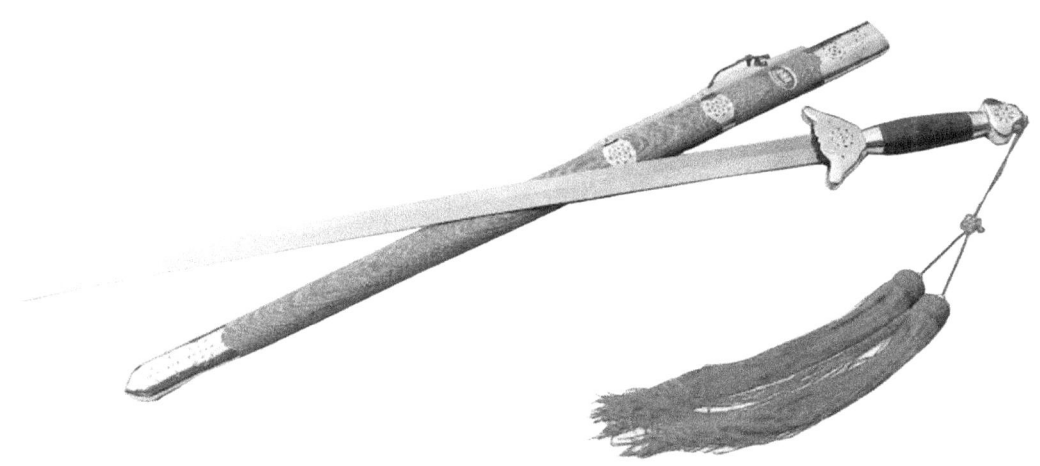

Giam

Sang Duan Bian

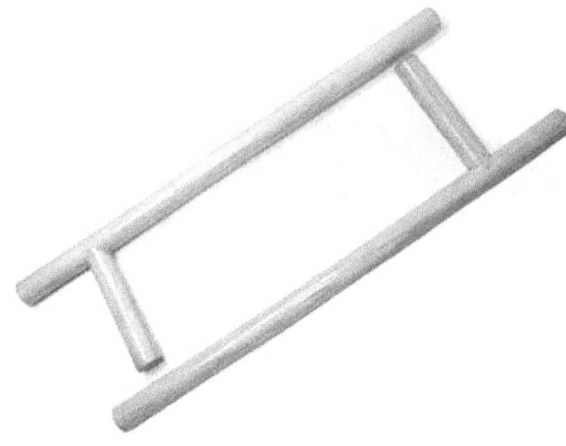

Sang Duan Guai

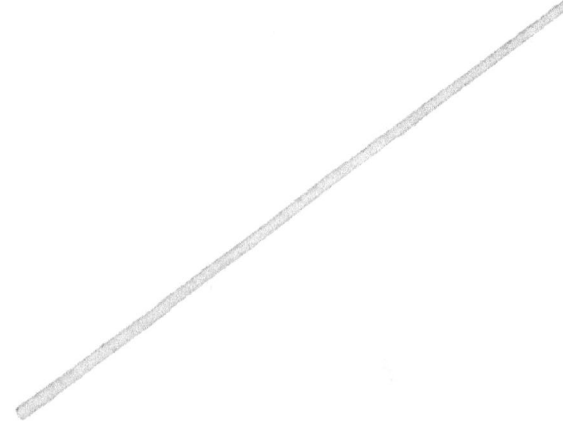

Gua

- **Sang Duan Bian** (雙短鞭): Double Short Whips
- **Sang Duan Guai** (雙短拐): Double Short Crutch
- **Gua** (杆): Staff
- **Guan Dou** (關刀): General Guan's Knife
- **Kai San Gao** (開山鉤): Cutting Mountain Hook or Trident
- **Giu Ti Zuê Bian** (九鐵截鞭) Nine Steel Section Whip

Forms are to be executed with what is referred to in Chinese as I, or intent. Without the "I" the forms are hollow, just a set of exercises. The intensity of training and focus are balanced with spiritual awareness, and enhances moral understanding. Therefore, the objective of Five Ancestor Fist practitioners is having control over their reactions; and knowing when to use deadly force and how to demonstrate mercy because one's skill is not meant for negative purpose, but as a last resort.

TECHNIQUES

Five Ancestor Fist is a discipline consisting of an average of 85 percent striking and 15 percent seizing techniques executed at close range. It can be perceived as an upright grappling style because an exponent does not mind being so close to his opponent and is able to use various

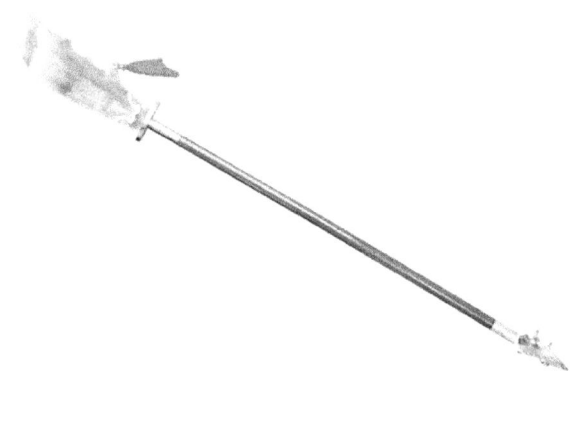

Guan Dou

Kai San Gao

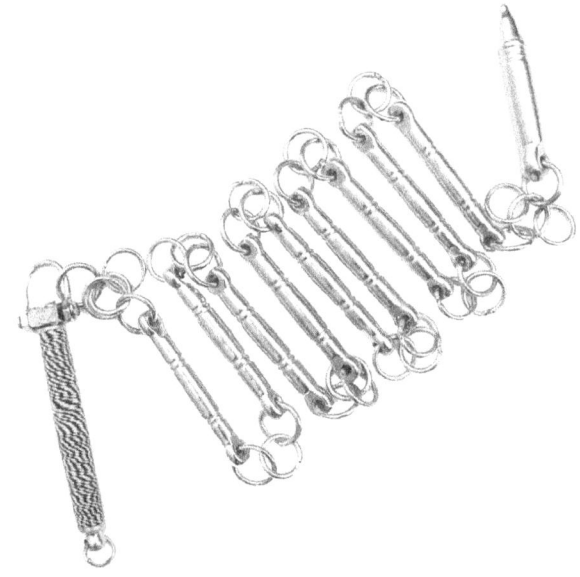

Giu Ti Zuê Bian

seizing techniques at this range as an added bonus. It allows effective throwing methods due to this range in fighting.

The objective is to keep the attacker off-balance and utilize his own action or attack against him. This allows the Five Ancestor exponent to employ a devastating technique that will quickly conclude the encounter.

As a striking art, Five Ancestor Fist emphasizes damaging strikes capable of dropping an attacker immediately. In delivering these strikes, an exponent must be able to generate the proper power to hit a specific target. Therefore, the strikes or techniques should be solid and powerful, with enough energy to penetrate and cause serious injury, which can lead to a hemorrhage or even a fracture.

IRON SKILLS

Five Ancestor Fist is referred to as a Short Boxing or Duan Kun because of its use of narrow stances and direct hand movements intended to strike at close range. Because of this, a Five Ancestor Fist practitioner needs to practice his Battle Forms to develop a method referred to as Iron Body Achievement, or Ti Sin Gong (aka Ti Pa Sho). Iron Body training allows an exponent to absorb strikes without sustaining internal injuries.

Piak Da Gong

Piak Da Gong

Piak Da Gong

To reinforce and test the Iron Body element of the Battle Forms, the practitioner utilizes a method referred to as the slapping and hitting skill, or Piak Da Gong, which consist of hitting one's body with one's own hand or having a partner strike certain areas, such as the forearms. Different apparatus are also used in this training, such as a bundle of chopsticks or sticks, to hit various sections of the body.

Ti Ziu Gong

Besides slapping and hitting, practitioners also use the method referred to as iron palm achievement, or Ti Ziu Gong (铁掌功), which conditions the hand for impact and at the same time increases its penetrating power.

The objective is to condition the whole body and the hands to absorb impact and reinforce the anatomical structures, which will complement the striking techniques of the art. As such, one's blocks possess the ability to injure an opponent because the bones have been strengthened, turning them into weapons.

SCATTER HANDS

Practitioners also train in the skill-sport of full-contact sparring called San Ciu or Sànshǒu in Mandarin, which means Scatter Hands or loose techniques. The tradition comes from public challenges when a new fighter would enter a town or city and challenge the established instructor on a Lui Dai, or better known by its Mandarin pronunciation, Lèitái, which is an open stage. Therefore, San Ciu is a crucial component within the Five Ancestor Fist's curriculums; it assists in testing practitioners' fighting ability to apply what they have acquired in their training. Also, it is conducted in a friendly and sportsmanlike manner because the intention is not to hurt one another, but to test one's martial arts skill and develop Martial Virtue, or Mu Diak, which is a code of etiquette; for example, respecting one's opponent, officials, elders and the general public.

Sànshŏu

As one can see, the art of Five Ancestor Fist possesses many intricate concepts that enhance one's body for combat or health purposes, which are an unsuspected benefit. Therefore, students need to be diligent and focus on achieving these rewards, which will enhance their lives on so many levels—even without them realizing it at times.

CHAPTER 8

KI GONG

Five Ancestor Fist is well known for its combative prowess; however, health is also a primary component, as mention within the Principle Chapter. The issuing of energy is based upon the use of Ki. Therefore, a practitioner has to practice the art of Ki Gong to excel within the discipline of Five Ancestor Fist. There is a basic adage: A weak body will not have the strength to train or become a good, strong fighter, nor reach its full potential.

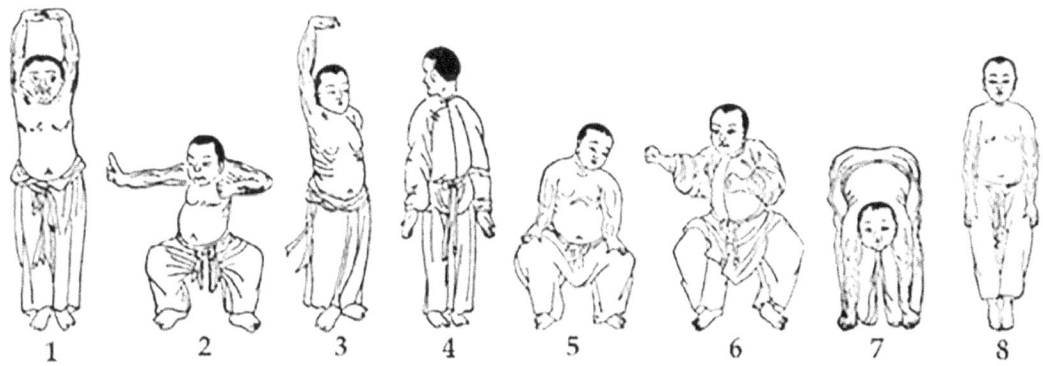

Ki Gong- Buê Dua Ngim (Eight Piece of Brocade)

Health development starts internally, which consist of tensing one's muscles, stimulating the internal organs like the kidneys, muscles, and tendons and improving one's blood circulation. This is accomplished syncing one's breath with tension.

Breathing provides the fresh air that is necessary to keep our bodies well nourished. A person with healthy and strong internal organs will be able to develop strength, stamina, and flexibility faster. This is accomplished through the training of hand and weapon forms.

Ngua Gong

In general, Five Ancestor is ideal for illness prevention because it strengthens the internal organs; thus, the risk of catching common illnesses is preventable. It also assists in the healing process after an injury.

DAN DIAN

The Dan Dian breathing is a natural way of cleansing one's body of toxic substances. Therefore, Dan Dian breathing helps preserve the body and at the same time assists in healing itself because it increases our Ki, vigor, and vitality.

Dan Dian breathing involves inhaling through the nose and directing fresh oxygen into the Dan Dian area, located beneath the navel, and slowly exhaling by applying pressure onto the abdomen to push the air out through the mouth.

The exhaling through the mouth removes the gaseous waste, which is followed by inhaling through the nose. This fills or condenses the

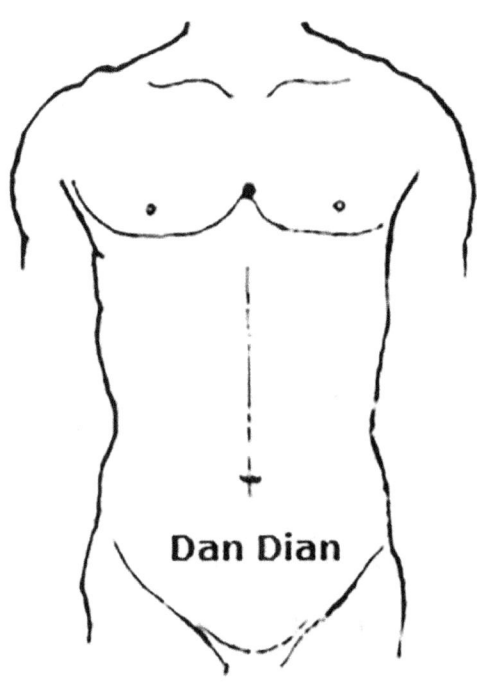

Dan Dian

Dan Dian with fresh oxygen that will vitalize the cells. The rhythmic inhaling and exhaling promotes proper blood and oxygen circulation throughout the entire body.

In performing the Dan Dian breathing, one must concentrate upon one's Ki flowing throughout the body, in particular the Governing meridian, which runs from the tailbone up the back to the head, then down anterior until it reaches the tailbone again. Therefore, use the notion of intention to assist the Ki in traveling throughout the body, sensing the rejuvenation and vigor. Make certain not to use unnecessary force and breathe naturally.

By performing the forms with intent and concentrated breathing, one can greatly improve blood and oxygen circulation. At the same time, this helps to focus Ki throughout the body, which is like meditation in motion. The added tension serves as an external force to aid the circulation by applying pressure in pumping the toxins from the body,

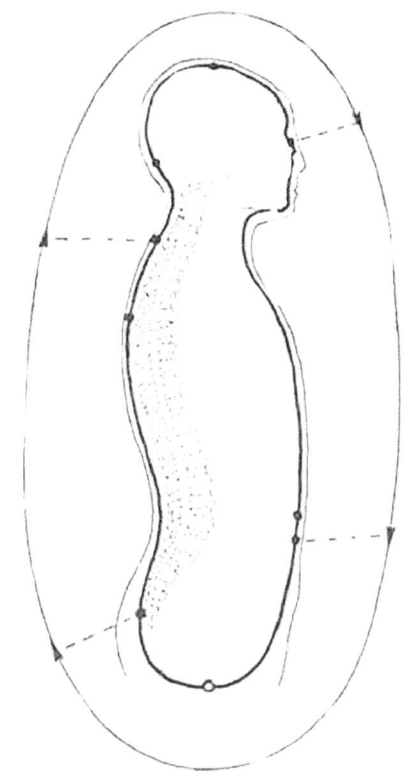

Breathing Pattern

which also stimulates and exercises the internal organs. This allows the body to properly distribute nourishment where it is needed.

Five Ancestor focus on the use of the core muscles, while implementing the Five Powers and the Four Methods; therefore, a student's core or midsection, lower back, and kidneys will become toned and stable. These attributes make Five Ancestor a well-rounded martial art for both men and women, regardless of body size or age, and whether for maintaining a healthy lifestyle or for actual combat.

ESSENCE

Essence, or spirit—referred to as Sin and Ki—are essential elements in martial arts training. Essence must be cultivated and resolved, whereas Ki must be thriving. For example, Three Battle form assists in this, especially by introducing the theory of swallow and spitting, which help to connect these elements into one unit. Breathing exercises gradually store energy and assist in releasing energy. For that reason, motions are stable and consistent, led by the head and guided by the eyes.

The gains are very profound: cultivating one's mind, elevating one's spirit to a sense of understanding, and pacifying one's energy. The techniques employed by someone with a clear mind and higher spirit are inherently better compared to someone whose spirit is muddled and inherently weaker.

If practitioners can utilize their intent to mobilize their Ki, they will be filled with an abundant amount of energy, which is capable of flowing freely throughout the channels of the body and filling it with vitality.

If the mind is kept still, like untouched water, and sufficient energy is accumulated and stored, it can be easily circulated throughout the body and when called upon to be useful.

CHAPTER 9

THE METHODS

Five Ancestor Fist consists of numerous strikes that employ the open hand, which can be also referred to as the palm, the clenched hand, or fist. However, it does not end there. The Five Ancestor exponents also use other parts of the body, such as the elbows, knees, and shoulders, for striking or bumping their opponents. Then there are kicks, which are direct and to the point. However, exponents possess the knowledge of seizing, or Kim La, which is popularly known by its Mandarin pronunciation: Qínná and the skill of throwing, or Sut.

This a brief introduction to various body methods found throughout Five Ancestor.

STRIKES

The execution of a Da or strike begins by opening into a Battle Stance, consisting of one leg in the front and the other leg roughly one foot behind; it should be one's shoulder length. This allows better mobility of body. The feet and the knees are facing slightly inside for better stability and balance. The hips are sunk down, similar to sitting on a stool, allowing the coccyx to be tucked in; hence, keeping the Ki stored within Dan Dian.

The shoulders are relaxed and the arm positioned in a posture referred to as time: Asking, Guarding Hand, or Mun Ho Ciu, which is commonly referred to in boxing as Cross-Arm Guard.

The strike is released like a projectile. For instance, the clenched fingers are facing upward and poised to one side of the chest. Slowly, it is launched horizontally, the fist and wrist torqueing. Now the clenched fingers face downward; the two first knuckles align with the wrist and forearm. The objective is for those two base knuckles—index and middle fingers—

to strike the intended target using the entire body to create momentum: a quick jerk, sinking forward with the entire arm and fist tensing up.

Striking the same area two or three consecutive times is ideal to make certain that the target goes down.

The chest-heart or sternum area is the ideal spot to aim for because it is a large target; it easier to hit and the chance of smashing the sternum may lead to a bone piercing the heart. The rest of the body presses forward and especially the legs are used to keep the attacker off balance, preventing the attacker from counterattacking effectively.

Various strikes can be found within the hand forms; however, one particular form stands out. Li Sip Gun, or Twenty Fist, was designed to develop explosive, penetrating punches, which is Five Ancestor's trademark.

1. Straight Strike

Fist Method

1. **Straight Strike:** *Dit Dui* (直搥)—or Straight Strike—is also referred to as Bing Dui (平搥) or Level Strike. As the name implies, it is a linear strike with a fully extended arm, supported by the energy stored within the Dan Dian. Therefore, the fist is aligned with the shoulder, keeping the fingers firmly clinched and using the first two base knuckles to hit the target.

2. **Hammer Back Fist:** *Dui Be Kun* (錘背拳)—or Whipping Strike— is also referred to as Gua Dui (挂搥) or Hanging-Up Strike. The objective of this strike is to hit with the back of the hand in a downward motion, similar to a hammer hitting a nail.

3. **Double Resonating Strike:** *Sang Zin Dui* (雙振搥)—or Double Resonating Strike—is also referred to as Sang Dong Strike (雙撞搥) or Double Colliding Fist. It is referred to in Western Boxing as an Upper Cut Punch. The objective is to strike in an upward motion, close to one's body.

2. Hammer Back Fist

3. Double Resonating Strike

4. **Hooking Strike:** *Gao Dui* (鉤搥)—or Hooking Strike—is also referred to as Passing-Through Fist or Guan Dui (贯搥). The objective is to hit the opponent's ear or temple.

5. **Double Planting Strike:** *Sang Zai Dui* (雙栽搥)—or Double Planting Strike—is also referred to Double Rock Strike or Sang Sia Dui (雙石搥). The objective is to strike in a downward motion.

6. **Baiting Strike:** *Siong Gao Dui* (上鉤搥)—or Baiting Strike—is a unique concept because it employs both arms. One arm is executing a Resonating Strike and the other is performing Seizing Fist or La Gun (拿拳). The rear hand grasps the opponent's wrist, while executing a Resonating Strike to the chin.

7. **Arhat's Double Hooking Strike:** *Lohan Sang Gao Dui* (羅漢雙鉤搥)—or Arhat's Double Hooking Strike—consists of a Hooking Strike and Planting Strike.

8. **Embracing Fist:** *Bao Kun* (包拳)—or the pulling and locking techniques, known as *La Sou Kun* (拉锁拳).

4. Hooking Strike

5. Double Rock Strike

6. Baiting Strike

7. Arhat's Double Hooking Strike

8. Embracing Fist

The Methods

9a. Giving Respect Fist

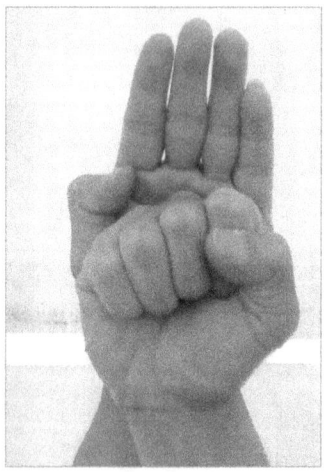

9b. Giving Respect Fist

9. **Giving Respect Fist:** *Meng Hiou Kun* (問候拳) is the Five Ancestor Fist Bow.

Hand/Arm Method

1. **Piercing Finger Hand:** *Cuan Zi Ciu* (穿指手)
2. **Poking Eye Socket:** *Tong Kong* (捅眶), also referred to as Double Finger Hand (Sang Zi Ciu 雙指手)
3. **Slicing Hand/Palm:** *Ciat Ciu/Ziu* (切手/掌)
4. **Tiger Claw Hand:** *Ho Dui Ciu* (虎搥手)
5. **Double Flank Defense:** *Sang Hiap Bou Ho* (雙脅保護)
6. **Double Covering Hand:** *Sang Gua Ciu/Ziu* (雙盖手掌) or Double Downward Defense (Sang Ge Bou Ho 雙低保護)
7. **Holding Shield Hand:** *Pou Bai Ciu* (抱牌手) or Butterflies Palm (O Diap Ziu 蝴蝶)
8. **Inward Arm:** *Lap Han Ciu* (內捍手) or Obstruction Arm (Ge Ciu 格手)
9. **Whipping Arm:** *Bi Ciu* (鞭手) or Chopping Arm (Kam Ciu 砍手)
10. **Thousand Character Arm:** *Cui Li Ciu* (千字手) or **Striking Chop Arm:** (Da Pi Ciu 打劈手)
11. **Double Epiphysis Poke:** *Sang Hiou Tong* (雙骺捅)
12. **Double Sweeping Hand:** *Sang Sou Ciu* (雙掃手)

1. Piercing Finger Hand

2. Poking Eye Socket

3. Slicing Hand/Palm

4. Tiger Claw Hand

5. Double Flank Defense

6. Double Covering Hand

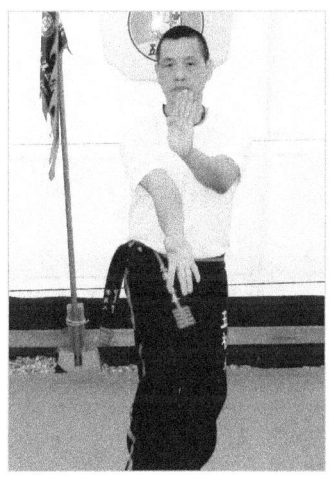
7. Holding Shield Hand

8. Inward Arm

9. Whipping Arm

10. Thousand Character Arm

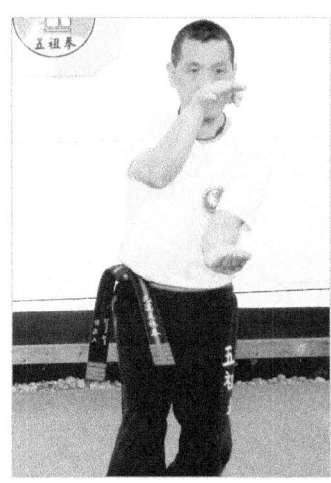
11. Double Epiphysis Poke

12. Double Sweeping Hand

Bridge Method

1. **Double Spreading Arm:** *Sang Lua Ciu* (雙攤手) or **Double Opening Arm** (*Sang Hai Ciu* 雙闓手)
2. **Joining Arm:** *Ping Bi* (拼臂); Sinking Bridge (Dim Giao 沉桥)
3. **Double Piercing Bridge:** *Sang Cuan Giao* (雙穿桥)

Elbow Method

1. **Vertical Elbow:** *Ziong Diu* (纵肘) also referred to as Dam Diu (担肘) or Lifting Elbow
2. **Level Elbow:** *Bing Diu* (平肘) or Propping-Up Elbow (Teng Diu 撑肘)
3. **Crushing Elbow:** *Zap Diu* (砸肘)

1. Double Spreading Arm

2. Joining Arm

3. Double Piercing Bridge

1. Vertical Elbow

2. Level Elbow

3. Crushing Elbow

Leg Method

1. **White Crane Jumping Kick:** *Pe Hoa Bao Di* (白鹤趵蹄)
2. **Golden Scissors Leg:** *Gim Zian Dou Tui* (金剪刀腿)
3. **Front Kick:** *Zui Tat* (前踢) can be referred to as Zui Ding Tui (前蹬腿) or In-Front Going-Up Leg
4. **Turning Side Kick:** *Hiong Ciak Tat* (向侧踢) can be referred to as Across Swing Leg (Hui Bai Tui 横摆腿)

1a. White Crane Jumping Kick

2. Golden Scissors Leg

1b. White Crane Jumping Kick

3. Front Kick

4. Turning Side Kick

5. **Side-Of Thread Leg:** *Ciak Suan Tui* (侧踹腿)
6. **Sweeping Leg:** *Sao Tui* (掃腿)

5. Side-Of Thread Leg

6. Sweeping Leg

CHAPTER 10

RISING FIST

Typically every form of Asian martial arts possesses some form of a bow or salutation. In the case of Chinese martial arts it can be referred to as Pou In or Embracing Seal; however, in the case of Five Ancestor, it is referred to as Qi Kun or Rising Fist.

This is done to acknowledge the elders that came before you and to greet the person before you; to show you come in peace. Therefore, Rising Fist is performed prior to all Five Ancestor Fist forms.

Originally Qi Kun was an elaborate system of coded messages hidden within the salutation, or Mun Hao Kun, to depict that you belonged to a secret society that was fighting against the Manchus.

The actual hand model salutation symbolizes the logogram for the Míng dynasty; the closed fist represents the sun and the open palm the moon. When the two logograms are placed together, they represent "Míng." Therefore, Qi Kun became prevalent within disciplines that were fighting against the Manchus. Each group had a variation of it, but each still signified the past glory of the Míng dynasty.

1. **Side-by-Side Stance, Both Side Fist**
   Stand at attention, breathing normally.

1. Side-by-Side Stance, Both Side Fist

2a. Lifting Knee, Embracing, Detain Fist

2b. Lifting Knee, Embracing, Detain Fist

2. **Lifting Knee, Embracing, Detain Fist**
   Inhale and lift the left leg up, knee slightly level with the waist. Pull with both hands, clenching them into fists, moving toward the right side of the chest. (The Eclipse)

3. **Four Level Stance, Double Flanking Defense**
   While exhaling, place the left leg parallel to the right leg and form Four Level Stance. The leg position should be as wide as one's shoulder; simultaneously push both hands toward the left hip area with an open palm, i.e., Double Flanking Defense. Exert 75 percent arm tension, while pressing down in conjunction with one's breathing.

4. **Four Level Stance, Double Planting Fist**
   Inhale; the two palms start to clench tightly into fists, i.e., Double Planting Fist. Apply 75 percent muscle tension in the arms.

5. **Four Level Stance, Embracing, Detain Fist**
   Maintaining the Four Level Stance, inhale and exhale while pulling the two fists toward the right side of the chest area; continue to apply 75 percent of tension in the arms.

3. Four Level Stance, Double Flanking Defense

4. Four Level Stance, Double Planting Fist

5. Four Level Stance, Embracing, Detain Fist

6. **Four Level Stance, Double Covering Palm**
   Exhale and throw the two fists out into the center into Double Covering Palm, again applying tension in the arms.

7. **Four Level Stance, Ten Character Arm**
   Inhale and exhale while lifting the arms to execute a Ten Character Arm.

8. **Four Level Stance, Double Spread Arm**
   Spread the arms open; it is also referred to as Double Opening Arm.

9. **Four Level Stance, Double Capturing Till Eyebrow Hand**
   From Double Spread Arm to Double Capturing Till Eyebrow Hand.

10. **Four Level Stance, Double Seizing Hand**
    Double Capturing Till Eyebrow Hand transformed into Double Seizing Hand.

6. Four Level Stance, Double Covering Palm

7. Four Level Stance, Ten Character Arm

8. Four Level Stance, Double Spread Arm

9. Four Level Stance, Double Capturing Till Eyebrow Hand

10. Four Level Stance, Double Seizing Hand

11. Four Level Stance, Double Embracing Fist

11. **Four Level Stance, Double Embracing Fist**
    While inhaling, pull the Double Seizing fist and rotate into Double Embracing Fist, which arrives at both sides of the body and slightly expands the chest, while breathing. Continue to apply 75 percent muscle tension.

12. **Four Level Stance, Giving Respect Fist**
    Slowly exhale while sliding both hands slowly from the upper chest to the hip area, keeping the right hand clenched and the left hand open. Then, placing the right fist in the left palm, i.e., Giving Respect Fist, continue to exhale while bringing the hands up to chin level. Again, continue to tense the arms.

12a. Four Level Stance, Giving Respect Fist

13. **Four Level Stance, Double Spread Arm**
    Inhale and then exhale while parting the hands, in the process executing a Double Spread Arm. The tips of the fingers are level with the eyebrows. (Opening the Gates of Palace or Heaven) [Photo:

14. **Four Level Stance, Double Joining Arm**
    Inhale and exhale while pressing down with both arms, slightly turning the forearm to execute Double Joining Palm. The elbows are tucked, protecting the rib area, while tensing the arms and sinking the Dan Dian. (Announcing the Emperor)

12b. Four Level Stance, Giving Respect Fist

13. Four Level Stance, Double Spreading Arm

14. Four Level Stance, Joining Arm

CHAPTER 11

GUARDING SKILL

Five Ancestor Fist possesses defensive or guarding positions that an exponent assumes to await an incoming strike from an opponent—to counter it or guard from an actual strike. There are three common defensive postures:

Zip Ciu Sang Ue (執手雙衛): Grasping Hand, Double Guard is a form of deception—a "Trojan Horse." One's arms are set low, leaving the upper body, especially the head, exposed. The objective is to entice the opponent to take the initiative or to attack your upper body, which will give the opponent a false sense of confidence, and when he lunges forward the exponent will be able to use the opponent's own power against him and take him off guard with an attack.

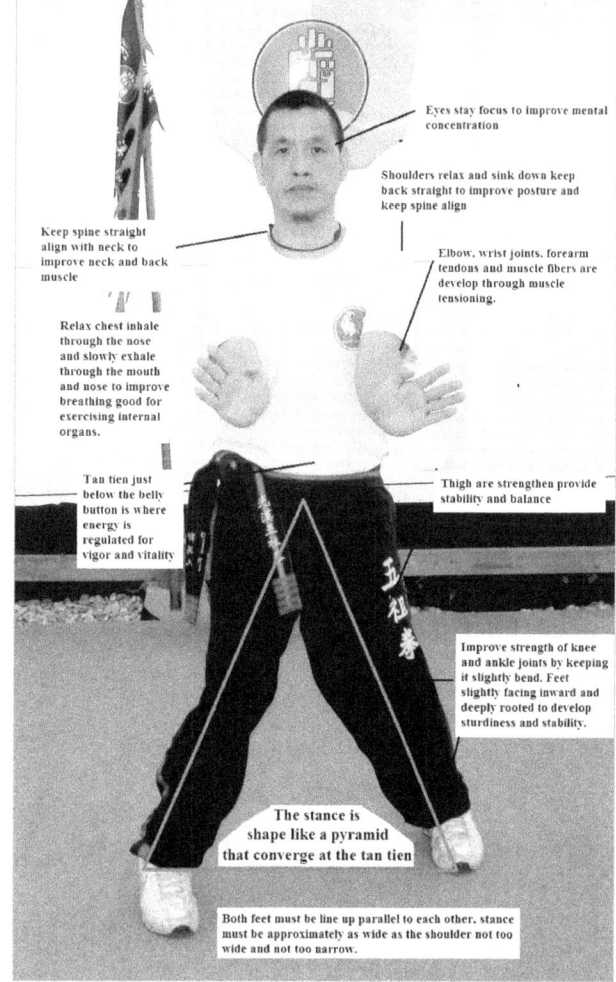

Grasping Hand, Double Guard

Pou Bai (抱牌): Embracing Tile is a full defensive posture that protects the entire body. For example, the hands are able to switch from clockwise to counter-clockwise, allowing them to defend against multiple strikes. The Empty Stance grants good mobility and counter attacking with a sweep, tripping, and kicks at a short range or confined space.

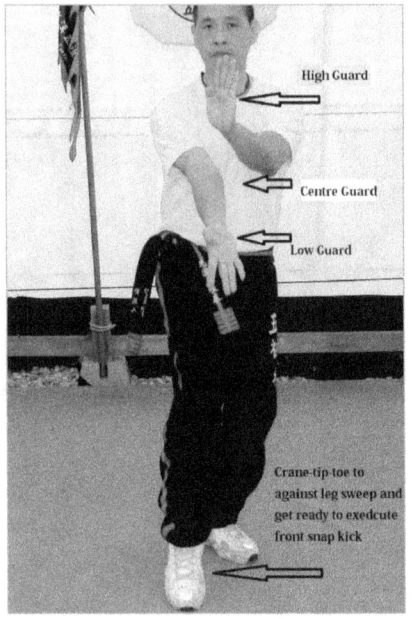

Embracing Tile

Embracing Tile-Ascending

Embracing Tile-Center

Embracing Tile-Descending

Bou Tê Diong (保中體): Protecting Center Body utilize the Three Battle Stance with both hands guarding the center, which is the most commonly used defensive or offensive posture within Five Ancestor Fist. It is also referred to as Asking, Guarding Hand.

Protecting Center Body

枝
SECTION THREE: BRANCHES

CHAPTER 12

THREE BATTLE WAY

Sam Chien, or Three Battles routine or Way, is considered the alpha and the omega of all routines in Five Ancestor Fist because it assists in developing proper breathing, or the Dan Dian breathing method, as mention in *Chapter 8: Ki Gong*.

The practitioner starts to use utilize isometric theory, which consist of tensing the muscles in coordination with one's breathing. At the same time this activates one's I, or Intent, which also enhances one's Sin or spirit. The byproduct will be manifested as Ging, or explosive energy.

Breathing is done by inhaling through the nose into the chest and exhaling by pushing down through the abdomen into the Dan Dian and then exhaling through the mouth while maintaining proper body structure. Proper structure helps strengthen the muscles, tendons, joints, and allows proper Ki to circulate.

The concept of "Iron shirt or Iron body" commences in Three Battle and continues within the other Battle routines. Iron Shirt or Ti Sam aids in strengthening the internal organs to be able to absorb physical distress. Such ability greatly improves the chances of a Five Ancestor exponent surviving in a physical altercation.

The body is strengthened through internal exercise; therefore, the ability to resist or recover from illnesses or injuries is also enhanced. Consequently, all practitioners of Five Ancestor Fist initiate their training with Three Battle because of these benefits.

Besides its health and conditioning benefits, Three Battle Way sets a solid foundation for fighting. Even though it is only three advancing steps and three retreating steps, it contains many intricate notions in its simplicity.

When doing the routine, the head and the face need to be upright; the neck must be straight and the chin pulled back, with an even gaze; the limbs of the body must stay even. The chest is slightly concave; consequently, the back is convex, like a turtle's shell. Then the shoulders sink and the joints tighten. The oblique muscles thrust forward and the spine sets; therefore, polar opposites meet at the center.

The stance needs to be stable, the pelvis must be tilted upward and the perineum (the space between the anus and genitals) must be pulled upward, which allows the *Xiyan* acupuncture point to open. Then the power is exerted through a notion referred to as Sam Dian Zing, or Three Field Essences, which can be perceived as earth, man, and heaven as one. Therefore, the weight is distributed toward the back and the body is rooted to the ground.

One's Battle stance must remain steady when advancing and retreating. The technique and the power executed must be focused, the body releasing and absorbing energy with a purpose. It's an even exchange between yin and yang, making certain to breathe deeply into the Dan Dian, which will assist the Ki in reaching the limbs.

Key Note: There are eight kinds of energy in the Three Battle Way: direct, parallel, hard, soft, stable, subtle, dense, and floating. All are within the scope of spitting, swallowing, sinking, and floating that have been comprehended; hard and soft Ging will flow like a rock tumbling from a hillside. Naturally exchanges between inhaling, exhaling, sinking, floating, essence, energy, and spirit aggregate into one and explode from both channels from the center of energy. Therefore, it is crucial to strengthen the body externally as well as internally.

As one can tell by now, Sam Chien goes beyond the obvious physical movements. For it to be "real," the practitioner needs to be conscious of the internal components. If not, the routine will be hollow, possessing no Issuing Energy to execute the techniques. However, this is only the beginning. After learning the single form, the practitioner learns to interact with others in a partner drill, which teaches the notions of defense and offense. Finally, this opens the doors to the techniques found within the form itself.

THREE BATTLE WAY

The following sections of the Sam Chien routine will be described and depicted in detail. Follow the photographs in sequence and the description for movement detail.

SECTION ONE: COMMENCEMENT FIST

1. **Side-by-Side Stance, Both Side Fist**
   Stand at attention, breathing normally.

2. **Lifting Knee, Embracing, Detain Fist**
   Inhale and lift the left leg up, the knee slightly level with waist. Pull with both hands, clenching them into fists, moving toward the right side of the chest. (The Eclipse)

3. **Four Level Stance, Double Flanking Defense**
   While exhaling, place the left leg parallel to the right leg and form Four Level Stance. The leg position should be as wide as one's shoulder; simultaneously push both hands toward the left hip area, open palm, i.e., Double Flanking Defense.

4. **Four Level Stance, Double Planting Fist**
   Inhale; the two palms start to clench tightly into fists, i.e., Double Planting Fist.

5. **Four Level Stance, Embracing, Detain Fist**
   Maintaining the Four Level Stance, inhale and exhale while pulling the two fists toward the right side of the chest area.

1. Side-by-Side Stance, Both Side Fist

2. Lifting Knee, Embracing, Detain Fist

3. Four Level Stance, Double Flanking Defense

4. Four Level Stance, Double Planting Fist

5. Four Level Stance, Embracing, Detain Fist

Three Battle Way

6. Four Level Stance, Double Covering Palm

7. Four Level Stance, Ten Character Arm

6. **Four Level Stance, Double Covering Palm**
   Exhale and throw the two fists out into the center into Double Covering Palm.

7. **Four Level Stance, Ten Character Arm**
   Inhale and exhale while lifting the arms to execute a Ten Character Arm.

8. **Four Level Stance, Double Spread Arm**
   Spread the arms open.

9. **Four Level Stance, Double Capturing Till Eyebrow Hand**
   From Double Spread Arm to Double Capturing Till Eyebrow Hand.

10. **Four Level Stance, Double Seizing Hand**
    Double Capturing Till Eyebrow Hand transformed into Double Seizing Hand.

8. Four Level Stance, Double Spread Arm

9. Four Level Stance, Double Capturing Till Eyebrow Hand

10. Four Level Stance, Double Seizing Hand

11. **Four Level Stance, Double Embracing Fist**
    While inhaling, pull the Double Seizing fist and rotate into Double Embracing Fist, which arrives at both sides of the body and slightly expanding the chest while breathing.

12. **Four Level Stance, Giving Respect Fist**
    Slowly exhale while sliding both hands slowly from the upper chest to hip area, keeping the right hand clenched and the left hand open (12a). Then, place the right fist in the left palm, i.e., Giving Respect Fist. Continue to exhale, while bringing the hands up to chin level (12b).

11. Four Level Stance, Double Embracing Fist

13. **Four Level Stance, Double Spread Arm**
    Inhale and exhale while parting the hands, in the process executing a Double Spread Arm. The tips of the fingers re level with the eyebrows. (Opening the Gates of Palace or Heaven)

14. **Four Level Stance, Double Joining Arm**
    Inhale and exhale while pressing down with both arms, slightly turning the forearms to execute Double Join Palm. The elbows are tucked, protecting the rib area, while tensing the arms and sinking the Dan Dian. (Announcing the Emperor)

12a. Four Level Stance, Giving Respect Fist

12b. Four Level Stance, Giving Respect Fist

13. Four Level Stance, Double Spread Arm

14. Four Level Stance, Double Joining Arm

Three Battle Way

15. Lifting Knee, Double Joining Arm

SECTION TWO: FIRST ASCENDING FOOTSTEP

15. **Lifting Knee, Double Joining Arm**
    Maintaining the arms in position, slowly start to lift the right leg four inches off the ground while stepping forward. Make certain to shift the body weight to the rear leg, i.e., left, maintaining the balance. The Three Battle Stance should be aligned with the shoulders.

16. **Three Battle Stance, Double Joining Palm**
    Set the front (right) leg down, making certain that you are rooted and the knees are tucked. The feet and toes should be slightly pointed inward to form the Three Battle Stance.

17. **Person Stance, Double Joining Palm**
    Lift the rear leg, i.e., the left, four inches of the ground and move it slowly forward toward the lead leg, i.e., right foot.

18. **Three Battle Stance, Double Joining Palm**
    Set the rear leg, i.e., the left, back down behind the lead leg, making certain to align the rear leg's toes with the lead leg's heel, which is aligned with the shoulder. Make certain that you are rooted and that the knees are tucked. The feet and toes should be slightly pointing inward, i.e., 15°. The body weight should distribute evenly between both legs, i.e., Three Battle Stance.

16. Three Battle Stance, Double Joining Palm

17. Person Stance, Double Joining Palm

18. Three Battle Stance, Double Joining Palm

19. **Three Battle Stance, Double Piercing Palm**
    Inhale while expanding the chest; pulling both hands toward the side of chest (19a). Exhale and thrust out with Double Piercing Palm (19b).

20. **Three Battle Stance, Double Joining Arm**
    Inhale and exhale while pressing down with both arms, slightly turning the forearms to execute Double Joining Arm. The elbows are tucked; protecting the rib area, while tensing the arms and sinking the Dan Dian. (Announcing the Emperor)

21. **Three Battle Stance, Double Spread Arm**
    Inhale deeply with reverse palm facing up, i.e., Double Joining Arm, while pulling the arms into the side of the chest. The chest expands and the oxygen and Ki rush into the body.

19a. Three Battle Stance, Double Piercing Palm

19b. Three Battle Stance, Double Piercing Palm

20. Three Battle Stance, Double Joining Arm

21. Three Battle Stance, Double Spread Arm

22a. Three Battle Stance, Double Joining Arm

22b. Three Battle Stance, Double Joining Arm

22. **Three Battle Stance, Double Joining Arm**
Exhale while parting the hands, the tips of the fingers are level with the eyebrows. (Opening the Gates of Palace or Heaven). Now press down with both arms. The elbows are tucked, protecting the rib area, while tensing the arms and sinking the Dan Dian. (Announcing the Emperor)

SECTION THREE: SECOND ASCENDING FOOTSTEP

23-30. Repeat the same sequence from Section One

SECTION FOUR: THIRD ASCENDING FOOTSTEP

31-39. Repeat the same sequence from Section One.

SECTION FIVE: FIRST DESCENDING FOOTSTEP

40. **Lifting Knee, Double Joining Arm**
    Shift body weight to the lead leg, i.e., the right. Now lift the rear leg, i.e., left, four inches off the ground and bring it toward the lead leg, while maintaining your Double Joining Arm.

41. **Three Battle Stance, Double Joining Arm**
    Set the left foot down toward your left shoulder and slowly shift your body weight onto it.

42. **Lifting Knee, Double Joining Arm**
    Maintaining the arms in position, slowly start to lift the right leg four inches off the ground while stepping forward. Make certain to shift the body weight to the rear leg, i.e., left, maintaining the balance. The Three Battle Stance should be aligned with the shoulders.

43. **Three Battle Stance, Double Joining Palm**
    Set the front (right) leg down, making certain that you are rooted and the knees are tucked. The feet and toes should be slightly pointed inward to form the Three Battle Stance.

40. Lifting Knee, Double Joining Arm

41. Three Battle Stance, Double Joining Arm

42. Lifting Knee, Double Joining Arm

43. Three Battle Stance, Double Joining Palm

44. Three Battle Stance, Double Joining Palm

44. Three Battle Stance, Double Joining Palm
Set the rear leg, i.e., the left, back down behind the lead leg, making certain to align the rear leg's toes with the lead leg's heel, which is aligned with the shoulder. Make certain that you are rooted and that the knees are tucked. The feet and toes should be slightly pointing inward, i.e., 15°. The body weight should distribute evenly between both legs, i.e., Three Battle Stance.

45. Three Battle Stance, Double Piercing Palm
Inhale while expanding the chest; pulling both hands toward the side of chest (45a). Exhale and thrust out with Double Piercing Palm (45b).

46. Three Battle Stance, Double Joining Arm
Inhale and exhale while pressing down with both arms, slightly turning the forearms to execute Double Joining Arm. The elbows are tucked; protecting the rib area, while tensing the arms and sinking the Dan Dian. (Announcing the Emperor)

45a. Three Battle Stance, Double Piercing Palm

45b. Three Battle Stance, Double Piercing Palm

46. Three Battle Stance, Double Joining Arm

47. **Three Battle Stance, Double Spread Arm**
    Inhale deeply with reverse palm facing up, i.e., Double Joining Arm, while pulling the arms into the side of the chest. The chest expands and the oxygen and Ki rush into the body.

48. **Three Battle Stance, Double Joining Arm**
    Exhale while parting the hands, the tips of the fingers are level with the eyebrows. (Opening the Gates of Palace or Heaven). Now press down with both arms. The elbows are tucked, protecting the rib area, while tensing the arms and sinking the Dan Dian. (Announcing the Emperor)

SECTION SIX: SECOND DESCENDING FOOTSTEP

49-56. Repeat the same sequence from Section Five.

SECTION SEVEN: THIRD DESCENDING FOOTSTEP

57-64. Repeat the same sequence from Section Five.

47. Three Battle Stance, Double Spread Arm

48a. Three Battle Stance, Double Joining Arm

48b. Three Battle Stance, Double Joining Arm

65. Lifting Knee, Double Joining Arm

SECTION EIGHT: STEP FORWARD 45° TO THREE BATTLE STANCE

65. **Lifting Knee, Double Joining Arm**
Maintaining the arms in position, slowly start to lift the right leg four inches off the ground while stepping forward. Make certain to shift the body weight to the rear leg, i.e., left, maintaining the balance. The Three Battle Stance should be aligned with the shoulders.

66. **Three Battle Stance, Double Joining Palm**
Set the front (right) leg down, making certain that you are rooted and the knees are tucked. The feet and toes should be slightly pointed inward to form the Three Battle Stance.

67. **Person Stance, Double Joining Palm**
Lift the rear leg, i.e., the left, four inches of the ground and move it slowly forward toward the lead leg, i.e., right foot.

68. **Three Battle Stance, Double Joining Palm**
Set the rear leg, i.e., the left, back down behind the lead leg, making certain to align the rear leg's toes with the lead leg's heel, which is aligned with the shoulder. Make certain that you are rooted and that the knees are tucked. The feet and toes should be slightly pointing inward, i.e., 15°. The body weight should distribute evenly between both legs, i.e., Three Battle Stance.

66. Three Battle Stance, Double Joining Palm

67. Person Stance, Double Joining Palm

68. Three Battle Stance, Double Joining Palm

69. **Three Battle Stance, Double Grasping Fist**
    While inhaling, simultaneously pulls both arms in while clinching them, which is referred as Grasping Fist.

70. **Three Battle Stance, Double Resonating Strike**
    Double Resonating Strike can be perceived as an elbow break that is simultaneously jerking and twisting with one's hips and body.

71. **Empty Stance, Double Resonating Strike**
    The left foot steps back, which allows you to convert the lead leg into Empty Stance. The body weight is distributed 80 percent in the rear leg and 20 percent in the front leg. Maintain the cross-arms.

72. **Empty Stance, Double Low Guard**
    Execute a descending Ten Character Arms while maintaining the Empty Stance and then convert into a Double Low Guard.

69. Three Battle Stance, Double Grasping Fist

70. Three Battle Stance, Double Resonating Strike

71. Empty Stance, Double Resonating Strike

72a. Empty Stance, Double Low Guard

72b. Empty Stance, Double Low Guard

Three Battle Way

73. Three Battle Stance, Double Low Guard

74. Three Battle Stance, Holding Shield Hands

73. **Three Battle Stance, Double Low Guard**
    Step forward to execute a Three Battle Stance.

74. **Three Battle Stance, Holding Shield Hands**
    The right hand executes a Patting Hand, while the left executes a Holding Shield Hands.

75. **Three Battle Stance, Spread Arm**
    The left arm executes a Spread Arm, while the right hand applies an Embracing Fist.

76. **Three Battle Stance, Propping-Up Elbow**
    The right arm executes a Propping-Up Elbow. The left hand clasps the forearm of the right arm. The elbow is aligned with the shoulder; one should be aiming for the sternum.

77. **Three Battle Stance, Whipping Arm**
    The right arm executes Whipping Arm.

75. Three Battle Stance, Spread Arm

76. Three Battle Stance, Propping-Up Elbow

77. Three Battle Stance, Whipping Arm

78. **Three Battle Stance, Slicing Palm**
    The right hand converges into Embracing Fist as the left hand executes a Slicing Palm.

79. **Three Battle Stance, Inward Arm**
    The right arm executes an Inward Arm.

80. **Three Battle Stance, Whipping Arm**
    The right arm quickly responds with a Whipping Arm once more.

81. **Empty Stance, Holding Shield Hand**
    Step back to create an Empty Stance (81a). The body weight is distributed 85 percent in the rear leg and 15 percent in the lead leg. Continue to slowly exhale and bring both hands to full shield, with palms facing out, the left palm at chin level guarding the upper body (81b). The right hand and palm facing out in the groin area guard the lower body. Keep both middle arms closely together to guard the center line.

78. Three Battle Stance, Slicing Palm

79. Three Battle Stance, Inward Arm

80. Three Battle Stance, Whipping Arm

81a. Empty Stance, Holding Shield Hand

81b. Empty Stance, Holding Shield Hand

82. **Four Level Stance, Embracing Fist**
    Execute a Ten Character Arm, but with the hands clenched and slowly the right foot steps back to form a Four Level Stance, while executing Embracing Fist to one's pectoral muscles.

83. **Side-by-Side Stance, Embracing Fist**
    Straighten the legs while the left leg slides against the right, which is referred as Side-By-Side Stance; exhale.

82a. Four Level Stance, Embracing Fist

82b. Four Level Stance, Embracing Fist

83. Side-by-Side Stance, Both Side Fist

Key Note: The stepping pattern consists of lifting one's knee and foot at least four to six inches from the ground. It was originally intended to avoid obstacles on the ground or to adjust to uneven surfaces. Also, it helps to lower one's Dan Dian, i.e., get rooted.

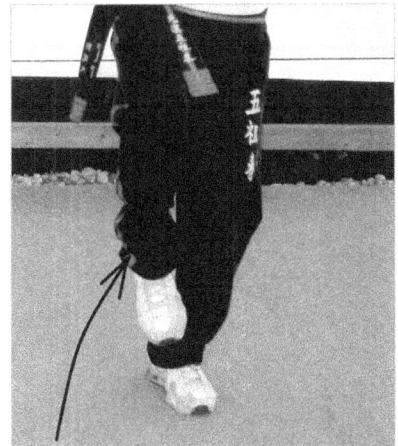

Three Battle Stance

CHAPTER 13

THREE BATTLE PARTNER DRILL

Traditionally practitioners learn an individual routine to teach them coordination, stamina, and the fighting methodology of their particular school. However, Five Ancestor Fist offers an added benefit: Partner Drill, commonly referred to as a Two-Man Set.

Therefore, Sam Chien Dui Lian, or Three Battle Partner Drill, strategy consists of familiarizing a practitioner with the four corners pattern, which consist of north, south, east, and west. This assists in developing concentration, sensitivity, and energy via muscle tension with both partners applying pressure against one another. In the process, it teaches timing, reinforces proper structure, and introduces the notion of counters.

The practitioners start by executing a three-steps-forward-and-three-steps-back sequence, which is referred to as: Sam Chien Cap Dim Dim Pu Huat, or the Three Battle Inserting, Sinking, Floating Method. The objective is to help develop the Five Bridges:

- **Swallowing** (Tun): Refers to the ability to absorb energy.
- **Spitting** (To): Manifested by executing techniques with decisiveness, explosiveness, and with precise accuracy.
- **Sinking** (Sim): Establishing strong and sturdy footwork.
- **Floating** (Pu): Unbalancing one's opponent.

After completing the first section, the practitioners move on to Sam Chien Si Siong Huat, or Three Battle Four Shape Method, consisting of a counter-clockwise motion that is repeated to the four corners until completed.

The opening section of Partner Drill is derived from the opening of Three Battle Way.

*The author Daniel Kun, is Exponent **A**; Joan Kun is Exponent **B**.*

THREE BATTLE PARTNER DRILL
SECTION ONE:

1. Side-by-Side Stance, Both Side Fist

2. Four Level Stance, Double Flank Defense

3. Four Level Stance, Double Planting Strike

4. Four Level Stance, Embracing, Detain Fist

1. **Side-by-Side Stance, Both Side Fist**
   Both standing at attention, breathing normally.

2. **Four Level Stance, Double Flank Defense**
   Inhale and lift the left leg up to step out, in the process forming a Four Level Stance, while simultaneously pushing both hands toward the left hip area; open palm, i.e., Double Flank Defense.

3. **Four Level Stance, Double Planting Strike**
   Inhaling, the two palms start to clench tightly into fists, i.e., Double Planting Strike.

4. **Four Level Stance, Embracing, Detain Fist**
   Maintaining the stance, inhale and exhale while pulling two fists toward the right side of the chest area.

5. **Four Level Stance, Double Covering Palm**
   Exhale while throwing two fists out into the center into Double Covering Palm.

6. **Four Level Stance, Double Seizing Hand**
   Life both hands and form into Double Seizing Hand.

7. **Four Level Stance, Double Embracing Fist**
   While inhaling, the Double Seizing fist rotates into Double Embracing Fist, which arrive at both sides of the body, while slightly expanding the chest and breathing.

8. **Four Level Stance, Giving Respect Fist**
   Slowly exhale while sliding both hands slowly from the upper chest to the chest area, keeping the right hand clenched and the left hand open. Then place the right fist in the left palm, i.e., Giving Respect Fist.

5. Four Level Stance, Double Covering Palm

6. Four Level Stance, Double Seizing Hand

7. Four Level Stance, Double Embracing Fist

8. Four Level Stance, Giving Respect Fist

9. Four Level Stance, Double Spread Arm

10. Four Level Stance, Double Joining Hand

9. **Four Level Stance, Double Spread Arm**
   Inhale and exhale while parting the hands, in the process executing a Double Spread Arm. The tips of the fingers are level with the eyebrows. (Opening the Gates of Palace or Heaven)

10. **Four Level Stance, Double Joining Hands**
    Inhale and exhale while pressing down with both arms, slightly turning the forearms to execute Double Joining Hands. The elbows are tucked, protecting the rib area, while tensing the arms and sinking the Dan Dian. (Announcing the Emperor)

SECTION TWO:
FIRST ASCENDING FOOTSTEP

1.

> A: **Three Battle Stance, Double Joining Hands**
> B: **Three Battle Stance, Double Joining Hands**
>
> A) Maintaining the arms in position, slowly start to lift the right leg off the ground, while stepping backward, in the process forming a Three Battle Stance while still maintaining Double Joining Hands.
>
> B) Maintaining the arms in position, slowly start to lift the right leg off the ground while stepping forward, forming a Three Battle Stance while still maintaining Double Joining Hands.

1A. Three Battle Stance, Double Joining Hand

1B. Three Battle Stance, Double Joining Hand

2.

A: Three Battle Stance, Double Joining Hands
B: Three Battle Stance, Double Joining Hands

A) Lift the right leg off the ground and move it slowly forward toward the opponent, while still maintaining Double Joining Hands.
B) Lift the left leg off the ground and move it slowly backward, away from the opponent, while still maintaining Double Joining Hands.

3.

A: Three Battle Stance, Double Spreading Arm
B: Three Battle Stance, Double Piercing Palm

A) Lift arms to form Double Spreading Arm to intercept the incoming strike.
B) Lift hands up to the pectoral muscles, converting them to Piercing Palm; then extend forward to strike Exponent **A**.

2A. Three Battle Stance, Double Joining Hand

3A. Double Spreading Arm-Double Piercing

2B. Three Battle Stance, Double Joining Hand

3B. Double Spreading Arm-Double Piercing

4.

A: **Three Battle Stance, Double Planting Strike**
B: **Three Battle Stance, Double Joining Hands**

A) Convert Double Scatter Arm into Double Planting Strike directed toward Exponent **B**'s rib cage.
B) Intercept incoming strike with Double Joining Hands.

4. Double Planting Strike-Double Joining Hand

5.

A: **Three Battle Stance, Double Hooking Strike**
B: **Three Battle Stance, Double Spreading Hand**

A) Convert Double Planting Strike into Double Hooking Strike directed toward Exponent **B**'s temples.
B) Intercept incoming strike with Double Spreading Hand.

5. Double Hooking Strike-Double Spread Arm

6.

A: **Three Battle Stance, Double Joining Hands**
B: **Three Battle Stance, Double Joining Hands**

A) The Double Hooking Strike converts to Double Joining Hand to neutralize Double Scattering Arms.
B) The Double Scattering Arms have converted to Double Joining Hands to neutralize the Double Joining Hands.

6. Double Joining Hand

Three Battle Partner Drill 107

SECTION THREE:
SECOND ASCENDING FOOTSTEP

Repeat the same sequence from Section One.

SECTION FOUR:
THIRD ASCENDING FOOTSTEP

Repeat the same sequence from Section One.

SECTION FIVE:
FIRST DESCENDING FOOTSTEP

1.

    A: **Three Battle Stance, Double Joining Hands**
    B: **Three Battle Stance, Double Joining Hands**

    A) Maintaining the arms in position, slowly start to lift the right leg off the ground while stepping forward, forming a Three Battle Stance while still maintaining Double Joining Hands.

    B) Maintaining the arms in position, slowly start to lift the right leg off the ground, while stepping backward, in the process forming a Three Battle Stance while still maintaining Double Joining Hands.

1A. Three Battle Stance, Double Joining Hand

1B. Three Battle Stance, Double Joining Hand

2.

A: **Three Battle Stance, Double Joining Hands**
B: **Three Battle Stance, Double Joining Hands**

A) Lift the left leg off the ground and move it slowly backward, away from the opponent, while still maintaining Double Joining Hands.

B) Lift the right leg off the ground and move it slowly forward toward the opponent, while still maintaining Double Joining Hands.

3.

A: **Three Battle Stance, Double Spreading Arm**
B: **Three Battle Stance, Double Piercing Palm**

A) Lift arms to form Double Spreading Arm to intercept the incoming strike.

B) Lift hands up to the pectoral muscles, converting them to Double Piercing Palm, then extend forward to strike Exponent **A**.

2A. Three Battle Stance, Double Joining Hand

3A. Double Spreading Arm-Double Piercing

2B. Three Battle Stance, Double Joining Hand

3B. Double Spreading Arm-Double Piercing

4.

A: **Three Battle Stance, Double Planting Strike**
B: **Three Battle Stance, Double Joining Hands**

A) Convert Double Scatter Arm into Double Planting Strike directed toward Exponent **B**'s rib cage.
B) Intercept incoming strike with Double Joining Hands.

4. Double Planting Strike-Double Joining Hand

5.

A: **Three Battle Stance, Double Hooking Strike**
B: **Three Battle Stance, Double Spreading Hand**

A) Convert Double Planting Strike into Double Hooking Strike directed toward Exponent **B**'s temples.
B) Intercept incoming strike with Double Spreading Arm.

5. Double Hooking Strike-Double Spread Arm

6.

A: **Three Battle Stance, Double Joining Hands**
B: **Three Battle Stance, Double Joining Hands**

A) The Double Hooking Strike converts to Double Joining Hands to neutralize Double Scattering Arms.
B) The Double Scattering Arms have converted to Double Joining Hands to neutralize the Double Joining Hands.

6. Double Joining Hand

SECTION SIX:
SECOND DESCENDING FOOTSTEP

Repeat the same sequence from Section Five.

SECTION SEVEN:
THIRD DESCENDING FOOTSTEP

Repeat the same sequence from Section Five.

SECTION EIGHT:

After the Third Descending Footstep, you will step forward in 45° Three Battle Stance

1.

   A: **Three Battle Stance, Slicing Palm**
   B: **Three Battle Stance, Double Embracing Fist**
   A) Lift the right leg off the ground and step backward, forming a Three Battle Stance while executing a Slicing Palm.
   B) Lift the right leg off the ground and step forward, forming a Three Battle Stance; however, the left leg is at a 45° angle

2.

1. Slicing Palm-Double Embracing Fist

   A: **Three Battle Stance, Straight Strike**
   B: **Three Battle Stance, Double Break**
   A) Execute a Straight Strike toward Exponent **B's** face.
   B) Intercept the incoming strike with a Double Break.

2. Straight Strike-Double Break

3.

A: **Three Battle Stance, Double Slicing Palm**

B: **Empty Stance, Double Hand Protecting the Gate**

A) Step forward with the right foot while executing Double Slicing Palm toward Exponent **B**'s kidneys.
B) Intercept the strikes with Double Hand Protecting the Gate, while stepping back and forming an Empty Stance.

3. Double Slicing Palm-Double Hand Protecting the Gate

4.

A: **Three Battle Stance, Hooking Strike**

B: **Three Battle Stance, Inward Arm**

A) Execute a right Hooking Strike toward Exponent **B**'s temple.
B) Step back in a 45° angle, forming again a Three Battle Stance while intercepting the strike with Inward Arm.

4. Hooking Strike-Inward Arm

5.

A: **Three Battle Stance, Asking, Guarding Hand**

B: **Three Battle Stance, Tray Elbow**

A) Intercept the incoming elbow strike with Asking, Guarding Hand.
B) Execute a Tray Elbow toward Exponent **A**'s temple.

5. Asking, Guarding Hand-Tray Elbow

6.

   A: **Three Battle Stance, Inward Arm**

   B: **Three Battle Stance, Whipping Arm**

   A) Intercept the incoming strike with Inward Arm.

   B) Execute a Whipping Arm toward Exponent **A**'s neck.

6. Inward Arm-Whipping Arm

7.

   A: **Three Battle Stance, Chopping Arm**

   B: **Three Battle Stance, Thousand Character Arm**

   A) Intercept the incoming strike with Chopping Arm.

   B) Execute a Thousand Character Arm toward Exponent **A**'s kidneys.

7. Chopping Arm-Thousand Character Arm

8.

   A: **Three Battle Stance, Straight Strike**

   B: **Three Battle Stance, Inward Arm**

   A) Execute a Straight Strike toward Exponent **B**'s Face.

   B) Intercept the incoming strike with Inward Arm.

8. Straight Strike-Inward Arm

9.

A: **Three Battle Stance, Spread Arm**
B: **Three Battle Stance, Specifying Fingers**

A) Intercept the incoming strike with Spread Arm.
B) Execute a Specifying Fingers toward Exponent **B**'s Face.

9. Spread Arm-Specifying Fingers

10.

A: **Empty Stance, Spread Arm**
B: **Intercepting Stance, Specifying Fingers**

A) Still maintaining the hand postures, the left leg steps forward into Empty Stance.
B) Still maintaining the hand postures, the left leg steps back in Intercepting Stance.

10. Spread Arm-Specifying Fingers

SECTION NINE: FIRST SHAPE

This is the beginning of Three Battle, Four Shape Method.

1.

A: **Three Battle Stance, Spread Arm**
B: **Three Battle Stance, Specifying Fingers**

A) Still maintaining the hand postures, the right leg steps forward into Three Battle Stance.
B) Still maintaining the hand postures, the right leg steps back, forming Three Battle Stance.

1. Spread Arm-Specifying Fingers

2.

A: **Three Battle Stance, Double Hooking Strike**
B: **Empty Stance, Double Seizing Hand**

A) Strike the opponent's temple with Double Hooking Strike.
B) Intercept the strikes with Double Seizing Hand, while the body leans back and the right leg converts to Empty Stance.

2. Double Hooking Strike-Double Seizing Hand

3.

A: **Three Battle Stance, Lifting Palm**
B: **Flicking Leg**

A) Intercept the incoming kick with Lifting Palm.
B) The hands pull back to the chest, i.e., Double Embracing Fist, while executing a right Flicking Leg.

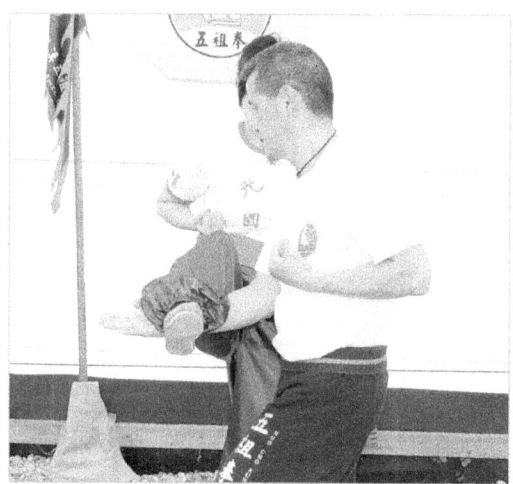

3. LIfting Palm-Flicking Leg

4.

A: **Three Battle Stance, Spread Arm**
B: **Three Battle Stance, Hook Strike**

A) Intercept the strike with Spread Arm.
B) Step down and forward into Three Battle Stance while executing a Hook Strike.

4. Spread Arm-Hooking Strike

Three Battle Partner Drill

5.

A: **Three Battle Stance, Straight Strike**
B: **Three Battle Stance, Spreading Arm**

A) Execute a Straight Strike toward Exponent **B**'s face.
B) Intercept the incoming strike with Spreading Arm.

5. Straight Strike-Spread Arm

6.

A: **Three Battle Stance, Asking, Guarding Hand**
B: **Three Battle Stance, Tray Elbow**

A) Intercept the incoming elbow strike with Asking, Guarding Hand.
B) Execute a Tray Elbow toward Exponent **A**'s face.

6. Asking, Guarding Hand-Tray Elbow

7.

A: **Three Battle Stance, Inward Arm**
B: **Three Battle Stance, Whipping Arm**

A) Intercept the incoming strike with Inward Arm.
B) Execute a Whipping Arm toward Exponent **A**'s neck.

7. Inward Arm-Whipping Arm

8.

A: **Three Battle Stance, Chopping Arm**

B: **Three Battle Stance, Thousand Character Arm**

A) Intercept the incoming strike with Chopping Arm.
B) Execute a Thousand Character Arm toward Exponent **A**'s kidneys.

8. Chopping Arm-Thousand Character Arm

9.

A: **Three Battle Stance, Straight Strike**

B: **Three Battle Stance, Inward Arm**

A) Execute a Straight Strike toward Exponent **B**'s Face.
B) Intercept the incoming strike with Inward Arm.

9. Straight Strike-Inward Arm

10.

A: **Three Battle Stance, Inward Arm**

B: **Three Battle Stance, Whipping Arm**

A) Intercept the incoming strike with Inward Arm.
B) Execute a Whipping Arm toward Exponent **A**'s neck.

10. Inward Arm-Whipping Arm

SECTION 10: SECOND SHAPE

1.

   A: Covering Stance, Inward Arm
   B: Empty Stance, Whipping Arm
   A) Still maintaining the hand postures, the left leg steps forward into Covering Stance.
   B) Still maintaining the hand postures, shifting the weight back and the left leg steps to form a right Empty Stance.

1. Inward Arm-Whipping Arm

2.

   A: Three Battle Stance, Double Slicing Palm
   B: Empty Stance, Double Protecting the Gate
   A) Step forward with the right foot while executing Double Slicing Palm toward Exponent **B**'s kidneys.
   B) Intercept the strikes with Double Hand Protecting the Gate, while stepping back and forming an Empty Stance.

2. Double Slicing Palm-Double Protecting the Gate

3.

   A: Three Battle Stance, Lifting Palm
   B: Flicking Leg
   A) Intercept the incoming kick with Lifting Palm.
   B) The hands pull back to the chest, i.e., Double Embracing Fist, while executing a right Flicking Leg.

3. Lifting Palm-Flicking Leg

4.

A: **Three Battle Stance, Seizing Hand**
B: **Three Battle Stance, Hook Strike**

A) Intercept the strike with Seizing Hand.
B) Step down and forward into Three Battle Stance while executing a Hook Strike.

4. Seizing Arm-Hook Strike

5.

A: **Three Battle Stance, Straight Strike**
B: **Three Battle Stance, Inward Arm**

A) Execute a Straight Strike toward Exponent **B**'s face.
B) Intercept the incoming strike with Inward Arm.

5. Straight Strike-Inward Arm

6.

A: **Three Battle Stance, Asking, Guarding Hand**
B: **Three Battle Stance, Tray Elbow**

A) Intercept the incoming elbow strike with Asking, Guarding Hand.
B) Execute a Tray Elbow toward Exponent **A**'s face.

6. Asking, Guarding Hand-Tray Elbow

7.

A: **Three Battle Stance, Inward Arm**

B: **Three Battle Stance, Whipping Arm**

A) Intercept the incoming strike with Inward Arm.

B) Execute a Whipping Arm toward Exponent **A**'s neck.

7. Inward Arm-Whipping Arm

8.

A: **Three Battle Stance, Chopping Arm**

B: **Three Battle Stance, Thousand Character Arm**

A) Intercept the incoming strike with Chopping Arm.

B) Execute a Thousand Character Arm toward Exponent **A**'s kidneys.

8. Chopping Arm-Thousand Character Hand

9.

A: **Three Battle Stance, Straight Strike**

B: **Three Battle Stance, Inward Arm**

A) Execute a Straight Strike toward Exponent **B**'s Face.

B) Intercept the incoming strike with Inward Arm.

9. Straight Strike-Inward Arm

10.

A: **Three Battle Stance, Inward Arm**
B: **Three Battle Stance, Whipping Arm**

A) Intercept the incoming strike with Inward Arm.
B) Execute a Whipping Arm toward Exponent **A**'s neck.

10. Inward Arm-Whipping Arm

SECTION 11: THIRD SHAPE

1.

A: **Covering Stance, Inward Arm**
B: **Empty Stance, Whipping Arm**

A) Still maintaining the hand postures, the left leg steps forward into Covering Stance.
B) Still maintaining the hand postures, the left leg steps back to form a right Empty Stance.

1. Inward Arm-Whipping Arm

2.

A: **Three Battle Stance, Double Hooking Strike**
B: **Empty Stance, Double Capturing Till Eyebrow Hand**

A) Step forward with the right foot while executing a Double Hooking Strike to Exponent **B**'s temple.
B) Intercept the strikes with Double Capturing Till Eyebrow Hand, while the body leans back and the right leg converts to Empty Stance.

2. Hooking Strike-Double Capturing Till Eyebrow Hand

Three Battle Partner Drill 121

3.

A: **Three Battle Stance, Lifting Palm**
B: **Flicking Leg**

A) Intercept the incoming kick with Lifting Palm.
B) The hands pull back to the chest, i.e., Double Embracing Fist, while executing a right Flicking Leg.

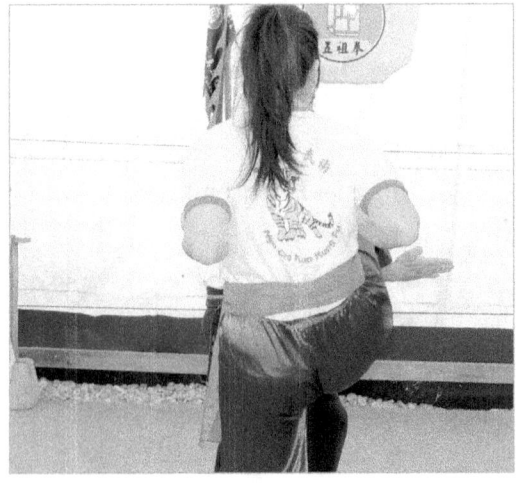

3. Lifting Palm-Flicking Leg

4.

A: **Three Battle Stance, Seizing Hand**
B: **Three Battle Stance, Hook Strike**

A) Intercept the strike with Seizing Hand.
B) Step down and forward into Three Battle Stance while executing a Hook Strike.

4. Seizing Hand-Hook Strike

5.

A: **Three Battle Stance, Straight Strike**
B: **Three Battle Stance, Spread Arm**

A) Execute a Straight Strike toward Exponent **B**'s face.
B) Intercept the incoming strike with Spread Arm.

5. Straight Strike-Spread Arm

6.

A: **Three Battle Stance, Asking, Guarding Hand**
B: **Three Battle Stance, Tray Elbow**

A) Intercept the incoming elbow strike with Asking, Guarding Hand.
B) Execute a Tray Elbow toward Exponent **A**'s face.

6. Asking, Guarding Hand-Tray Elbow

7.

A: **Three Battle Stance, Inward Arm**
B: **Three Battle Stance, Whipping Arm**

A) Intercept the incoming strike with Inward Arm.
B) Execute a Whipping Arm toward Exponent **A**'s neck.

7. Inward Arm-Whipping Arm

8.

A: **Three Battle Stance, Chopping Arm**
B: **Three Battle Stance, Thousand Character Arm**

A) Intercept the incoming strike with Chopping Arm.
B) Execute a Thousand Character Arm toward Exponent **A**'s kidneys.

8. Chopping Arm-Thousand Character Hand

Three Battle Partner Drill

9.

A: **Three Battle Stance, Straight Strike**
B: **Three Battle Stance, Inward Arm**
A) Execute a Straight Strike toward Exponent **B**'s Face.
B) Intercept the incoming strike with Inward Arm.

9. Straight Strike-Inward Arm

10.

A: **Three Battle Stance, Inward Arm**
B: **Three Battle Stance, Whipping Arm**
A) Intercept the incoming strike with Inward Arm.
B) Execute a Whipping Arm toward Exponent **A**'s neck.

10. Inward Arm-Whipping Arm

SECTION 12: FOURTH SHAPE

1.

A: **Empty Stance, Inward Arm**
B: **Empty Stance, Whipping Arm**
A) Still maintaining the hand postures, the left leg steps forward into Empty Stance.
B) Still maintaining the hand postures, the left leg steps back to form a right Empty Stance.

1. Inward Arm-Whipping Arm

2.

A: **Three Battle Stance, Double Slicing Palm**
B: **Empty Stance, Double Hand Protecting the Gate**

A) Step forward with the right foot while executing Double Slicing Palm toward Exponent **B**'s kidneys.
B) Intercept the strikes with Double Hand Protecting the Gate while stepping back and forming an Empty Stance.

2. Double Slicing Palm-Double Hand Protecting the Gate

3.

A: **Three Battle Stance, Lifting Palm**
B: **Flicking Leg**

A) Intercept the incoming kick with Lifting Palm.
B) The hands pull back to the chest, i.e., Double Embracing Fist, while executing a right Flicking Leg.

3. Lifting Palm-Flicking Leg

4.

A: **Three Battle Stance, Spread Arm**
B: **Three Battle Stance, Hook Strike**

A) Intercept the strike with Spread Arm.
B) Step down and forward into Three Battle Stance while executing a Hook Strike.

4. Spread Arm-Hook Strike

Three Battle Partner Drill

5.

A: **Three Battle Stance, Asking, Guarding Hand**

B: **Three Battle Stance, Tray Elbow**

A) Intercept the incoming elbow strike with Asking, Guarding Hand.

B) Execute a Tray Elbow toward Exponent **A**'s face.

5. Asking, Guarding Hand-Tray Elbow

6.

A: **Three Battle Stance, Inward Arm**

B: **Three Battle Stance, Whipping Arm**

A) Intercept the incoming strike with Inward Arm.

B) Execute a Whipping Arm toward Exponent **A**'s neck.

6. Inward Arm-Whipping Arm

7.

A: **Three Battle Stance, Chopping Arm**

B: **Three Battle Stance, Thousand Character Arm**

A) Intercept the incoming strike with Chopping Arm.

B) Execute a Thousand Character Arm toward Exponent **A**'s kidneys.

7. Chopping Arm-Thousand Character Hand

8.

A: **Three Battle Stance, Straight Strike**
B: **Three Battle Stance, Inward Arm**

A) Execute a Straight Strike toward Exponent **B**'s Face.
B) Intercept the incoming strike with Inward Arm.

8. Straight Strike-Inward Arm

9.

A: **Three Battle Stance, Inward Arm**
B: **Three Battle Stance, Whipping Arm**

A) Intercept the incoming strike with Inward Arm.
B) Execute a Whipping Arm toward Exponent **A**'s neck.

9. Inward Arm-Whipping Arm

Empty Stance, Holding Shield

Step back to create a right Empty Stance while executing Holding Shield.

Empty Stance, Holding Shield

Four Level Stance, Embracing Fist

Right leg steps back, forming a Four Level Stance, while executing Embracing Fist.

Four Level Stance, Embracing Fist

Side-by-Side Stance, Embracing Fist

Straighten the legs while the left leg slides against the right, referred to as Side-By-Side Stance; exhale.

Side-by-Side Stance, Embracing Fist

Side-by-Side Stance, Both Side Fist

Lower the fists to the sides of the body.

Side-by-Side Stance, Both Side Fist

CHAPTER 14

THREE BATTLE WAY TECHNIQUES

The Sam Chien solo routine introduces the outline for the core techniques, or methods, within Five Ancestor Fist. The Partner Drilling routine introduces the techniques in a structured format to familiarize practitioners with the notions of intent, timing, and technique. Then practitioners are able to extract those techniques and expand upon them in a conceptual way.

Therefore, Sam Chien introduces practitioners to the primary techniques, which make up Five Ancestor Fist's fighting syllabus. For example, the practitioner is introduced to the straight strike, which is the number-one striking method employed throughout the whole system. Then practitioners are introduced to the various intercepts and blocks that are crucial when engaging in close-range fighting. This leads to the introduction of the art of Seizing, with its various grasping methods, and Elbow Presses.

1. Double Flank Defense

Double Flank Defense

1. The author is executing a Double Flank Defense, or Palms.
2. The opponent hurls a Horizontal Swinging Leg, which the author intercepts with the Double Flank Defense.

2. Double Flank Defense

Double Covering Palm

1. The author executes a Double Covering Palm.
2. The opponent executes a Flicking Leg, which the author intercepts with a Double Covering Palm.

1. Double Covering Palm

2. Double Covering Palm

Double Seizing Hand to Double Embracing Fist

1. The author demonstrates the Double Seizing Hand posture.
2. The author demonstrates Double Embracing Fist.
3. Double Seizing Hand was designed to counter against two arms toward coming toward you, be it grab or choke. The objective is to intercept with the dorsal side of the forearm, while the hands execute a Double Crane Wing Hand, allowing you to grasp the opponent's arms.

1. Double Seizing Hand to Double Embracing Fist

2. Double Seizing Hand to Double Embracing Fist

3. Double Seizing Hand to Double Embracing Fist

4. Double Seizing Hand to Double Embracing Fist

However, you quickly start to shift the hands to actually grasp the opponent's elbows and squeeze the elbow joint. Your elbows are tucked against your body while pinning the opponent's hands against your ribcage. This particular movement can hyperextended the opponent's elbow, which can lead to a break.

Double Spreading Arm to Double Piercing Palm

1. The opponent grasps the author's shoulder. The author leans back.
2. The author then executes a Double Spreading Arm to force the opponent's grasp off.
3. The author counters with Double Piercing Palm in the armpit or throat.

1. Double Spreading Arm to Double Piercing Palm

2. Double Spreading Arm to Double Piercing Palm

3. Double Spreading Arm to Double Piercing Palm

4. Double Spreading Arm to Double Piercing Palm

Double Spreading Arm to Double Joining Hands

1. The opponent grasps the author's wrists.
2. The author executes a Double Spreading Arm to twist out of the grasp.
3. The author now rotates the wrist in the process executing a Double Capturing Till Eyebrow Hand.
4. The author executes the Double Joining Hands.

1. Double Spreading Arm to Double Joining Hand

2. Double Spreading Arm to Double Joining Hand

3. Double Spreading Arm to Double Joining Hand

4. Double Spreading Arm to Double Joining Hand

Double Break

1. The opponent's grasp the author's shoulder.
2. The author extends both his arm forward; attempting to cross them, which allows him to lock his opponent's arm.
3. At which point the author starts to twist into Single Butterfly Stance, while adding pressure to the opponent's elbow.
4. Finally the author shifts his lead hand in the process forming a Covering Palm, which continues to add pressure to the opponent's elbow.

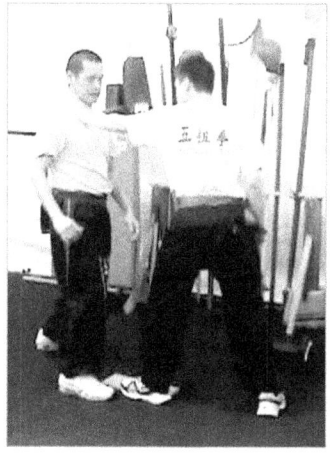

1. Double Break

2. Double Break

3. Double Break

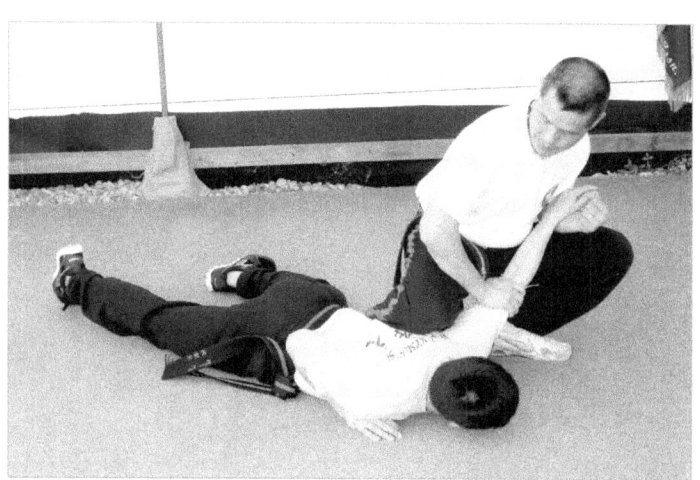

4. Double Break

Three Battle Way Techniques

Double Hand Protecting the Gate

1. The author illustrates the Double Low Guard in Empty Stance.
2. The opponent grasps the author's shoulder, which the author quickly response by twisting in his arms, while executing an Empty Stance, which grants him leverage. This is the first stage of executing Low Guard Palms.
3. The author concludes with a Flicking Leg.

1. Double Hand Protecting the Gate

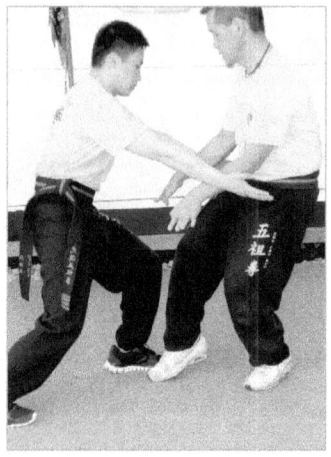

2. Double Hand Protecting the Gate

3. Double Hand Protecting the Gate

Spreading Arm, Tray Elbow, to Whipping Arm

1. The author demonstrating Spread Arm.
2. The author demonstrating Tray Elbow.
3. The author executing a Whipping Arm
4. The author executes Spread Arm, which intercepts the opponent's Level Strike.
5. The author quickly responds with a Tray Elbow to the opponent's sternum area.
6. To finalize it the author strikes the opponent's neck with a Whipping Arm.

1. Spreading Arm, Tray Elbow, to Whipping Arm

2. Spreading Arm, Tray Elbow, to Whipping Arm

3. Spreading Arm, Tray Elbow, to Whipping Arm

4. Spreading Arm, Tray Elbow, to Whipping Arm

5. Spreading Arm, Tray Elbow, to Whipping Arm

6. Spreading Arm, Tray Elbow, to Whipping Arm

Slicing Palm

1. The author demonstrating Slicing Palm.
2. The author executes a Slicing Palm to the opponent's kidney or rib cage.

1. Slicing Palm

2. Slicing Palm

Inward Arm to Whipping Arm

1. The author demonstrating Inward Arm.
2. The author executing a Whipping Arm
3. The opponent executes a Level Strike, which the author intercepts with Inward Arm. [
4. The author has secured the opponent's wrist with Seizing Hand, while executing Whipping Arm.

1. Inward Arm to Whipping Arm

2. Inward Arm to Whipping Arm

3. Inward Arm to Whipping Arm

4. Inward Arm to Whipping Arm

Chopping Hand

1. The opponent's grasp the author's wrist.
2. The author executes a Chopping Hand to the opponent's wrist.

1. Inward Arm to Whipping Arm

2. Inward Arm to Whipping Arm

3. Inward Arm to Whipping Arm

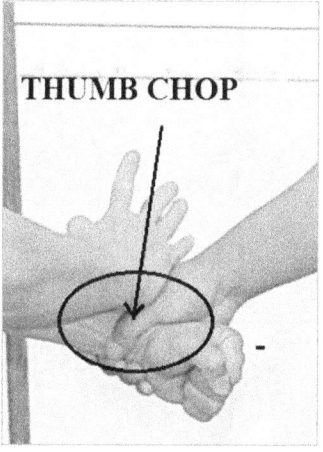

4. Inward Arm to Whipping Arm

Three Battle Way Techniques

CHAPTER 15

TWENTY PUNCHES
DI SIP KUN (二十拳)

Di Sip Kun, or Twenty Punches, was designed for practitioners to master the core strikes and blocks-intercepts found throughout the Five Ancestor Fist system, expanding beyond the rudiment of Three Battle Way, where the methods were executed while stationary. However, now the practitioner needs to coordinate the strikes and intercepts while utilizing footwork. In the process, the practitioner begins to develop a sense of timing, focus, and the generation of power.

The first thing that a practitioner will notice is that Twenty Fist is performed in a cross pattern, which corresponds to the compass points of north, south, east, and west. This particular pattern is referred to as the Ten Character Pattern. The Chinese logograms for the number ten is a cross, hence its name.

This is the first major footwork pattern taught to practitioners because it introduces them to notions of angles, or corners, which is a strategy that can be used against multiple attackers. Therefore, Twenty Fist focuses on mobility and the execution of effective and explosive strikes, or blocks, that can drop an attacker immediately with minimum effort. This effectiveness is crucial in surviving when attacked by multiple attackers, especially if they are coming from different angles. By using this tactic, the number of attackers will be reduced quickly.

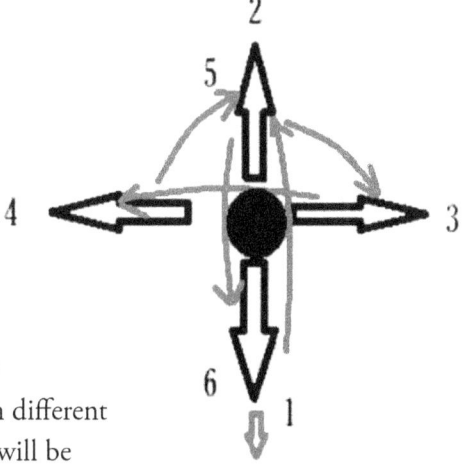

Ten Character Pattern

STRAIGHT STRIKE

The execution of the Straight Strike is based on the development of the explosiveness of Huat Ging, which combines speed and focus. The use of the "Five Powers" comes into play, which consist of the legs rooting, the hips torqueing, the shoulders cocking, and the arms and hands issuing the energy. This physical action is enhanced by Dan Dian breathing, and all of these together produce a sound and effective technique.

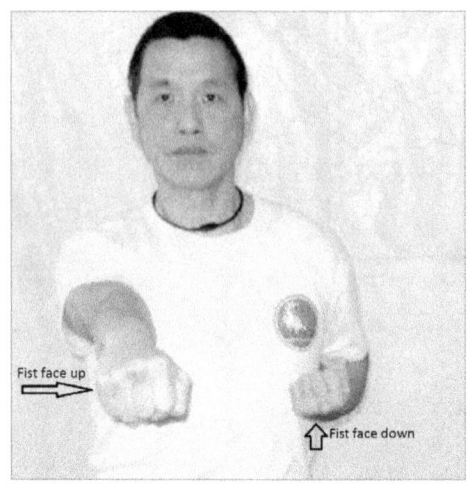

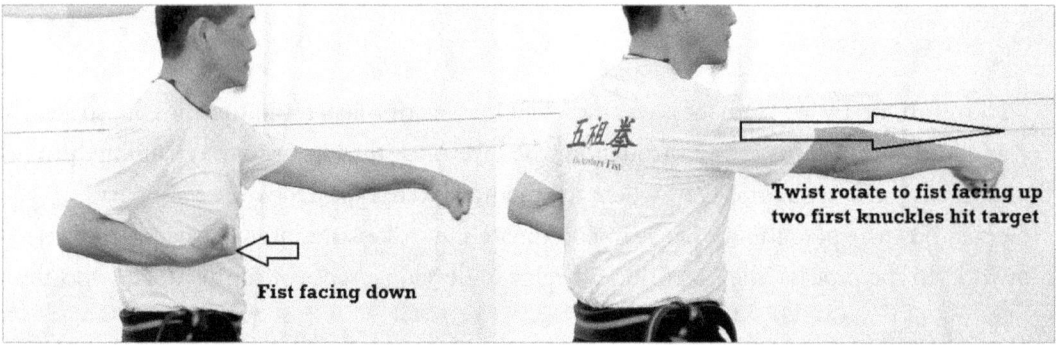

The Straight Strike travels in a spiral motion, similar to a bullet going down the barrel of a gun. Therefore, practitioners should focus on the first two knuckles, which are the intended striking area. In the beginning the strikes originate below the pectoral muscles, while the back of the fist is facing down and the Fist Heart is facing up. Then the arm starts to extend, while the clenched hand starts to turn, i.e., Fist Heart facing down.

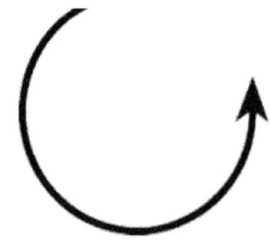

Straight Strike Spiral

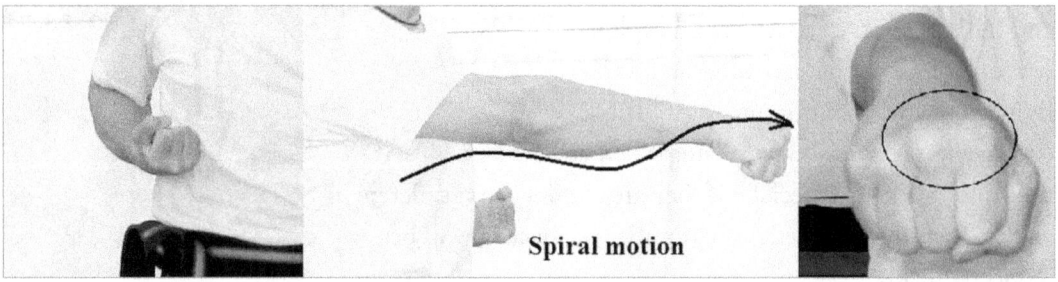

Straight Strike-Two Knuckles

In releasing the strike, the opposite arm pulls back into Embracing Fist to create a counterbalance effect, which increases the striking arm's power and speed. But make certain the stance is rooted and that the eyes are focused upon the target and not the opponent's eyes. The intended target is the sternum or the heart.

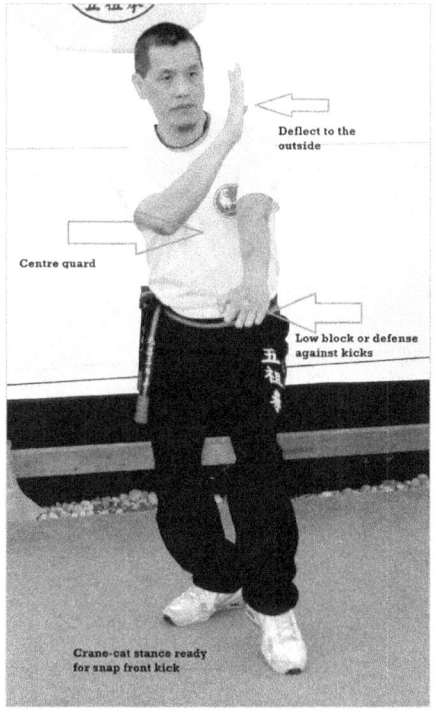

Straight Strike-Embracing Fist

The strike is also amplified by the torque of the hip and cocking of the shoulder, as mentioned previously. Also, keeping the arm firm and fingers clenched tight is the secret in developing explosive, penetrating strikes.

As mentioned before, the straight strike targets the sternum or heart area. The torso is a large target and by aiming at the heart, the results can be damaging.

CONDITIONING

For the Straight Strike to be effective beyond practicing the patterns, practitioners need to condition the fist itself. This is done by striking a solid object with the fist and becoming familiar with the sensations and alignments needed for the strike.

Conditioning the Fist

Twenty Punches Di Sip Kun (二十拳)   141

The solid object assists in conditioning the knuckles and securing the alignment of the wrist, elbow, and shoulder. However, it requires careful supervision and the use of Chinese liniment, better known by its Cantonese pronunciation as Dit Da Jáu, i.e., Diat Da Ziu in Mǐnnányǔ. It is essential in stimulating blood circulation, and reducing pain and swelling. This is a crucial element in the training of Iron Body or, in this case, Iron Fist.

Key Note: Use Dit Da Jáu prior to and after training; however, do not immediately wash your hands, especially in cold water, for at least forty-five minutes, as it can possibly cause nerve damage.

SEIZING

The skill of seizing consists of two principles: One is to intercept and then grasp, i.e., seize. The second takes into account that the forearm is meant to intercept if needed, by striking the opponent's arm.

Seizing

Our natural instinct when attacked is to use our arms to protect ourselves, either by covering up or whaling away. Therefore, training in Five Ancestor Fist allows practitioners to develop proper intercepting and blocking techniques without wasting energy. This grants them better success in defending themselves.

Inward Arm is derived from the same source as Straight Strike, which is the Five Powers. Making it powerful, especially when Issuing Energy, is based on Dan Dian breathing, which assists in extracting energy from the ground that is torqued in the hips, then cocked into the shoulder, and finally issued through the arms.

Like the Straight Strike, the practitioner needs to partake in Iron Arm training. This can consist of a two-person drill, which is referred to as "Striking Three Star," or Three Star Blocking. The objective is to condition the dorsal side of the forearm by striking one another. Practitioners can train by themselves as well, using an apparatus; for example, hitting a solid object, i.e., pillar or pole.

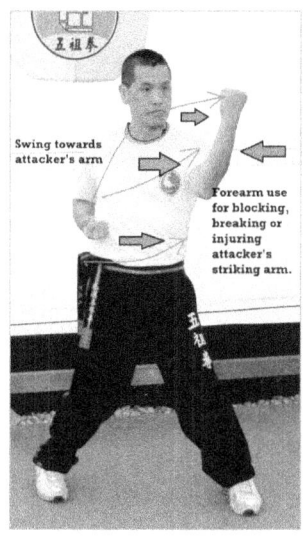

Inward Arm

Striking Three Star

Striking Three Star on a Pole

Twenty Punches Di Sip Kun (二十拳)

DI SIP KUN FORM
SECTION ONE:

1. **Side-by-Side Stance, Both Side Fist**
   Stand at attention, breathing normally.

2. **Lifting Knee, Embracing, Detain Fist**
   Inhale and lift the left leg up, with the knee slightly level with the waist. Pull with both hands, clenching them into fists, moving toward the right side of the chest. (The Eclipse)

3. **Four Level Stance, Double Flanking Defense**
   While exhaling, place the left leg parallel to the right leg and form Four Level Stance. The legs should be as wide as or slightly wider than the shoulders. Simultaneously push both hands toward the left hip area; open palm, i.e., Double Flank Defense.

1. Side-by-Side Stance, Both Side Fist

2. Lifting Knee, Embracing, Detain Fist

3. Four Level Stance, Double Flanking Defense

4. **Four Level Stance, Double Planting Fist**
   Inhale as the two palms start to clench tightly into fists, i.e., Double Planting Fist.

5. **Four Level Stance, Embracing, Detain Fist**
   Maintaining Four Level Stance, inhale and exhale while pulling the two fists toward the right side of the chest area.

4. Four Level Stance, Double Planting Fist

5. Four Level Stance, Embracing, Detain Fist

6. **Four Level Stance, Double Covering Palm**
   Exhale and throw the two fists out into the center into Double Covering Palm.

7. **Four Level Stance, Ten Character Arm**
   Inhale and exhale while lifting the arms to execute a Ten Character Arm.

6. Four Level Stance, Double Covering Pal

7. Four Level Stance, Ten Character Arm

Twenty Punches Di Sip Kun (二十拳)

8. **Four Level Stance, Double Spread Arm**
   Spread the arms open; this is also referred to as Double Opening Arm.

9. **Four Level Stance, Double Capturing Till Eyebrow Hand**
   Spread the arms, in the process executing Double Capturing Till Eyebrow Hand.

10. **Four Level Stance, Double Seizing Hand**
    Double Capturing Till Eyebrow Hand transformed into Double Seizing Hand.

11. **Four Level Stance, Double Embracing Fist**
    While inhaling, pull the Double Seizing fist and rotate into Double Embracing Fist, which arrives at both sides of the body, and slightly expand the chest while breathing.

8. Four Level Stance, Double Spread Arm

9. Four Level Stance, Double Capturing Till Eyebrow Hand

10. Four Level Stance, Double Seizing Hand

11. Four Level Stance, Double Embracing Fist

12. **Four Level Stance, Giving Respect Fist**
    Slowly exhale while sliding both hands slowly from the upper chest to the hip area, keeping the right hand clenched and the left hand open. Then place the right fist in the left palm, i.e., Giving Respect Fist. Continue to exhale while bringing the hands up to chin level.

13. **Four Level Stance, Double Spread Arm**
    Inhale and then exhale while parting the hands, in the process executing a Double Spread Arm. The tips of the fingers are level with the eyebrows. (Opening the Gates of Palace or Heaven)

12a. Four Level Stance, Giving Respect Fist

12b. Four Level Stance, Giving Respect Fist

13. Four Level Stance, Giving Respect Fist

14. Four Level Stance, Double Spread Arm

14. **Four Level Stance, Double Joining Hands**
    Inhale and exhale while pressing down with both arms, slightly turning the forearms to execute Double Joining Hands. The elbows are tucked, protecting the rib area, while tensing the arms and sinking the Dan Dian. (Announcing the Emperor)

Twenty Punches Di Sip Kun (二十拳)

SECTION TWO:

1. **Three Battle Stance, Bridging Arm**
   Lift the left leg to step forward, in the process forming a Three Battle Stance, while executing a right Bridging Arm.

2. **Three Battle Stance, Bridging Arm**
   Lift the right leg to step forward, in the process forming a Three Battle Stance, while executing a left Bridging Arm.

3. **Three Battle Stance, Straight Strike**
   While maintaining the stance, execute a right Straight Strike.

4. **Three Battle Stance, Straight Strike**
   Execute a left Straight Strike.

1. Three Battle Stance, Bridging Arm

2. Three Battle Stance, Bridging Arm

3. Three Battle Stance, Straight Strike

4. Three Battle Stance, Straight Strike

5. **Three Battle Stance, Straight Strike**
   Execute a right Straight Strike.

6. **Three Battle Stance, Hammer Back Strike**
   Lift the left leg to step forward, in the process forming a Three Battle Stance, while executing a right Hammer Back Strike.

7. **Empty Stance, Holding Shield Hands**
   Slowly turn back, i.e., south, while shifting the body weight to the right leg, which allows the formation of a left Empty Stance, and at the same time execute a Holding Shield Hands.

5. Three Battle Stance, Straight Strike

6. Three Battle Stance, Hammer Back Strike

7a. Empty Stance, Holding Shield Hands

7b. Empty Stance, Holding Shield Hands

Twenty Punches Di Sip Kun (二十拳)

SECTION THREE:

1. **Three Battle Stance, Inward Arm**
   Step forward with the left leg, in the process forming a Three Battle Stance, while executing a left Inward Arm.

2. **Three Battle Stance, Straight Strike**
   While maintaining the stance, execute a right Straight Strike.

3. **Three Battle Stance, Straight Strike**
   Execute a left Straight Strike.

4. **Three Battle Stance, Straight Strike**
   Execute a right Straight Strike.

1. Three Battle Stance, Inward Arm

2. Three Battle Stance, Straight Strike

3. Three Battle Stance, Straight Strike

4. Three Battle Stance, Straight Strike

5. **Three Battle Stance, Hammer Back Strike**

   Execute a right Hammer Back Strike.

6. **Empty Stance, Holding Shield Hand**

   Slowly turn toward the right side, i.e., west, while shifting the body weight to the left leg, which allows the formation of a right Empty Stance, and at the same time execute a Holding Shield Hand.

5. Three Battle Stance, Hammer Back Strike

6a. Empty Stance, Holding Shield Hand

6b. Empty Stance, Holding Shield Hand

SECTION FOUR:

1. **Three Battle Stance, Inward Arm**
   Step forward with the right leg, in the process forming a Three Battle Stance, while executing a right Inward Arm.

2. **Three Battle Stance, Straight Strike**
   While maintaining the stance, execute a left Straight Strike.

3. **Three Battle Stance, Straight Strike**
   Execute a right Straight Strike.

4. **Three Battle Stance, Straight Strike**
   Execute a left Straight Strike.

1. Three Battle Stance, Inward Arm

2. Three Battle Stance, Straight Strike

3. Three Battle Stance, Straight Strike

4. Three Battle Stance, Straight Strike

5. **Three Battle Stance, Hammer Back Strike**
   Execute a left Hammer Back Strike.

6. **Empty Stance, Holding Shield Hand**
   Slowly turn toward the left side, i.e., east, while shifting the body weight to the right leg, which allows the formation of a left Empty Stance, and at the same time execute a Holding Shield Hand.

5. Three Battle Stance, Hammer Back Strike

6a. Empty Stance, Holding Shield Hand

6b. Empty Stance, Holding Shield Hand

SECTION FIVE:

1. **Three Battle Stance, Inward Arm**
   Step forward with the left leg, in the process forming a Three Battle Stance, while executing a left Inward Arm.

2. **Three Battle Stance, Straight Strike**
   While maintaining the stance, execute a right Straight Strike.

3. **Three Battle Stance, Straight Strike**
   Now execute a left Straight Strike.

4. **Three Battle Stance, Straight Strike**
   Execute a right Straight Strike.

1. Three Battle Stance, Inward Arm

2. Three Battle Stance, Straight Strike

3. Three Battle Stance, Straight Strike

4. Three Battle Stance, Straight Strike

5. **Three Battle Stance, Hammer Back Strike**
   Execute a Hammer Back Strike.

6. **Empty Stance, Holding Shield Hand**
   Slowly turn toward the right side, i.e., south, while shifting the body weight to the left leg, which allows the formation of a right Empty Stance, and at the same time execute a Holding Shield Hand.

5. Three Battle Stance, Hammer Back Strike

6a. Empty Stance, Holding Shield Hand

6b. Empty Stance, Holding Shield Hand

Twenty Punches Di Sip Kun (二十拳)

SECTION SIX:

1. **Three Battle Stance, Inward Strike**
   Step forward with the right leg, in the process forming a Three Battle Stance, while executing a right Inward Arm.

2. **Three Battle Stance, Straight Strike**
   While maintaining the stance, execute a left Straight Strike.

3. **Three Battle Stance, Straight Strike**
   Execute a right Straight Strike.

4. **Three Battle Stance, Straight Strike**
   Execute a left Straight Strike.

1. Three Battle Stance, Inward Arm

2. Three Battle Stance, Straight Strike

3. Three Battle Stance, Straight Strike

4. Three Battle Stance, Straight Strike

5. **Three Battle Stance, Hammer Back Strike**
   Execute a left Hammer Back Strike.

6. **Empty Stance, Holding Shield Hand**
   Slowly turn toward the right side, i.e., north, while shifting the body weight to the right leg, which allows the formation of a left Empty Stance, and at the same time execute a Holding Shield Hand.

5. Three Battle Stance, Hammer Back Strike

6a. Empty Stance, Holding Shield Hand

6b. Empty Stance, Holding Shield Hand

SECTION SEVEN:

1. **Three Battle Stance, Inward Arm**
   Step forward with the left leg, in the process forming a Three Battle Stance, while executing a left Inward Arm. [Photo: 15.68]

2. **Three Battle Stance, Straight Strike**
   While maintaining the stance, execute a right Straight Strike. [Photo: 15.69]

3. **Three Battle Stance, Straight Strike**
   Execute a left Straight Strike. [Photo: 15.70]

4. **Three Battle Stance, Straight Strike**
   Execute a right Straight Strike. [Photo: 15.71]

1. Three Battle Stance, Inward Arm

2. Three Battle Stance, Straight Strike

3. Three Battle Stance, Straight Strike

4. Three Battle Stance, Straight Strike

5. **Three Battle Stance, Hammer Back Strike**
   Execute a right Hammer Back Strike.

6. **Empty Stance, Holding Shield Hand**
   Shift the body weight to the left leg, which allows the formation of a right Empty Stance, and at the same time execute a Holding Shield Hand.

5. Three Battle Stance, Hammer Back Strike

6. Empty Stance, Holding Shield Hand

7. **Three Battle Stance, Seizing Hand**
   The right leg steps forward to form Three Battle Stance, while executing a right Seizing Hand.

8. **Three Battle Stance, Straight Strike**
   While maintaining the stance, execute a left Straight Strike.

7. Three Battle Stance, Seizing Hand

8. Three Battle Stance, Straight Strike

9. **Three Battle Stance, Straight Strike**
   Execute a right Straight Strike.

10. **Three Battle Stance, Hammer Back Strike**
    Execute a left Hammer Back Strike.

11. **Empty Stance, Hammer Back Strike**
    Shift the weight back to form a right Empty Stance.

9. Three Battle Stance, Straight Strike

10. Three Battle Stance, Hammer Back Strike

11. Empty Stance, Hammer Back Strike

12. **Empty Stance, Cutting-Off Bridge**
While in Empty Stance, execute Cutting-Off Bridge.

13. **Empty Stance, Double Hanging-Up Hand**
Now the hands convert to Double Hanging-Up Hand, also referred to as Asking, Guarding Hand.

12a. Empty Stance, Cutting-Off Bridge

12b. Empty Stance, Cutting-Off Bridge

12c. Empty Stance, Cutting-Off Bridge

13. Empty Stance, Double Hanging-Up Hand

14. **Four Level Stance, Ten Character Arm**

    Execute a Ten Character Arm, but with the hands clenched, while the right leg steps back to form a Four Level Stance.

15. **Four Level Stance, Double Embracing Fist**

    Slowly bring Double Embracing Fist to the pectoral muscles.

16. **Side-by-Side Stance, Double Embracing Fist**

    Straighten up the legs while the left leg slides against the right, which is referred as Side-By-Side Stance; exhale.

14a. Four Level Stance, Ten Character Arm

14b. Four Level Stance, Ten Character Arm

15. Four Level Stance, Double Embracing Fist

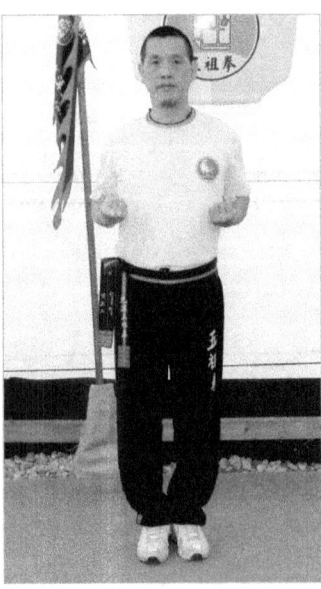

16. Side-by-Side Stance, Double Embracing Fist

17. **Side-by-Side Stance, Both Side Fist**
Lower the fists to the side of the body.

17. Side-by-Side Stance, Both Side Fist

CHAPTER 16

TWENTY PUNCHES PARTNER DRILL
DI SIP KUN DUI LIAN (二十對練)

Five Ancestor Fist is an ideal art because it encourages a step-by-step learning process compared to other disciplines. For example, each routine introduces a certain number of techniques for the practitioner to master and then gradually introduces more. However, the most remarkable learning processes that Five Ancestor Fist possesses are the Partner Drill for corresponding solo routines, which illustrates and enhances the practitioner's skill.

Twenty Fist Partner Drill continues where Three Battle Partner Drill left off. Again stressing primary techniques like Straight Strike, it introduces the use of quick strikes that are designed for close range fighting; for example, the Hammer Back Strike. It also continues to the Five Power theory, especially swallowing, as demonstrate by Holding Shield Hands.

*The author, i.e., Daniel Kun, is Exponent **A**; Abigail Kun is Exponent **B**.*

DI SIP KUN DUI LIAN

SECTION ONE:

1. **Side-by-Side Stance, Both Side Fist**

    Stand at attention, breathing normally.

2. **Lifting Knee, Embracing, Detain Fist**

    Inhale and lift the left leg up, the knee slightly level with the waist. Pull with both hands, clenching them into fists, moving toward the right side of the chest. (The Eclipse)

3. **Four Level Stance, Double Flank Defense**

    While exhaling, place the left leg parallel to the right leg and form Four Level Stance. The legs should be as wide as or slightly wider than the shoulders. Simultaneously push both hands toward the left hip area; open palm, i.e., Double Flank Defense.

1. Side-by-Side Stance, Both Side Fist

2. Lifting Knee, Embracing, Detain Fist

3. Four Level Stance, Double Flank Defense

4. **Four Level Stance, Double Planting Strike**

   Inhale as the two palms start to clench tightly into fists, i.e., Double Planting Fist.

5. **Four Level Stance, Embracing, Detain Fist**

   Maintaining Four Level Stance, inhale and exhale while pulling the two fists toward the right side of the chest area.

6. **Four Level Stance, Double Covering Palm**

   Exhale and throw the two fists out into the center into Double Covering Palm.

7. **Four Level Stance, Ten Character Arm**

   Inhale and exhale while lifting the arms to execute a Ten Character Arm.

4. Four Level Stance, Double Planting Strike

5. Four Level Stance, Embracing, Detain Fist

6. Four Level Stance, Double Covering Palm

7. Four Level Stance, Ten Character Arm

8. **Four Level Stance, Double Spread Arm**
   Inhale and then exhale while parting the hands, in the process executing a Double Spread Arm. The tips of the fingers are level with the eyebrows. (Opening the Gates of Palace or Heaven)

9. **Four Level Stance, Double Capturing Till Eyebrow Hand**
   Spread the arms, in the process executing Double Capturing Till Eyebrow.

10. **Four Level Stance, Double Seizing Hand**
    Double Capturing Till Eyebrow transformed into Double Seizing Hand.

11. **Four Level Stance, Double Embracing Fist**
    While inhaling, pull the Double Seizing fist and rotate into Double Embracing Fist, which arrives at both sides of the body and slightly expands the chest, while breathing.

8. Four Level Stance, Double Spread Arm

9. Four Level Stance, Double Capturing Till Eyebrow Hand

10. Four Level Stance, Double Seizing Hand

11. Four Level Stance, Double Embracing Fist

12. **Four Level Stance, Giving Respect Fist**

    Slowly exhale while sliding both hands slowly from the upper chest to the hip area, keeping the right hand clenched and the left hand open. Then place the right fist in the left palm, i.e., Giving Respect Fist. Continue to exhale while bringing the hands up to chin level.

13. **Four Level Stance, Double Spread Arm**

    Inhale and then exhale while parting the hands, in the process executing a Double Spread Arm. The tips of the fingers are level with the eyebrows. (Opening the Gates of Palace or Heaven)

14. **Four Level Stance, Double Joining Hands**

    Lower the arms, forming Double Joining Hands.

12a. Four Level Stance, Giving Respect Fist

12b. Four Level Stance, Giving Respect Fist

13. Four Level Stance, Double Spread Arm

14. Four Level Stance, Double Joining Hand

Twenty Punches Partner Drill Di Sip Kun Dui Lian (二十對練)

SECTION TWO:

1.
   A: **Three Battle Stance, Straight Strike**
   B: **Three Battle Stance, Patting Hand**
   A) Lift the left leg to step forward, in the process forming a Three Battle Stance, while executing a left Straight Strike.
   B) Lift the right leg and step back to form a Three Battle Stance, while intercepting the strike with a right Patting Hand.

1. Three Battle Stance, Straight Strike-Three Battle Stance, Patting Hand

2.
   A: **Three Battle Stance, Straight Strike**
   B: **Three Battle Stance, Patting Hand**
   A) Lift the right leg to step forward, in the process forming a Three Battle Stance, while executing a right Straight Strike.
   B) Lift the left leg and step back to form a Three Battle Stance, while intercepting the strike with a left Patting Hand.

2. Three Battle Stance, Straight Strike-Three Battle Stance, Patting Hand

3.
   A: **Three Battle Stance, Thousand Character Arm**
   B: **Three Battle Stance, Planting Strike**
   A) Intercept the incoming strike with a right Thousand Character Arm.
   B) Execute a right Planting Strike toward Exponent **A**'s rib cage.

3. Three Battle Stance, Thousand Character Arm-Three Battle Stance, Planting Strike

4.

A: **Three Battle Stance, Thousand Character Arm**
B: **Three Battle Stance, Planting Strike**

A) Intercept the incoming strike with a left Thousand Character Arm.
B) Execute a left Planting Strike toward Exponent **A**'s rib cage.

5.

A: **Three Battle Stance, Thousand Character Arm**
B: **Three Battle Stance, Planting Strike**

A) Intercept the incoming strike with a right Thousand Character Arm.
B) Execute a right Planting Strike toward Exponent **A**'s rib cage.

6.

A: **Three Battle Stance, Intercepting Strike**
B: **Three Battle Stance, Intercepting Strike**

A) Execute a right Intercepting Strike.
B) Execute a right Intercepting Strike.

4. Three Battle Stance, Thousand Character Arm-Three Battle Stance, Planting Strike

5. Three Battle Stance, Thousand Character Arm-Three Battle Stance, Planting Strike

6. Three Battle Stance, Intercepting Strike-Three Battle Stance, Intercepting Strike

Twenty Punches Partner Drill Di Sip Kun Dui Lian (二十對練)

7.

A: **Three Battle Stance, Hammer Back Strike**

B: **Three Battle Stance, Hammer Back Strike**

A) Intercepting strike converts into Hammer Back Strike, which is intended to press down Exponent **B**'s forearm.

B) Intercepting strike converts into Hammer Back Strike, which is intended to press down Exponent **A**'s forearm.

7. Three Battle Stance, Hammer Back Strike-Three Battle Stance, Hammer Back Strike

8.

A: **Horse Stance, Hammer Back Strike**

B: **Horse Stance, Hammer Back Strike**

A) At this point one's wrist is sticking to Exponent **B**'s wrist, while the right leg steps forward, i.e., giving one's back to the exponent.

B) At this point one's wrist is sticking to Exponent **A**'s wrist, while the right leg steps forward, i.e., giving one's back to the exponent.

8. Horse Stance, Hammer Back Strike-Horse Stance, Hammer Back Strike

SECTION THREE:

1.

A: **Empty Stance, Hammer Back Strike**

B: **Empty Stance, Hammer Back Strike**

A) Facing once more Exponent **B** in left Empty Stance, while still maintaining Hammer Back Strike posture.

B) Facing once more Exponent **A** in left Empty Stance, while still maintaining Hammer Back Strike posture.

1. Empty Stance, Hammer Back Strike-Empty Stance, Hammer Back Strike

2.

A: **Three Battle Stance, Arhat Double Hooking**
B: **Empty Stance, Holding Shield Hand**

A) Step forward into Three Battle Stance, while executing Arhat Double Hooking Strike.
B) Still maintaining the left Empty Stance, execute Holding Shield Hand to intercept the incoming strikes.

2. Three Battle Stance, Arhat Double Hooking-Empty Stance, Holding Shield Hand

3.

A: **Three Battle Stance, Straight Strike**
B: **Three Battle Stance, Inward Arm**

A) Execute a left Straight Strike toward Exponent **B**'s face.
B) Step forward to form a left Three Battle Stance, while intercepting the incoming strike with a left Inward Arm.

3. Three Battle Stance, Straight Strike-Three Battle Stance, Inward Arm

4.

A: **Three Battle Stance, Planting Strike**
B: **Three Battle Stance, Planting Strike**

A) Intercept the incoming strike with a right Planting Strike.
B) Execute a right Planting Strike toward Exponent **A**'s rib cage.

4. Three Battle Stance, Planting Strike-Three Battle Stance, Planting Strike

Twenty Punches Partner Drill Di Sip Kun Dui Lian (二十對練)

5.

   A: **Three Battle Stance, Planting Strike**

   B: **Three Battle Stance, Planting Strike**

   A) Intercept the incoming strike with a left Planting Strike.

   B) Execute a left Planting Strike toward Exponent **A**'s rib cage.

6.

   A: **Three Battle Stance, Planting Strike**

   B: **Three Battle Stance, Planting Strike**

   A) Intercept the incoming strike with a right Planting Strike.

   B) Execute a right Planting Strike toward Exponent **A**'s rib cage.

7.

   A: **Three Battle Stance, Intercepting Strike**

   B: **Three Battle Stance, Intercepting Strike**

   A) Execute a right Intercepting Strike.

   B) Execute a right Intercepting Strike.

5. Three Battle Stance, Planting Strike-Three Battle Stance, Planting Strike

6. Three Battle Stance, Planting Strike-Three Battle Stance, Planting Strike

7. Three Battle Stance, Intercepting Strike-Three Battle Stance, Intercepting Strike

8.

A: **Three Battle Stance, Hammer Back Strike**
B: **Three Battle Stance, Hammer Back Strike**

A) Intercepting strike converts into Hammer Back Strike, which is intended to press down Exponent **B**'s forearm.
B) Intercepting strike converts into Hammer Back Strike, which is intended to press down Exponent **A**'s forearm.

8. Three Battle Stance, Hammer Back Strike-Three Battle Stance, Hammer Back Strike

9.

A: **Three Battle Stance, Whipping Arm**
B: **Empty Stance, Holding Shield Hand**

A) Step forward with the left foot at a 90° angle to create a Three Battle Stance, while setting up a right Whipping Arm. Then execute a Whipping Arm toward Exponent **B**'s neck.
B) Moving body weight to the rear leg, i.e., left, form a right Empty Stance and move the waist in a 45° angle, while maintaining a Holding Shield Hand. Then execute a Holding Shield Hand to intercept the incoming strike.

9a. Three Battle Stance, Whipping Arm-Empty Stance, Holding Shield Hand

9b. Three Battle Stance, Whipping Arm-Empty Stance, Holding Shield Hand

SECTION FOUR:

1.

   A: Three Battle Stance, Straight Strike
   B: Three Battle Stance, Inward Arm
   A) Execute a left Straight Strike toward Exponent **B**'s face.
   B) Step forward to form a right Three Battle Stance, while intercepting the incoming strike with a left Inward Arm.

2.

   A: Three Battle Stance, Planting Strike
   B: Three Battle Stance, Planting Strike
   A) Intercept the incoming strike with a right Planting Strike.
   B) Execute a right Planting Strike toward Exponent **A**'s rib cage.

3.

   A: Three Battle Stance, Planting Strike
   B: Three Battle Stance, Planting Strike
   A) Intercept the incoming strike with a left Planting Strike.
   B) Execute a left Planting Strike toward Exponent **A**'s rib cage.

1. Three Battle Stance, Straight Strike-Three Battle Stance, Inward Arm

2. Three Battle Stance, Planting Strike-Three Battle Stance, Planting Strike

3. Three Battle Stance, Planting Strike-Three Battle Stance, Planting Strike

4.
   A: **Three Battle Stance, Planting Strike**
   B: **Three Battle Stance, Planting Strike**
   A) Intercept the incoming strike with a right Planting Strike.
   B) Execute a right Planting Strike toward Exponent **A**'s rib cage.

5.
   A: **Three Battle Stance, Intercepting Strike**
   B: **Three Battle Stance, Intercepting Strike**
   A) Execute a right Intercepting Strike.
   B) Execute a right Intercepting Strike.

6.
   A: **Three Battle Stance, Hammer Back Strike**
   B: **Three Battle Stance, Hammer Back Strike**
   A) Intercepting strike converts into Hammer Back Strike, which is intended to press down Exponent **B**'s forearm.
   B) Intercepting strike converts into Hammer Back Strike, which is intended to press down Exponent **A**'s forearm.

4. Three Battle Stance, Planting Strike-Three Battle Stance, Planting Strike

5. Three Battle Stance, Intercepting Strike-Three Battle Stance, Intercepting Strike

6. Three Battle Stance, Hammer Back Strike-Three Battle Stance, Hammer Back Strike

7.

A: **Horse Stance, Hammer Back Strike**
B: **Empty Stance, Hammer Back Strike**

A) At this point, one's wrist is sticking to Exponent **B**'s wrist, while the left leg steps forward, i.e., giving one's back to the exponent.
B) At this point, one's wrist is sticking to Exponent **A**'s wrist, while the left leg steps forward, i.e., giving one's back to the exponent.

SECTION FIVE:

1.

A: **Empty Strike, Hammer Back Strike**
B: **Empty Strike, Hammer Back Strike**

A) Face Exponent **B** in left Empty Stance, while still maintaining Hammer Back Strike posture.
B) Facing Exponent **A** in left Empty Stance, while still maintaining Hammer Back Strike posture.

2.

A: **Three Battle Stance, Arhat Double Hooking Strike**
B: **Empty Stance, Holding Shield Hand**

A) Step forward into Three Battle Stance, while executing Arhat Double Hooking Strike.
B) Still maintaining the left Empty Stance, execute Holding Shield Hand to intercept the incoming strikes.

7. Three Battle Stance, Hammer Back Strike-Empty Stance, Hammer Back Strike

1. Empty Stance, Hammer Back Strike-Empty Stance, Hammer Back Strike

2. Three Battle Stance, Arhat Double Hooking-Empty Stance, Holding Shield Hand

3.

A: **Three Battle Stance, Straight Strike**
B: **Three Battle Stance, Inward Arm**
A) Execute a left Straight Strike toward Exponent **B**'s face.
B) Step forward to form a left Three Battle Stance, while intercepting the incoming strike with a left Inward Arm.

4.

A: **Three Battle Stance, Planting Strike**
B: **Three Battle Stance, Planting Strike**
A) Intercept the incoming strike with a right Planting Strike.
B) Execute a right Planting Strike toward Exponent **A**'s rib cage.

5.

A: **Three Battle Stance, Planting Strike**
B: **Three Battle Stance, Planting Strike**
A) Intercept the incoming strike with a Left Planting Strike.
B) Execute a left Planting Strike toward Exponent **A**'s rib cage.

3. Three Battle Stance, Straight Strike-Three Battle Stance, Inward Arm

4. Three Battle Stance, Planting Strike-Three Battle Stance, Planting Strike

5. Three Battle Stance, Planting Strike-Three Battle Stance, Planting Strike

Twenty Punches Partner Drill Di Sip Kun Dui Lian (二十對練)

6.

A: **Three Battle Stance, Planting Strike**
B: **Three Battle Stance, Planting Strike**
A) Intercept the incoming strike with a right Planting Strike.
B) Execute a right Planting Strike toward Exponent **A**'s rib cage.

7.

A: **Three Battle Stance, Intercepting Strike**
B: **Three Battle Stance, Intercepting Strike**
A) Execute a right Intercepting Strike.
B) Execute a right Intercepting Strike.

8.

A: **Three Battle Stance, Hammer Back Strike**
B: **Three Battle Stance, Hammer Back Strike**
A) Intercepting strike converts into Hammer Back Strike, which is intended to press down Exponent **B**'s forearm.
B) Intercepting strike converts into Hammer Back Strike, which is intended to press down Exponent **A**'s forearm.

6. Three Battle Stance, Planting Strike-Three Battle Stance, Planting Strike

7. Three Battle Stance, Intercepting Strike-Three Battle Stance, Intercepting Strike

8. Three Battle Stance, Hammer Back Strike-Three Battle Stance, Hammer Back Strike

9.

A: **Three Battle Stance, Whipping Arm**

B: **Empty Stance, Holding Shield Hand**

A) Step forward with the right foot at a 90° angle to create a Three Battle Stance, while setting up a right Whipping Arm. Now execute a Whipping Arm toward Exponent **B**'s neck.

B) Moving body weight toward the rear leg, i.e., right, form a right Empty Stance and move the waist in a 45° angle, while maintaining a Hammer Back Strike posture. Now execute a Holding Shield Hand to intercept the incoming strike.

9a. Three Battle Stance, Whipping Arm-Empty Stance, Holding Shield Hand

9b. Three Battle Stance, Whipping Arm-Empty Stance, Holding Shield Hand

SECTION SIX:

1.
    A: **Three Battle Stance, Straight Strike**
    B: **Three Battle Stance, Inward Arm**
    A) Execute a left Straight Strike toward Exponent **B**'s face.
    B) Step forward to form a right Three Battle Stance, while intercepting the incoming strike with a left Inward Arm.

1. Three Battle Stance, Straight Strike-Three Battle Stance, Inward Arm

2.
    A: **Three Battle Stance, Planting Strike**
    B: **Three Battle Stance, Planting Strike**
    A) Intercept the incoming strike with a right Planting Strike.
    B) Execute a right Planting Strike toward Exponent **A**'s rib cage.

2. Three Battle Stance, Planting Strike-Three Battle Stance, Planting Strike

3.
    A: **Three Battle Stance, Planting Strike**
    B: **Three Battle Stance, Planting Strike**
    A) Intercept the incoming strike with a left Planting Strike.
    B) Execute a left Planting Strike toward Exponent **A**'s rib cage.

3. Three Battle Stance, Planting Strike-Three Battle Stance, Planting Strike

4.

A: **Three Battle Stance, Planting Strike**

B: **Three Battle Stance, Planting Strike**

A) Intercept the incoming strike with a right Planting Strike.
B) Execute a right Planting Strike toward Exponent **A**'s rib cage.

5.

A: **Three Battle Stance, Intercepting Strike**

B: **Three Battle Stance, Intercepting Strike**

A) Execute a right Intercepting Strike.
B) Execute a right Intercepting Strike.

6.

A: **Three Battle Stance, Hammer Back Strike**

B: **Three Battle Stance, Hammer Back Strike**

A) Intercepting strike converts into Hammer Back Strike, which is intended to press down Exponent **B**'s forearm.
B) Intercepting strike converts into Hammer Back Strike, which is intended to press down Exponent **A**'s forearm.

4. Three Battle Stance, Planting Strike-Three Battle Stance, Planting Strike

5. Three Battle Stance, Intercepting Strike-Three Battle Stance, Intercepting Strike

6. Three Battle Stance, Hammer Back Strike-Three Battle Stance, Hammer Back Strike

7.

A: **Horse Stance, Hammer Back Strike**
B: **Empty Stance, Hammer Back Strike**

A) At this point, one's wrist is sticking to Exponent **B**'s wrist, while the left leg steps forward, i.e., giving one's back to the exponent.

B) At this point, one's wrist is sticking to Exponent **A**'s wrist, while the left leg steps forward, i.e., giving one's back to the exponent.

7. Three Battle Stance, Hammer Back Strike-Empty Stance, Hammer Back Strike

8.

A: **Three Battle Stance, Arhat Double Hooking Strike**
B: **Empty Stance, Holding Shield Hand**

A) At this point, one's wrist is sticking to Exponent **B**'s wrist, while the right leg steps forward, i.e., giving one's back to the exponent. Now step forward into Three Battle Stance, while executing Arhat Double Hooking Strike.

B) At this point, one's wrist is sticking to Exponent **A**'s wrist, while the left leg steps forward, i.e., giving one's back to the exponent. Still maintaining the left Empty Stance, execute Holding Shield Hand to intercepting the incoming strikes.

8a. Three Battle Stance, Arhat Double Hooking-Empty Stance, Holding Shield Hand

8b. Three Battle Stance, Arhat Double Hooking-Empty Stance, Holding Shield Hand

SECTION SEVEN:

1.
   A: **Three Battle Stance, Straight Strike**
   B: **Three Battle Stance, Inward Arm**
   A) Execute a left Straight Strike toward Exponent **B**'s face.
   B) Step forward to form a left Three Battle Stance, while intercepting the incoming strike with a left Inward Arm.

1. Three Battle Stance, Straight Strike-Three Battle Stance, Inward Arm

2.
   A: **Three Battle Stance, Planting Strike**
   B: **Three Battle Stance, Planting Strike**
   A) Intercept the incoming strike with a right Planting Strike.
   B) Execute a right Planting Strike toward Exponent **A**'s rib cage.

2. Three Battle Stance, Planting Strike-Three Battle Stance, Planting Strike

3.
   A: **Three Battle Stance, Planting Strike**
   B: **Three Battle Stance, Planting Strike**
   A) Intercept the incoming strike with a Left Planting Strike.
   B) Execute a left Planting Strike toward Exponent **A**'s rib cage.

3. Three Battle Stance, Planting Strike-Three Battle Stance, Planting Strike

Twenty Punches Partner Drill Di Sip Kun Dui Lian (二十對練)

4.

A: **Three Battle Stance, Planting Strike**
B: **Three Battle Stance, Planting Strike**

A) Intercept the incoming strike with a right Planting Strike.
B) Execute a right Planting Strike toward Exponent **A**'s rib cage.

5.

A: **Three Battle Stance, Intercepting Strike**
B: **Three Battle Stance, Intercepting Strike**

A) Execute a right Intercepting Strike.
B) Execute a right Intercepting Strike.

6.

A: **Three Battle Stance, Hammer Back Strike**
B: **Three Battle Stance, Hammer Back Strike**

A) Intercepting strike converts into Hammer Back Strike, which is intended to press down Exponent **B**'s forearm.
B) Intercepting strike converts into Hammer Back Strike, which is intended to press down Exponent **A**'s forearm.

4. Three Battle Stance, Planting Strike-Three Battle Stance, Planting Strike

5. Three Battle Stance, Intercepting Strike-Three Battle Stance, Intercepting Strike

6. Three Battle Stance, Hammer Back Strike-Three Battle Stance, Hammer Back Strike

7.

A: **Three Battle Stance, Straight Strike**
B: **Empty Stance, Holding Shield Hand**

A) Execute a right Straight Strike toward Exponent **B**'s face.
B) Leaning back to form a right Empty Stance, execute Holding Shield Hand to intercepting the incoming strike.

8.

A: **Three Battle Stance, Straight Strike**
B: **Three Battle Stance, Seizing Hand**

A) Execute a left Straight Strike toward Exponent **B**'s face.
B) Intercept the incoming strike with a right Seizing Hand.

9.

A: **Three Battle Stance, Planting Strike**
B: **Three Battle Stance, Planting Strike**

A) Intercept the incoming strike with a Left Planting Strike.
B) Execute a left Planting Strike toward Exponent **A**'s rib cage.

7. Three Battle Stance, Straight Strike-Empty Stance, Holding Shield Hand

8. Three Battle Stance, Straight Strike-Three Battle Stance, Seizing Hand

9. Three Battle Stance, Planting Strike-Three Battle Stance, Planting Strike

Twenty Punches Partner Drill Di Sip Kun Dui Lian (二十對練)

10.

A: **Three Battle Stance, Planting Strike**

B: **Three Battle Stance, Planting Strike**

A) Intercept the incoming strike with a right Planting Strike.
B) Execute a right Planting Strike toward Exponent **A**'s rib cage.

11.

A: **Three Battle Stance, Intercepting Strike**

B: **Three Battle Stance, Intercepting Strike**

A) Execute a right Intercepting Strike.
B) Execute a right Intercepting Strike.

12.

A: **Three Battle Stance, Hammer Back Strike**

B: **Three Battle Stance, Hammer Back Strike**

A) Intercepting strike converts into Hammer Back Strike, which is intended to press down Exponent **B**'s forearm.
B) Intercepting strike converts into Hammer Back Strike, which is intended to press down Exponent **A**'s forearm.

10. Three Battle Stance, Planting Strike-Three Battle Stance, Planting Strike

11. Three Battle Stance, Intercepting Strike-Three Battle Stance, Intercepting Strike

12. Three Battle Stance, Hammer Back Strike-Three Battle Stance, Hammer Back Strike

13.

A: **Empty Stance, Hammer Back Strike**

B: **Empty Stance, Hammer Back Strike**

A) Lean back to form a right Empty Stance, while still maintaining Hammer Back Strike posture.

B) Lean back to form a right Empty Stance, while still maintaining Hammer Back Strike posture.

14. **Empty Stance, Cutting-Off Bridge**
    While in Empty Stance, execute Cutting-Off Bridge.

13. Empty Stance, Hammer Back Strike-Empty Stance, Hammer Back Strike

14a. Empty Stance, Cutting-Off Bridge

14b. Empty Stance, Cutting-Off Bridge

Twenty Punches Partner Drill Di Sip Kun Dui Lian (二十對練)

15. **Empty Stance, Double Hanging-Up Hand**

   The hands convert to Double Hanging-Up Hand.

16. **Four Level Stance, Double Hanging-Up Hand**

   The right leg steps out to form a Four Level Stance, while maintaining the Double Hanging-Up Hand.

17. **Four Level Stance, Ten Character Arm**

   Execute a Ten Character Arm while the right leg steps back to form a Four Level Stance.

15. Empty Stance, Double Hanging-Up Hand

16. Four Level Stance, Double Hanging-Up Hand

17. Four Level Stance, Ten Character Arm

18. **Four Level Stance, Double Embracing Fist**
   Slowly bring Double Embracing Fist to one's pectoral muscles.

19. **Side-by-Side Stance, Double Embracing Hand**
   Straighten up the legs while the left leg slides against the right, which is referred as Side-By-Side Stance; exhale.

20. **Side-by-Side Stance, Both Side Fist**
   Lower the fists to the side of the body.

18. Four Level Stance, Double Embracing Fist

19. Side-by-Side Stance, Double Embracing Hand

20. Side-by-Side Stance, Both Side Fist

CHAPTER 17

DI SIP KUN TECHNIQUES

Patting Hand to Straight Strike

Opponent executes a Straight Strike, while the author intercepts the strike with Patting Hand. The author executes a Straight Strike.

Patting Hand to Straight Strike

The opponent executes a strike; by intercepting it with Patting Hand, you are able to alter its course and be able to step out of way, allowing you to execute a Straight Strike. However, a practitioner should be aware that moving forward or sideways allows you to close the gap and deny your opponent the room to efficiently execute an offensive technique. It also keeps him off balance and on the defensive. This method is also referred to as "bridging and breaking down the gates."

Holding Shield Hand to Straight Strike

Deflect and parry the attacker's Straight Strike and at the same time step forward and follow through with a Straight Strike.

Holding Shield Hand to Straight Strike

Holding Shield Hand to Straight Strike

Detain Hand-Slicing Palm

Intercept with Detain Hand, while executing a Slicing Palm strike to the kidney.

Seizing Hand to Straight Strike

Intercept a strike with Seizing Hand and then execute a Straight Strike.

Detain Hand-Slicing Palm

Seizing Hand to Straight Strike

Seizing Hand to Straight Strike

Inward Arm to Straight Strike

The Inward Arm intercepts and blocks by using the outer dorsal side of the forearm to intercept; however, it possesses the ability to damage and possibly break an attacker's striking arm, especially a Hook Strike. That is one of the reasons why Five Ancestor Boxing practitioners condition the forearms. After intercepting, follow through with three Straight Strikes aimed toward the sternum or heart.

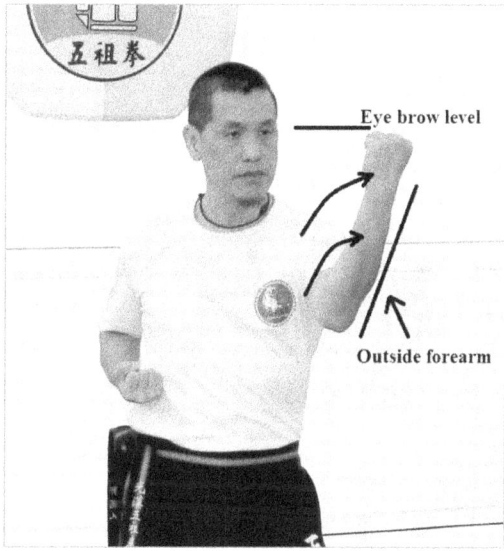

Hammer Back Strike to Straight Strike

As the name implies, Hammer Back Strike is a downward pattern strike. However, it possesses secondary uses; for instance, the actual motion enables the ability to escape from a wrist grab, which may prevent you from striking an opponent, or your arm being manipulated, e.g., twisted, struck, etc. Therefore, the objective is to torque the arm in an outwardly, i.e., half-clockwise, twist to break the grasp.

Four Corners

The purpose of the four corners movement is to condition yourself to be aware of your surroundings and defend yourself against multiple attackers. The ability to drop attackers with one or two well-focused strikes is the key to survival.

Four corners concept is design against multiple attackers

The forearm blocking and punch must be explosive, accurate and powerful

Body, mind and spirit must be decisive and one

CHAPTER 18

FOUR GATE STRIKING CORNER FIST
SI MUN DA KAK LO (四門打角)

Four Gate Striking Corner is an entry form to the dynamic fighting principles of Five Ancestor Fist and introduces the practitioner to more intricate techniques compared to the two prior routines, i.e., Three Battle and Twenty Fist. These techniques consist of combinations that synchronize the hands, feet, and eyes, and originate from Arhat Boxing. They also enhance the notion of the four angles as introduced in Twenty Fist by using Monkey Boxing's elements, such as jumping.

Just like Twenty Punches, the Four Gate Striking Angle, or simply the Four Gates, utilizes the Five Power theory. However, it is taken to the next level by employing Piercing Palm, knee strikes, Resonating Strike, Hammer Back Strike, etc. These strikes are extracted from Grand Ancestor Fist, but also contain the whipping skill of White Crane Boxing and always at the center is Damo breathing principles, which enhance all the movements.

SI MUN DA KAK
SECTION ONE:

1. **Side-by-Side Stance, Both Side Fist**
   Stand at attention, breathing normally.

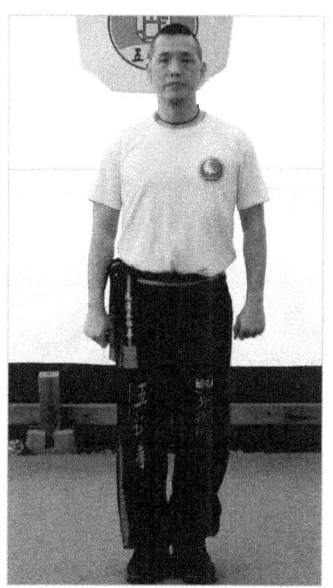

1. Side-by-Side Stance, Both Side Fist

2. Lifting Knee, Embracing, Detain Fist

3. Four Level Stance, Double Flanking Defense

2. **Lifting Knee, Embracing, Detain Fist**
   Inhale and lift the left leg up, the knee slightly level with the waist. Pull with both hands, clenching them into fists, moving toward the right side of the chest. (The Eclipse)

3. **Four Level Stance, Double Flanking Defense**
   While exhaling, place the left leg parallel to the right leg and form the Four Level Stance. The legs should be as wide as or slightly wider than the shoulders; simultaneously push both hands toward the left hip area, open palm, i.e., Double Flank Defense.

4. **Four Level Stance, Double Planting Fist**
   Inhale as the two palms start to clench tightly into fists, i.e., Double Planting Fist.

5. **Four Level Stance, Embracing, Detain Fist**
   Maintaining Four Level Stance, inhale and exhale while pulling the two fists toward the right side of the chest area.

6. **Four Level Stance, Double Covering Palm**
   Exhale and throw the two fists out into the center into Double Covering Palm.

4. Four Level Stance, Double Planting Fist

5. Four Level Stance, Embracing, Detain Fist

6. Four Level Stance, Double Covering Palm

7. **Four Level Stance, Ten Character Arm**
   Inhale and exhale while lifting the arms to execute a Ten Character Arm.

8. **Four Level Stance, Double Spread Arm**
   Inhale and then exhale while parting the hands, in the process executing a Double Spread Arm. The tips of the fingers are level with the eyebrows. (Opening the Gates of Palace or Heaven)

9. **Four Level Stance, Double Capturing Till Eyebrow Hand**
   Spread the arms, in the process executing Double Capturing Till Eyebrow Hand.

10. **Four Level Stance, Double Seizing Hand**
    Double Capturing Till Eyebrow transformed into Double Seizing Hand.

11. **Four Level Stance, Double Embracing Fist**
    While inhaling, pull the Double Seizing fist and rotate into Double Embracing Fist, which arrive at both sides of the body and slightly expand the chest, while breathing.

7. Four Level Stance, Ten Character Arm

8. Four Level Stance, Double Spread Arm

9. Four Level Stance, Double Capturing Till Eyebrow Hand

10. Four Level Stance, Double Seizing Hand

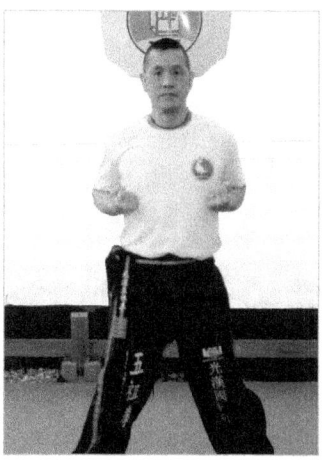

11. Four Level Stance, Double Embracing Fist

12a. Four Level Stance, Giving Respect Fist

12b. Four Level Stance, Giving Respect Fist

12. **Four Level Stance, Giving Respect Fist**
    Slowly exhale while sliding both hands slowly from the upper chest to hip area; keep the right hand clenched and the left hand open. Then place the right fist in the left palm, i.e., Giving Respect Fist. Continue to exhale, while bringing the hands up to chin level.

13. **Four Level Stance, Double Spread Arm**
    Inhale and then exhale while parting the hands, in the process executing a Double Spread Arm. The tips of the fingers are level with the eyebrows. (Opening the Gates of Palace or Heaven)

14. **Four Level Stance, Double Joining Hands**
    Inhale and then exhale while dropping the hands toward the Dan Dian in Double Joining Hands pattern.

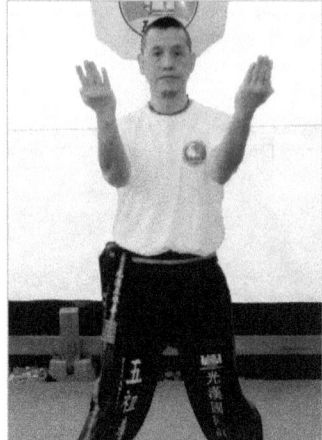

13. Four Level Stance, Double Spread Arm

14. Four Level Stance, Double Joining Hands

SECTION TWO:

1. **Three Battle Stance, Patting Hand**
   Lift the left leg to step forward, in the process forming a Three Battle Stance, while executing a right Patting Hand.

2. **Three Battle Stance, Patting Hand**
   Lift the right leg to step forward, in the process forming a Three Battle Stance, while executing a left Patting Hand.

3. **Three Battle Stance, Piercing Palm**
   While maintaining the stance, execute a right Piercing Palm.

4. **Three Battle Stance, Piercing Palm**
   Step the right leg back to form a Three Battle Stance, while maintaining the right Piercing Palm.

5. **Lifting Knee, Crushing Elbow**
   Simultaneously lift the left knee up while executing a Crushing Elbow.

1. Four Level Stance, Double Joining Hand

2. Three Battle Stance, Patting Hand

3. Three Battle Stance, Patting Hand

4. Three Battle Stance, Piercing Palm

5. Lifting Knee, Crushing Elbow

6. Three Battle Stance, Thousand Character Arm

7. Empty Stance, Holding Shield Hand

6. **Three Battle Stance, Thousand Character Arm**
   Drop the left foot forward, forming a Three Battle Stance, while executing a Thousand Character Arm.

7. **Empty Stance, Holding Shield Hand**
   Shift the weight toward the right leg, in the process forming a left Empty Stance, while executing Holding Shield Hand.

8. **Three Battle Stance, Seizing Hand**
   Step forward into a left Three Battle Stance while executing a left Seizing Hand.

9. **Three Battle Stance, Seizing Hand**
   While still maintaining Seizing Hand posture, step forward with a right Three Battle Stance.

10. **Three Battle Stance, Straight Strike**
    Execute a right Straight Strike.

11. **Three Battle Stance, Straight Strike**
    Execute a left Straight Strike.

12. **Three Battle Stance, Straight Strike**
    Execute a right Straight Strike.

13. **Three Battle Stance, Hammer Back Strike**
    Finally, execute a right Hammer Back Strike.

8. Three Battle Stance, Seizing Hand

9. Three Battle Stance, Seizing Hand

10. Three Battle Stance, Straight Strike

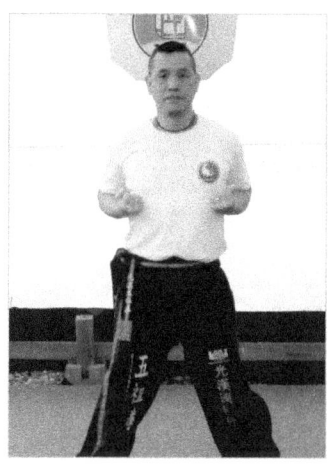

11. Three Battle Stance, Straight Strike

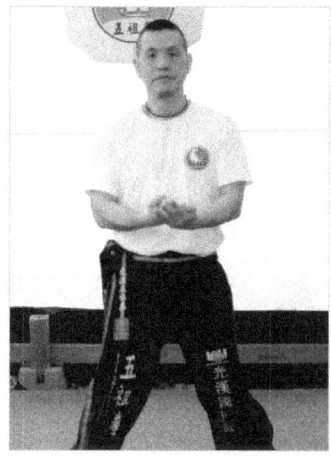

12. Three Battle Stance, Straight Strike

13. Three Battle Stance, Hammer Back Strike

SECTION THREE:

1. **Empty Stance, Holding Shield Hand**
   Turn the body toward the left, i.e., west, forming a left Empty Stance, while executing a Holding Shield Hand.

2. **Three Battle Stance, Seizing Hand**
   Step forward into a Three Battle Stance, while executing a left Seizing Hand.

1a. Empty Stance, Holding Shield Hand

1b. Empty Stance, Holding Shield Hand

2. Three Battle Stance, Seizing Hand

3. Three Battle Stance, Seizing Hand

3. **Three Battle Stance, Seizing Hand**
   Step forward with the right leg, forming a Three Battle Stance, while still maintaining Seizing Hand.

4. **Four Level Stance, Ascending Hook Strike, Seizing Hand**
   Turn the waist, i.e., torso facing south, and execute a right Ascending Hook Strike, while maintaining the Seizing Hand pattern.

5. **Single Butterfly Stance, Thousand Character Arm**
   Leap back, forming a left Single Butterfly Stance, while executing a left Thousand Character Arm.

4. Four Level Stance, Ascending Hook Strike, Seizing Hand

5a. Single Butterfly Stance, Thousand Character Arm

6. **Empty Stance, Holding Shield Hand**
   Rise up into a left Empty Stance while executing a Holding Shield Hand.

7. **Three Battle Stance, Seizing Hand**
   Step forward into a Three Battle Stance, while executing a left Seizing Hand.

5b. Single Butterfly Stance, Thousand Character Arm

6. Empty Stance, Holding Shield Hand

7. Three Battle Stance, Seizing Hand

8. **Three Battle Stance, Intercepting Strike**
   Step forward with the right leg, forming a Three Battle Stance, while maintaining Seizing Hand and executing an Intercepting Strike.

9. **Three Battle Stance, Hammer Back Strike**
   Execute a Hammer Back Strike.

10. **Three Battle Stance, Inside Hanging-Up**
    Execute a Holding Shield Hand; however, the lower hand, i.e., right, is clenched into a fist, which is referred to Inside Hanging-Up.

11. **Three Battle Stance, Resonating Strike**
    The right arm rises while executing a right Resonating Strike.

12. **Three Battle Stance, Slicing Palm**
    Finally, execute a left Slicing Palm.

8a. Three Battle Stance, Intercepting Strike

8b. Three Battle Stance, Intercepting Strike

9. Three Battle Stance, Hammer Back Strike

10. Three Battle Stance, Inside Hanging-Up

11. Three Battle Stance, Resonating Strike

12. Three Battle Stance, Slicing Palm

Four Gate Striking Corner Fist Si Mun Da Kak Lo (四門打角)

SECTION FOUR:

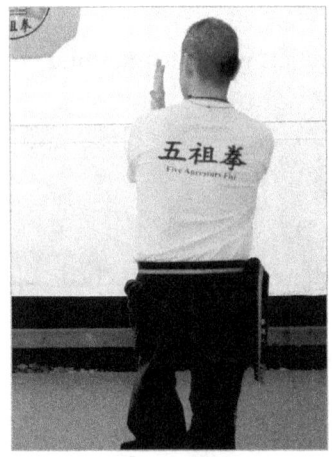

1. Empty Stance, Holding Shield Hand

2. Three Battle Stance, Seizing Hand

1. **Empty Stance, Holding Shield Hand**
   Turn the body toward the left, i.e., south, forming a left Empty Stance, while executing a Holding Shield Hand.

2. **Three Battle Stance, Seizing Hand**
   Step forward into a Three Battle Stance, while executing a left Seizing Hand.

3. **Three Battle Stance, Seizing Hand**
   Step forward with the right leg, forming a Three Battle Stance, while still maintaining Seizing Hand.

4. **Three Battle Stance, Straight Strike**
   Execute a right Straight Strike.

5. **Three Battle Stance, Straight Strike**
   Execute a left Straight Strike.

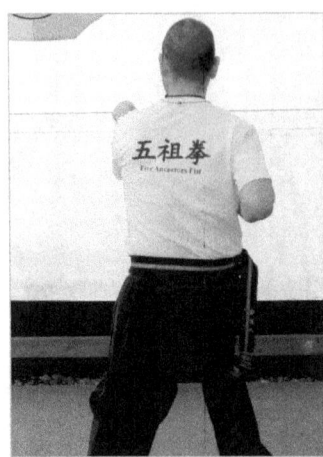

3. Three Battle Stance, Seizing Hand

4. Three Battle Stance, Straight Strike

5. Three Battle Stance, Straight Strike

6. **Three Battle Stance, Straight Strike**
   Execute a right Straight Strike.

7. **Three Battle Stance, Hammer Back Strike**
   While maintaining the Three Battle Stance, execute a Hammer Back Strike.

6. Three Battle Stance, Straight Strike

7. Three Battle Stance, Hammer Back Strike

SECTION FIVE:

1. **Empty Stance, Holding Shield Hand**
   Turn the body toward the left, i.e., east, forming a left Empty Stance, while executing a Holding Shield Hand.

2. **Three Battle Stance, Seizing Hand**
   Step forward into a Three Battle Stance while executing a left Seizing Hand.

3. **Three Battle Stance, Seizing Hand**
   Now step forward with the right leg, forming a Three Battle Stance, while still maintaining Seizing Hand.

1. Empty Stance, Holding Shield Hand

2. Three Battle Stance, Seizing Hand

3. Three Battle Stance, Seizing Hand

4. Four Level Stance, Ascending Hook Strike, Seizing Hand

4. **Four Level Stance, Ascending Hook Strike, Seizing Hand**
   Turn the waist, i.e., torso facing south, and execute a right Ascending Hook Strike, while maintaining the Seizing Hand pattern.

5. **Single Butterfly Stance, Thousand Character Arm**
   Leap back, forming a left Single Butterfly Stance, while executing a left Thousand Character Arm.

6. **Empty Stance, Holding Shield Hand**
   Rise up into a left Empty Stance while executing a Holding Shield Hand.

5a. Single Butterfly Stance, Thousand Character Arm

5b. Single Butterfly Stance, Thousand Character Arm

6. Empty Stance, Holding Shield Hand

7. **Three Battle Stance, Seizing Hand**
   Step forward into a Three Battle Stance while executing a left Seizing Hand.

8. **Three Battle Stance, Intercepting Strike**
   Step forward with the right leg, forming a Three Battle Stance, while maintaining Seizing Hand and executing Intercepting Strike. [Photos: 18.58-69]

9. **Three Battle Stance, Hammer Back Strike**
   Step forward with the right leg, forming a Three Battle Stance, while still maintaining Seizing Hand, and at the same time raising the right arm and then executing a Hammer Back Strike.

10. **Three Battle Stance, Inside Hanging-Up**
    Now execute a Holding Shield Hand; however, the lower hand, i.e., right, is clenched into a fist, which is referred to as Inside Hanging-Up. [

11. **Three Battle Stance, Resonating Strike**
    Raise the right arm and execute a right Resonating Strike.

12. **Three Battle Stance, Slicing Palm**
    Finally, execute a left Slicing Palm.

7. Three Battle Stance, Seizing Hand

8a. Three Battle Stance, Intercepting Strike

8b. Three Battle Stance, Intercepting Strike

9. Three Battle Stance, Hammer Back Strike

10. Three Battle Stance, Inside Hanging-Up

11. Three Battle Stance, Resonating Strike

12. Three Battle Stance, Slicing Palm

SECTION SIX:

1. Tiger Stance, Spread Arm

2. Four Level Stance, Spread Arm

1. **Tiger Stance, Spread Arm**
   Step over the right leg with the left foot, forming a Tiger Stance, while maintaining a left Spread Arm.

2. **Four Level Stance, Spread Arm**
   The right leg steps out to form a Four Level Stance, while maintaining a left Spread Arm.

3. **Double Bow Stance, Shoulder Bridge**
   Turn the torso to the left side, forming a left Double Bow Stance, while executing a right Shoulder Bridge.

4. **Double Bow Stance, Coiling Bridge**
   Execute a right Coiling Bridge.

5. **Double Bow Stance, Seizing Hand**
   The Coiling Bridge has transformed into Seizing Hand.

3. Double Bow Stance, Shoulder Bridge

4. Double Bow Stance, Coiling Bridge

5. Double Bow Stance, Seizing Hand

6. **Double Bow Stance, Straight Strike**
   Switch the body to the right, forming a right Double Bow Stance, while executing a left Straight Strike.

7. **Double Bow Stance, Shoulder Bridge**
   Shift the weight onto the right leg while executing a right Shoulder Bridge.

8. **Double Bow Stance, Coiling Bridge**
   Execute a left Coiling Bridge.

9. **Double Bow Stance, Seizing Hand**
   The Coiling Bridge has transformed into Seizing Hand.

10. **Double Bow Stance, Straight Strike**
    Switch the body to the left, forming a left Double Bow Stance, while executing a right Straight Strike.

6. Double Bow Stance, Straight Strike

7. Double Bow Stance, Shoulder Bridge

8. Double Bow Stance, Coiling Bridge

9. Double Bow Stance, Seizing Hand

10. Double Bow Stance, Straight Strike

11a. Three Battle Stance, Double Piercing Hand

11b. Three Battle Stance, Double Piercing Hand

11c. Three Battle Stance, Double Piercing Hand

12. Empty Stance, Ten Character Hand

11. **Three Battle Stance, Double Piercing Hand**
    The right hand transforms into a Seizing, while crossing the other arm, i.e., Ten Character, and at the same time lifting the right knee. Then the right leg steps forward, forming a Three Battle Stance, while executing a Double Piercing Hand.

12. **Empty Stance, Ten Character Hand**
    The left foot steps forward into a left Empty Stance, while doing Ten Character Hand.

13. **Three Battle Stance, Double Slicing Hand**
    Part the hands into Double Spreading Hands while lifting the left knee. Step down into a left Three Battle Stance while still maintaining the Double Spreading Hand. Now step forward with the right leg, forming a Three Battle Stance, while executing Double Slicing Hand.

14. **Three Battle Stance, Head Bump**
    Clench the fist and move the head forward.

13a. Three Battle Stance, Double Slicing Hand

13b. Three Battle Stance, Double Slicing Hand

13c. Three Battle Stance, Double Slicing Hand

14a. Three Battle Stance, Head Bump

14b. Three Battle Stance, Head Bump

SECTION SEVEN:

1. **Empty Stance, Holding Shield Hand**
   Turn the body toward the left, i.e., south, forming a left Empty Stance, while executing a Holding Shield Hand.

2. **Three Battle Stance, Seizing Hand**
   The leg steps forward, forming a Three Battle Stance, while executing a left Seizing Hand.

3. **Three Battle Stance, Straight Strike**
   While maintaining the Seizing Hand, the right knee lifts. The right foot steps down into a right Three Battle Stance while executing a right Straight Strike.

1a. Empty Stance, Holding Shield Hand

1b. Empty Stance, Holding Shield Hand

2. Three Battle Stance, Seizing Hand

3a. Three Battle Stance, Straight Strike

3b. Three Battle Stance, Straight Strike

4. **Three Battle Stance, Straight Strike**
   Execute a left Straight Strike.

5. **Three Battle Stance, Straight Strike**
   Execute a right Straight Strike.

6. **Three Battle Stance, Hammer Back Strike**
   While maintaining the Three Battle Stance, execute a Hammer Back Strike.

4. Three Battle Stance, Straight Strike

5. Three Battle Stance, Straight Strike

6a. Three Battle Stance, Hammer Back Strike

6b. Three Battle Stance, Hammer Back Strike

SECTION EIGHT:

1. **Empty Stance, Holding Shield Hand**
   Turn the body toward the left, i.e., north, forming a left Empty Stance, while executing Holding Shield Hand.

2. **Three Battle Stance, Seizing Hand**
   Left leg steps forward, forming a Three Battle Stance, while executing a left Seizing Hand.

3. **Three Battle Stance, Straight Strike**
   Execute a right Straight Strike.

4. **Empty Stance, Holding Shield Hand**
   The left leg steps back, forming a right Empty Stance, while executing Holding Shield Hand.

1a. Empty Stance, Holding Shield Hand

1b. Empty Stance, Holding Shield Hand

2. Three Battle Stance, Seizing Hand

3. Three Battle Stance, Straight Strike

4. Empty Stance, Holding Shield Hand

5. **Three Battle Stance, Spreading Arm**
   The right leg steps forward, forming a right Three Battle Stance, while executing a right Spreading Arm.

6. **Empty Stance, Holding Shield Hand**
   The left foot steps forward, forming a left Empty Stance, while executing a Holding Shield Hand.

7. **Three Battle Stance, Spreading Arm**
   The leg steps forward, forming a left Three Battle Stance, while executing a left Spreading Arm.

8. **Empty Stance, Holding Shield Hand**
   The right leg goes forward, forming a right Empty Stance, while executing a Holding Shield Hands.

9. **Horse Stance, Ten Character Hand**
   The torso turns to the left, i.e., west, while the stance converts into a Horse Stance, while executing Ten Character Hand.

5. Three Battle Stance, Spreading Arm

6. Empty Stance, Holding Shield Hand

7. Three Battle Stance, Spreading Arm

8. Empty Stance, Holding Shield Hand

9. Horse Stance, Ten Character Hand

10. Double Bow Stance, Willow Leaf Palm

10. **Double Bow Stance, Willow Leaf Palm**
    Shift the weight into a right Double Bow Stance while executing a right Willow Leaf Palm.

11. **Horse Stance, Willow Leaf Palm**
    While maintaining the Willow Leaf Palm, lift the left knee. Now set down the left foot back where you started, forming a Horse Stance once more, while still maintaining the Willow Leaf Palm.

12. **Single Standing Stance, Willow Leaf Palm**
    While still maintaining the Willow Leaf Palm, lift the right knee.

13. **Empty Stance, Willow Leaf Palm**
    Step the right foot down into a right Empty Stance; again maintaining the Willow Leaf Palm.

14. **Empty Stance, Cutting-Off Bridge**
    While in Empty Stance, execute Cutting-Off Bridge.

15. **Empty Stance, Double Hanging-Up Hand**
    The hands convert into Double Hanging-Up Hand.

11a. Horse Stance, Willow Leaf Palm

11b. Horse Stance, Willow Leaf Palm

12. Single Standing Stance, Willow Leaf Palm

13. Empty Stance, Willow Leaf Palm

14a. Empty Stance, Cutting-Off Bridge

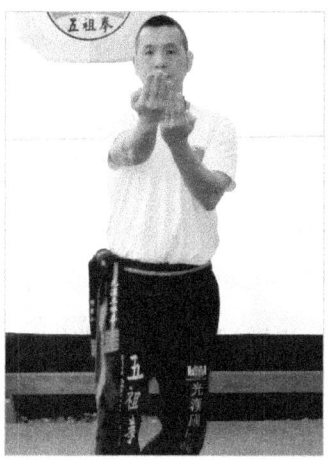

14b. Empty Stance, Cutting-Off Bridge

15. Empty Stance, Double Hanging-Up Hand

16. **Four Level Stance, Double Embracing Fist**
    Cross the arms while the right leg steps back to form a Four Level Stance. Slowly bring Double Embracing Fist to one's pectoral muscles.

17. **Side-by-Side, Double Embracing Fist**
    Straighten up the legs while the left leg slides against the right, which is referred as Side-By-Side Stance; exhale.

18. **Side-by-Side Stance, Both Side Fist**
    Lower the fists to the sides of the body.

16a. Four Level Stance, Double Embracing Fist

16b. Four Level Stance, Double Embracing Fist

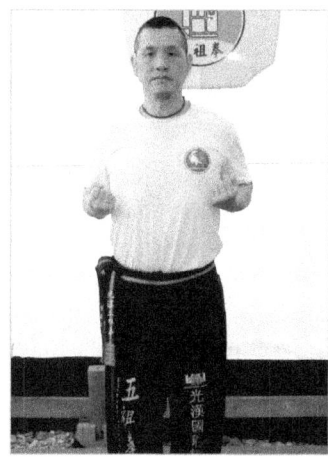

17. Side-by-Side, Double Embracing Fist

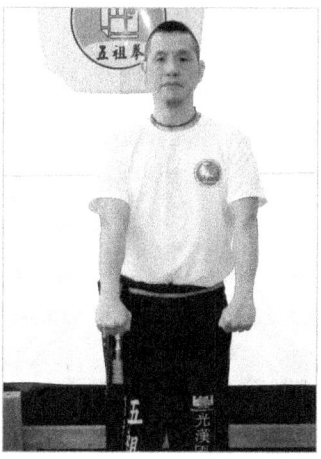

18. Side-by-Side Stance, Both Side Fist

CHAPTER 19

FOUR GATE STRIKING CORNER FIST PARTNER DRILL SI MUN DA GAK DUI LIAN (四門打角對練)

The intent behind Four Gate Striking Corner Partner Drill is to expand practitioners' understanding of close-quarter combat, which was already begun with Three Battle Partner Drill, in which practitioners were introduced to being up and close to their opponent. Therefore, Twenty Fist takes it one level higher by introducing the use of continuous mobility. For example, a two-step forward teaches practitioners to move it and shorten the distance between them and the opponent. However, at the same time it teaches the opponent and practitioner how to deflect and counter an incoming assault.

This principle also introduces practitioners to the ability to defend themselves from multiple attacks by being conscious of the space around them and using devastating strikes that are direct and to the point. For example, the strikes are solid, while the hand motions possess the whipping skill, which is inherited from White Crane Boxing. Therefore, the lead arm act like a shield, intercepting, while the other arm strikes out. However, these motions are supported by solid footwork.

Another intricate aspect that is stressed is intercepting, which is again supported with solid footwork and stances. For instance, turning, sliding, and jumping to intercept an incoming strike and at the same time stepping into a countering strike, which is the cornerstone of Grand Ancestor Boxing and Monkey Boxing.

Therefore, practitioners should be aware that the drill will impart focus, timing, distancing, reaction, conditioning, and confidence, all crucial for close-quarter combat.

*The author, i.e., Daniel Kun, is Exponent **A**; Andy Chan is Exponent **B**.*

SI MUN DA GAK DUI LIAN
SECTION ONE:

1. **Side-by-Side Stance, Both Side Fist**
   Stand at attention, breathing normally.

2. **Lifting Knee, Embracing, Detain Fist**
   Inhale and lift the left leg up, the knee slightly level with the waist. Pull with both hands, clenching them into fists, moving toward the right side of the chest. (The Eclipse)

3. **Four Level Stance, Double Flanking Defense**
   While exhaling, place the left leg parallel to the right leg and form Four Level Stance. The legs should be as wide as or slightly wider than the shoulders; simultaneously push both hands toward the left hip area, open palm, i.e., Double Flank Defense.

1. Side-by-Side Stance, Both Side Fist

2. Lifting Knee, Embracing, Detain Fist

3. Four Level Stance, Double Flanking Defense

4. **Four Level Stance, Double Planting Fist**

   Inhale as the two palms start to clench tightly into fists, i.e., Double Planting Fist.

5. **Four Level Stance, Embracing, Detain Fist**

   Maintaining Four Level Stance, inhale and exhale while pulling the two fists toward the right side of the chest area.

6. **Four Level Stance, Double Covering Palm**

   Exhale and throw the two fists out into the center into Double Covering Palm.

7. **Four Level Stance, Ten Character Arm**

   Inhale and exhale while lifting the arms to execute a Ten Character Arm.

4. Four Level Stance, Double Planting Fist

5. Four Level Stance, Embracing, Detain Fist

6. Four Level Stance, Double Covering Palm

7. Four Level Stance, Ten Character Arm

8. **Four Level Stance, Double Spread Arm**
   Inhale and then exhale while parting the hands, in the process executing a Double Spread Arm. The tips of the fingers are level with the eyebrows. (Opening the Gates of Palace or Heaven)

9. **Four Level Stance, Double Capturing Till Eyebrow Hand**
   Spread the arms, in the process executing Double Capturing Till Eyebrow.

10. **Four Level Stance, Double Seizing Hand**
    Double Capturing Till Eyebrow transforms into Double Seizing Hand.

11. **Four Level Stance, Double Embracing Fist**
    While inhaling, pull the Double Seizing fist and rotate into Double Embracing Fist, which arrives at both sides of the body, and slightly expand the chest while breathing.

8. Four Level Stance, Double Spread Arm

9. Four Level Stance, Double Capturing Till Eyebrow Hand

10. Four Level Stance, Double Seizing Hand

11. Four Level Stance, Double Embracing Fist

12. **Four Level Stance, Giving Respect Fist**

    Slowly exhale while sliding both hands slowly from the upper chest to the hip area, keeping the right hand clenched and the left hand open. Then place the right fist in the left palm, i.e., Giving Respect Fist. Continue to exhale while bringing the hands up to chin level.

13. **Four Level Stance, Double Spread Arm**

    Inhale and then exhale while parting the hands, in the process executing a Double Spread Arm. The tips of the fingers are level with the eyebrows. (Opening the Gates of Palace or Heaven)]

14. **Four Level Stance, Double Joining Hands**

    Inhale and then exhale while dropping the hands toward the Dan Dian in Double Joining Hands pattern.

12. Four Level Stance, Giving Respect Fist

13. Four Level Stance, Giving Respect Fist

14. Four Level Stance, Double Spread Arm

15. Four Level Stance, Double Joining Arm

SECTION TWO:

1.
   A: Three Battle Stance, Straight Strike
   B: Three Battle Stance, Patting Hand
   A) Lift the left leg to step forward, in the process forming a Three Battle Stance, while executing a left Straight Strike.
   B) Lift the left leg to step forward, in the process forming a Three Battle Stance, while executing a right Patting Hand to intercept the incoming strike.

1. Three Battle Stance, Straight Strike-Three Battle Stance, Patting Hand

2.
   A: Three Battle Stance, Straight Strike
   B: Three Battle Stance, Patting Hand
   A) Lift the right leg to step forward, in the process forming a Three Battle Stance, while executing a left Straight Strike.
   B) Lift the right leg to step forward, in the process forming a Three Battle Stance, while executing a left Patting Hand to intercept the incoming strike.

2. Three Battle Stance, Straight Strike-Three Battle Stance, Patting Hand

3.
   A: Three Battle Stance, Seizing Hand
   B: Three Battle Stance, Piercing Palm
   A) Step back with the right leg, forming a left Three Battle Stance, while executing a left Seizing Hand on an incoming strike.
   B) Execute a right Piercing Palm.

3. Three Battle Stance, Seizing Hand-Three Battle Stance, Piercing Palm

4.

A: **Three Battle Stance, Arhat's Double Hooking Strike**
B: **Single Standing Leg, Hammer Back Strike**

A) Intercept both incoming strikes by employing Arhat's Double Hooking Strike.
B) Lift the knee to strike Exponent A's, while executing a Hammer Back Strike.

4. Three Battle Stance, Arhat's Double Hooking Strike-Single Standing Leg, Hammer Back Strike

5.

A: **Three Battle Stance, Thousand Character Arm**
B: **Three Battle Stance, Thousand Character Arm**

A) Intercept the incoming strike with a left Thousand Character Arm.
B) Step down and forward into a left Three Battle Stance while executing a left Thousand Character Arm.

5. Three Battle Stance, Thousand Character Arm-Three Battle Stance, Thousand Character Arm

6.

A: **Empty Stance, Bridge Arm**
B: **Empty Stance, Holding Shield Hand**

A) Lean back to form a right Empty Stance while executing a left Bridge Arm.
B) Lean back to form a left Empty Stance while executing Holding Shield Hand.

6. Empty Stance, Bridge Arm-Empty Stance, Holding Shield Hand

7.
   A: **Three Battle Stance, Straight Strike**
   B: **Three Battle Stance, Seizing Hand**
   A) Step forward into a right Three Battle Stance while executing a right Straight Strike to Exponent **B**'s face.
   B) Step forward into a right Three Battle Stance while executing a right Seizing Hand to intercept the incoming strike.

7. Three Battle Stance, Straight Strike-Three Battle Stance, Seizing Hand

8.
   A: **Three Battle Stance, Straight Strike**
   B: **Three Battle Stance, Seizing Hand**
   A) Step back into a left Three Battle Stance.
   B) Step forward into a right Three Battle Stance while maintaining the Seizing Hand.

9.
   A: **Three Battle Stance, Thousand Character Arm**
   B: **Three Battle Stance, Planting Strike**
   A) Intercept an incoming strike with a right Thousand Character Arm.
   B) Execute a right Planting Strike.

8. Three Battle Stance, Straight Strike-Three Battle Stance, Seizing Hand

9. Three Battle Stance, Thousand Character Arm-Three Battle Stance, Planting Strike

10.

A: **Three Battle Stance, Thousand Character Arm**
B: **Three Battle Stance, Planting Strike**

A) Intercept an incoming strike with a left Thousand Character Arm.
B) Execute a left Planting Strike.

11.

A: **Three Battle Stance, Thousand Character Arm**
B: **Three Battle Stance, Planting Strike**

A) Intercept an incoming strike with a right Thousand Character Arm.
B) Execute a right Planting Strike.

10. Three Battle Stance, Thousand Character Arm-Three Battle Stance, Planting Strike

11. Three Battle Stance, Thousand Character Arm-Three Battle Stance, Planting Strike

SECTION THREE:

1.

   A: Tiger Stance, Thousand Character Arm
   B: Tiger Stance, Planting Strike
   A) While maintaining the Thousand Character Arm, the left leg steps over the right foot, forming a left Tiger Stance.
   B) While maintaining the Planting Strike, the left leg steps over the right foot, forming a left Tiger Stance.

1. Tiger Stance, Thousand Character Arm-Tiger Stance, Planting Strike

2.

   A: Three Battle Stance, Thousand Character Arm
   B: Empty Stance, Holding Shield Hand
   A) The right leg steps back to form a left Three Battle Stance while maintaining the Thousand Character Arm.
   B) The right leg step forward, which allows the leg to form into a left Empty Stance, while executing Holding Shield Hand.

2. Three Battle Stance, Thousand Character Arm-Empty Stance, Holding Shield Hand

3.

   A: Three Battle Stance, Straight Strike
   B: Three Battle Stance, Seizing Hand
   A) Execute a right Straight Strike to Exponent **B**'s face.
   B) Step forward into a left Three Battle Stance while executing a left Seizing Hand to intercept the incoming strike.

3. Three Battle Stance, Straight Strike-Three Battle Stance, Seizing Hand

4.

A: **Three Battle Stance, Straight Strike**
B: **Three Battle Stance, Seizing Hand**

A) Still maintaining the Straight Strike, step back with the left leg to form a right Three Battle Stance.
B) Step forward into a right Three Battle Stance while still maintaining the Seizing Hand.

5.

A: **Empty Stance, Descending Ten Character Hand**
B: **Horse Stance, Resonating Strike**

A) Lean back to form a right Empty Stance while executing a Descending Ten Character Hand to intercept the incoming strike.
B) Turn the torso to form a Horse Stance while executing a Resonating Strike.

6.

A: **Three Battle Stance, Bridge Arm**
B: **Single Butterfly Stance, Thousand Character Hand**

A) Execute a right Flicking Leg. Then step forward into a right Three Battle Stance while executing a left Bridge Arm.
B) Lift the arms while lifting the right knee, then jump back to form a left Single Butterfly Stance while executing a left Thousand Character Hand.

4. Three Battle Stance, Straight Strike-Three Battle Stance, Seizing Hand

5. Empty Stance, Descending Ten Character Hand-Horse Stance, Resonating Strike

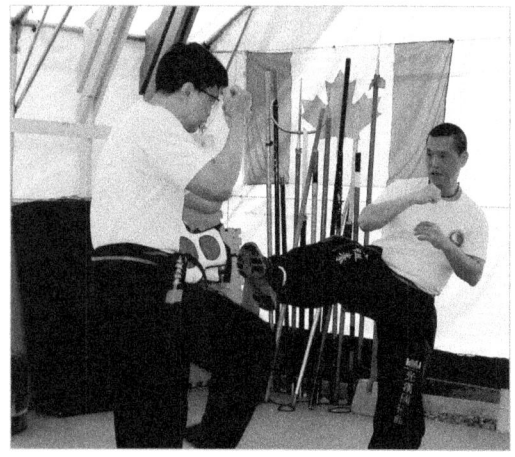

6a. Three Battle Stance, Bridge Arm-Single Butterfly Stance, Thousand Character Hand

6b. Three Battle Stance, Bridge Arm-Single Butterfly Stance, Thousand Character Hand

7. Three Battle Stance, Bridge Arm-Empty Stance, Holding Shield Hand

7.

    A: **Three Battle Stance, Bridge Arm**
    B: **Empty Stance, Holding Shield Hand**

    A) Maintain the left Bridge Arm.
    B) Rise up into a left Empty Stance while executing a Holding Shield Hand.

8.

    A: **Three Battle Stance, Straight Strike**
    B: **Three Battle Stance, Seizing Hand**

    A) Execute a right Straight Strike.
    B) Step forward into a left Three Battle Stance while executing a left Seizing Hand.

8. Three Battle Stance, Bridge Arm-Empty Stance, Holding Shield Hand

9.

A: **Three Battle Stance, Straight Strike**
B: **Three Battle Stance, Hammer Back Strike**

A) The right leg step back to form a left Three Battle Stance while executing a left Straight Strike.
B) Step forward with the right leg, forming a Three Battle Stance, while executing a right Hammer Back Strike.

9. Three Battle Stance, Straight Strike-Three Battle Stance, Hammer Back Strike

10.

A: **Three Battle Stance, Straight Strike**
B: **Three Battle Stance, Hammer Back Strike**

A) The right leg step back to form a left Three Battle Stance while executing a left Straight Strike.
B) Step forward with the right leg, forming a Three Battle Stance, while executing a right Hammer Back Strike.

10. Three Battle Stance, Straight Strike-Three Battle Stance, Hammer Back Strike

11.

A: **Three Battle Stance, Thousand Character Arm**
B: **Three Battle Stance, Slicing Palm**

A) Intercept the incoming strike with a right Thousand Character Arm.
B) Execute a left Slicing Palm direct to Exponent **A**'s rib cage.

11. Three Battle Stance, Thousand Character Arm-Three Battle Stance, Slicing Palm

SECTION FOUR:

1.

   A: **Tiger Stance, Thousand Character Arm**
   B: **Tiger Stance, Holding Shield Hands**

   A) While maintaining the Thousand Character Arm, the left leg steps over the right foot, forming a left Tiger Stance.
   B) Convert the hands into Holding Shield Hands while the left leg steps over the right foot, forming a left Tiger Stance.

1. Tiger Stance, Thousand Character Arm-Tiger Stance, Holding Shield Hand

2.

   A: **Three Battle Stance, Thousand Character Arm**
   B: **Empty Stance, Holding Shield Hands**

   A) The right leg steps back to form a left Three Battle Stance, while maintaining the Thousand Character Arm.
   B) The right leg step forward, which allows the leg to form a left Empty Stance, while executing Holding Shield Hands.

2. Three Battle Stance, Thousand Character Arm-Empty Stance, Holding Shield Hand

3.

   A: **Three Battle Stance, Straight Strike**
   B: **Three Battle Stance, Seizing Hand**

   A) Execute a right Straight Strike to Exponent **B**'s face.
   B) Step forward into a left Three Battle Stance while executing a left Seizing Hand to intercept the incoming strike.

3. Three Battle Stance, Straight Strike-Three Battle Stance, Seizing Hand

4.

A: **Three Battle Stance, Thousand Character Hand**

B: **Three Battle Stance, Planting Strike**

A) Intercept the incoming strike with the right Thousand Character Hand.

B) The right leg steps forward into a right Three Battle Stance, while executing a right Planting Strike toward Exponent **A**'s rib cage.

4. Three Battle Stance, Thousand Character Arm- Three Battle Stance, Planting Strike

5.

A: **Three Battle Stance, Thousand Character Hand**

B: **Three Battle Stance, Planting Strike**

A) Intercept an incoming strike with the left Thousand Character Hand.

B) Execute a left Planting Strike toward Exponent **A**'s rib cage.

5. Three Battle Stance, Thousand Character Arm- Three Battle Stance, Planting Strike

6.

A: **Three Battle Stance, Thousand Character Hand**

B: **Three Battle Stance, Planting Strike**

A) Intercept an incoming strike with the right Thousand Character Hand.

B) Execute a right Planting Strike toward Exponent **A**'s rib cage.

6. Three Battle Stance, Thousand Character Arm- Three Battle Stance, Planting Strike

SECTION FIVE:

1.
   A: **Tiger Stance, Thousand Character Arm**
   B: **Tiger Stance, Holding Shield Hands**
   A) While maintaining the Thousand Character Arm, the left leg steps over the right foot, forming a left Tiger Stance.
   B) Convert the hands into Holding Shield Hands while the left leg steps over the right foot, forming a left Tiger Stance.

1. Tiger Stance, Thousand Character Arm-Tiger Stance, Holding Shield Hand

2.
   A: **Three Battle Stance, Thousand Character Arm**
   B: **Empty Stance, Holding Shield Hands**
   A) The right leg steps forward to form a right Three Battle Stance, while maintaining the Thousand Character Arm.
   B) The right leg steps forward, which allows the leg to form a left Empty Stance, while executing Holding Shield Hands.

2. Three Battle Stance, Thousand Character Arm-Empty Stance, Holding Shield Hand

3.
   A: **Three Battle Stance, Straight Strike**
   B: **Three Battle Stance, Seizing Hand**
   A) Execute a right Straight Strike to Exponent **B**'s face.
   B) Step forward into a left Three Battle Stance while executing a left Seizing Hand to intercept the incoming strike.

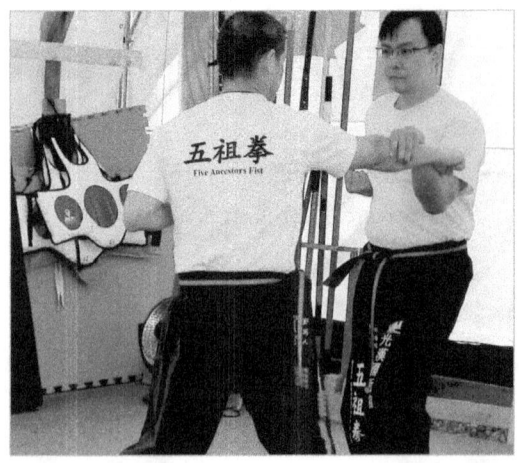

3. Three Battle Stance, Straight Strike-Three Battle Stance, Seizing Hand

4.

A: **Empty Stance, Descending Ten Character Hand**
B: **Horse Stance, Resonating Strike**

A) Lean back to form a right Empty Stance while executing a Descending Ten Character Hands to intercept the incoming strike.

B) Turn the torso to form a Horse Stance while executing a Resonating Strike.

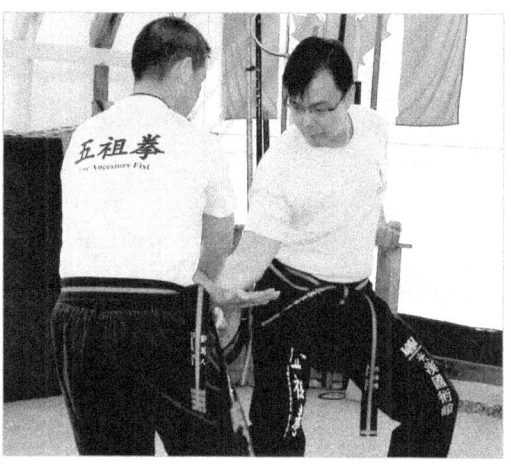

4. Empty Stance, Descending Ten Character Hand-Horse Stance, Resonating Strike

5.

A: **Three Battle Stance, Bridge Arm**
B: **Single Butterfly Stance, Thousand Character Hand**

A) Execute a right Flicking Leg. Step forward into a right Three Battle Stance while executing a left Bridge Arm.

B) Lift the arms while lifting the right knee, and jump back to form a left Single Butterfly Stance while executing a left Thousand Character Hand.

5a. Three Battle Stance, Bridge Arm-Single Butterfly Stance, Thousand Character Hand

5b. Three Battle Stance, Bridge Arm-Single Butterfly Stance, Thousand Character Hand

6.

A: **Three Battle Stance, Bridge Arm**
B: **Empty Stance, Holding Shield Hand**

A) Maintain the left Bridge Arm.
B) Rise up into a left Empty Stance while executing a Holding Shield Hand.

7.

A: **Three Battle Stance, Straight Strike**
B: **Three Battle Stance, Seizing Hand**

A) Execute a right Straight Strike.
B) Step forward into a left Three Battle Stance while executing a left Seizing Hand.

8.

A: **Horse Stance, Straight Strike**
B: **Three Battle Stance, Hammer Back Strike**

A) The right leg steps back to form a left Horse Stance while executing a left Straight Strike.
B) Step forward with the right leg, forming a Three Battle Stance, while executing a right Hammer Back Strike.

6. Three Battle Stance, Bridge Arm-Empty Stance, Holding Shield Hand

7. Three Battle Stance, Straight Strike-Three Battle Stance, Seizing Hand

8. Three Battle Stance, Straight Strike-Three Battle Stance, Hammer Back Strike

9.

A: **Three Battle Stance, Straight Strike**
B: **Three Battle Stance, Hammer Back Strike**

A) The right leg steps back to form a left Three Battle Stance while executing a left Straight Strike.
B) Step forward with the right leg, forming a Three Battle Stance, while executing a right Hammer Back Strike.

9. Three Battle Stance, Straight Strike-Three Battle Stance, Hammer Back Strike

10.

A: **Three Battle Stance, Thousand Character Arm**
B: **Three Battle Stance, Slicing Palm**

A) Intercept the incoming strike with a right Thousand Character Arm.
B) Execute a left Slicing Palm direct to Exponent **A**'s rib cage.

10. Three Battle Stance, Thousand Character Arm-Three Battle Stance, Slicing Palm

SECTION SIX:

1.

    A: **Tiger Stance, Thousand Character Arm**
    B: **Tiger Stance, Holding Shield Hands**
    A) While maintaining the Thousand Character Arm, the left leg steps over the right foot, forming a left Tiger Stance.
    B) Convert the hands into Holding Shield Hands while the left leg steps over the right foot, forming a left Tiger Stance.

1. Tiger Stance, Thousand Character Arm-Tiger Stance, Holding Shield Hand

2.

    A: **Tiger Stance, Thousand Character Arm**
    B: **Tiger Stance, Thousand Character Arm**
    A) Maintain the stance and Thousand Character Arm.
    B) Convert the Holding Shield Hands into a left Thousand Character Arm.

2. Tiger Stance, Thousand Character Arm-Tiger Stance, Thousand Character Arm

3.

    A: **Three Battle Stance, Thousand Character Arm**
    B: **Three Battle Stance, Thousand Character Arm**
    A) The right leg steps forward to form a right Three Battle Stance while maintaining the Thousand Character Arm.
    B) The right leg step forward to form a right Three Battle Stance while still maintaining the Thousand Character Arm.

3. Three Battle Stance, Thousand Character Arm-Three Battle Stance, Thousand Character Arm

4.

A: **Three Battle Stance, Straight Strike**
B: **Three Battle Stance, Seizing Hand**

A) Execute a right Straight Strike to Exponent **B**'s face, while shifting the stance to a left Three Battle Stance.

B) Shift to the right Three Battle Stance while executing a left Seizing Hand to intercept the incoming strike.

4. Three Battle Stance, Straight Strike-Three Battle Stance, Seizing Hand

5.

A: **Three Battle Stance, Thousand Character Hand**
B: **Three Battle Stance, Planting Strike**

A) Intercept an incoming strike with a right Thousand Character Hand.

B) Shift the weight to right side while executing a left Planting Strike.

5. Three Battle Stance, Thousand Character Arm-Three Battle Stance, Planting Strike

6.

A: **Three Battle Stance, Straight Strike**
B: **Three Battle Stance, Seizing Hand**

A) Execute a left Straight Strike to Exponent **B**'s face while shifting the stance to a right Three Battle Stance.

B) Shift to the right Three Battle Stance while executing a left Seizing Hand to intercept the incoming strike.

6. Three Battle Stance, Straight Strike-Three Battle Stance, Seizing Hand

Four Gate Striking Corner Fist Partner Drill Si Mun Da Gak Dui Lian (四門打角對練)

7.

A: Three Battle Stance, Thousand Character Hand
B: Three Battle Stance, Planting Strike

A) Intercept an incoming strike with a left Thousand Character Hand.
B) Shift the weight to the right side while executing a right Planting Strike.

8.

A: Three Battle Stance, Spread Arm
B: Three Battle Stance, Double Spreading Arm

A) Intercept an incoming strike with a left Spreading Arm.
B) The right leg steps forward into a right Three Battle Stance while maintaining a Double Spreading Arms.

9.

A: Three Battle Stance, Spread Arm
B: Three Battle Stance, Double Piercing Arm

A) Intercept an incoming strike with a right Spreading Arm Hand.
B) The left leg steps forward into a left Three Battle Stance while executing a Double Piercing Palm.

7. Three Battle Stance, Thousand Character Arm- Three Battle Stance, Planting Strike

8. Three Battle Stance, Spread Arm-Three Battle Stance, Double Spreading Arm

9. Three Battle Stance, Spread Arm-Three Battle Stance, Double Piercing Arm

10.

A: **Three Battle Stance, Double Thousand Character Hand**
B: **Three Battle Stance, Double Cutting Palm**

A) Lift the arms and intercept incoming strikes with a Double Thousand Character Hand.
B) The right leg steps forward into a right Three Battle Stance while lowering Double Spread Palm. Execute Double Cutting Palm to Exponent A's rib cage.

11.

A: **Three Battle Stance, Double Resonating Strike**
B: **Three Battle Stance, Double Spreading Palm**

A) Intercept the incoming strikes with a Double Resonating Strike.
B) Execute a Double Spreading Palm.

10a. Three Battle Stance, Double Thousand Character Hand-Three Battle Stance, Double Cutting Palm

10b. Three Battle Stance, Double Thousand Character Hand-Three Battle Stance, Double Cutting Palm

11. Three Battle Stance, Double Resonating Strike-Three Battle Stance, Double Spreading Palm

12.

    A: **Three Battle Stance, Double Hammer Back Strike**
    B: **Three Battle Stance, Double Hammer Back Strike**

    A) Lower the arms to form a Double Hammer Back Strike.
    B) Lower the arms to form a Double Hammer Back Strike.

12. Three Battle Stance, Double Hammer Back Strike-Three Battle Stance, Double Hammer Back Strike

SECTION SEVEN:

1.

    A: **Tiger Stance, Bridging Arm**
    B: **Empty Stance, Holding Shield Hand**

    A) The right leg steps over the left foot, forming a right Tiger Stance, while maintaining a left Bridging Arm.
    B) Turn the torso, giving Exponent A your side, while forming a left Empty Stance and executing a Holding Shield Hands.

1. Tiger Stance, Bridge Arm-Tiger Stance, Holding Shield Hand

2.

    A: **Three Battle Stance, Thousand Character Arm**
    B: **Horse Stance, Holding Shield Hands**

    A) The left leg moves around to form a right Three Battle Stance, while executing a left Thousand Character Arm.
    B) Maintain the Holding Shield Hands and left Horse Stance.

2. Tiger Stance, Bridge Arm-Horse Stance, Holding Shield Hand

3.

A: **Three Battle Stance, Thousand Character Arm**
B: **Empty Stance, Holding Shield Hands**

A) The left leg moves around to form a right Three Battle Stance, while executing a left Thousand Character Arm.
B) Maintain the Holding Shield Hands while placing the body weight onto the right leg to form left Empty Stance.

3. Three Battle Stance, Thousand Character Arm-Empty Stance, Holding Shield Hand

4.

A: **Three Battle Stance, Straight Strike**
B: **Three Battle Stance, Seizing Hand**

A) Execute a right Straight Strike toward Exponents **B**'s face.
B) Step forward into a left Three Battle Stance while executing a left Seizing Hand.

4. Three Battle Stance, Straight Strike-Three Battle Stance, Seizing Hand

5.

A: **Three Battle Stance, Straight Strike**
B: **Three Battle Stance, Seizing Hand**

A) Step forward with the left leg, forming a left Three Battle Stance, while maintaining the Straight Strike.
B) Step back into a right Three Battle Stance while maintaining the Seizing Hand.

5. Three Battle Stance, Straight Strike-Three Battle Stance, Seizing Hand

6.

A: Three Battle Stance, Thousand Character Hand
B: Three Battle Stance, Planting Strike

A) Intercept an incoming strike with a right Thousand Character.
B) Execute a right Planting Strike.

7.

A: Three Battle Stance, Thousand Character Hand
B: Three Battle Stance, Planting Strike

A) Intercept an incoming strike with a left Thousand Character.
B) Execute a left Planting Strike.

8.

A: Three Battle Stance, Thousand Character Hand
B: Three Battle Stance, Planting Strike

A) Intercept an incoming strike with a right Thousand Character.
B) Execute a right Planting Strike.

6. Three Battle Stance, Thousand Character Arm- Three Battle Stance, Planting Strike

7. Three Battle Stance, Thousand Character Arm- Three Battle Stance, Planting Strike

8. Three Battle Stance, Thousand Character Arm- Three Battle Stance, Planting Strike

9.

A: **Three Battle Stance, Intersecting Strike**

B: **Three Battle Stance, Intersecting Strike**

A) Execute a right Intersecting Strike.

B) Execute a right Intersecting Strike.

10.

A: **Three Battle Stance, Hammer Back Strike**

B: **Three Battle Stance, Hammer Back Strike**

A) Convert the Intersecting Strike into a Hammer Back Strike.

B) Convert the Intersecting Strike into a Hammer Back Strike.

9. Three Battle Stance, Intersecting Strike-Three Battle Stance, Intersecting Strike

10. Three Battle Stance, Hammer Back Strike-Three Battle Stance, Hammer Back Strike

SECTION EIGHT:

1.

   A: **Tiger Stance, Bridging Arm**
   B: **Empty Stance, Holding Shield Hands**
   - A) The right leg steps over the left foot, forming a right Tiger Stance, while maintaining a left Bridging Arm.
   - B) Turn the torso, giving Exponent A your side, while forming a left Empty Stance and executing a Holding Shield Hands.

1. Tiger Stance, Bridge Arm-Empty Stance, Holding Shield Hand

2.

   A: **Three Battle Stance, Bridging Arm**
   B: **Empty Stance, Holding Shield Hands**
   - A) The left leg moves around to form a right Three Battle Stance, while executing a left Bridge Arm.
   - B) Maintain the Holding Shield Hands and left Empty Stance.

2. Three Battle Stance, Bridging Arm-Empty Stance, Holding Shield Hand

3.

   A: **Three Battle Stance, Straight Strike**
   B: **Three Battle Stance, Seizing Hand**
   - A) Execute a right Straight Strike toward Exponents **B**'s face.
   - B) Step forward into a left Three Battle Stance while executing a left Seizing Hand.

3. Three Battle Stance, Straight Strike-Three Battle Stance, Seizing Hand

4.

A: **Three Battle Stance, Thousand Character Hand**
B: **Three Battle Stance, Planting Strike**

A) Intercept an incoming strike with a right Thousand Character Hand.
B) Execute a left Planting Strike.

5.

A: **Empty Stance, Holding Shield Hands**
B: **Empty Stance, Holding Shield Hands**

A) Shifting the weight back to form a right Empty Stance while executing a Holding Shield Hands.
B) The right leg steps forward, forming a right Empty Stance, while executing a Holding Shield Hands.

6.

A: **Three Battle Stance, Spread Arm**
B: **Three Battle Stance, Spread Arm**

A) Step forward with the right leg, forming a right Three Battle Stance, while executing a right Spread Arm.
B) Step forward with the right leg, forming a right Three Battle Stance, while executing a right Spread Arm.

4. Three Battle Stance, Thousand Character Arm- Three Battle Stance, Planting Strike

5. Empty Stance, Holding Shield Hands- Empty Stance, Holding Shield Hands

6. Three Battle Stance, Spread Arm-Three Battle Stance, Spread Arm

7.

A: **Empty Stance, Holding Shield Hands**

B: **Empty Stance, Holding Shield Hands**

A) Step forward with the left leg, forming a left Empty Stance, while executing a Holding Shield Hands.
B) Step forward with the left leg, forming a left Empty Stance, while executing a Holding Shield Hands.

7. Empty Stance, Holding Shield Hands- Empty Stance, Holding Shield Hands

8.

A: **Three Battle Stance, Spread Arm**

B: **Three Battle Stance, Spread Arm**

A) Step forward with the left leg, forming a left Three Battle Stance, while executing a left Spread Arm.
B) Step forward with the left leg, forming a left Three Battle Stance, while executing a left Spread Arm.

8. Three Battle Stance, Spread Arm-Three Battle Stance, Spread Arm

9.

A: **Empty Stance, Holding Shield Hands**

B: **Empty Stance, Holding Shield Hands**

A) Step forward with the right leg, forming a right Empty Stance, while executing a Holding Shield Hands.
B) Step forward with the right leg, forming a right Empty Stance, while executing a Holding Shield Hands.

9. Empty Stance, Holding Shield Hands- Empty Stance, Holding Shield Hands

10.

A: **Three Battle Stance, Willow Leaf Palm**
B: **Three Battle Stance, Willow Leaf Palm**
  A) Step forward with the right leg, forming a right Three Battle Stance, while executing a right Willow Leaf Palm.
  B) Step forward with the right leg, forming a right Three Battle Stance, while executing a right Willow Leaf Palm.

10. Three Battle Stance, Willow Leaf Palm-Three Battle Stance, Willow Leaf Palm

11.

A: **Empty Stance, Willow Leaf Palm**
B: **Empty Stance, Willow Leaf Palm**
  A) Shift the weight back to form a right Empty Stance while executing a right Willow Leaf Palm.
  B) Shift the weight back to form a right Empty Stance while executing a right Willow Leaf Palm.

11. Empty Stance, Willow Leaf Palm-Empty Stance, Willow Leaf Palm

12. **Empty Stance, Cutting-Off Bridge**
    While in Empty Stance, execute Cutting-Off Bridge.

13. **Empty Stance, Double Hanging-Up Hand**
    The hands convert to Double Hanging-Up Hand.

14. **Four Level Stance, Ten Character Arm**
    Execute a Ten Character Arm, i.e., clenched hands, while the right leg steps back to form a Four Level Stance.

12a. Empty Stance, Cutting-off Bridge-Empty Stance, Cutting-Off Bridge

12b. Empty Stance, Cutting-Off Bridge-Empty Stance, Cutting-Off Bridge

13. Empty Stance, Double Hanging-Up Hand

14. Four Level Stance, Ten Character Arm

15. **Four Level Stance, Double Embracing Fist**
Slowly bring Double Embracing Fist to one's pectoral muscles.

16. **Side-by-Side Stance, Double Embracing Fist**
Straighten up the legs while the left leg slides against the right, which is referred as Side-By-Side Stance; exhale.

17. **Side-by-Side Stance, Both Side Fist**
Lower the fists to the sides of the body.

15. Four Level Stance, Double Embracing Fist

16. Side-by-Side Stance, Double Embracing Fist

17. Side-by-Side Stance, Both Side Fist

CHAPTER 20

FOUR GATE STRIKING CORNER FIST TECHNIQUES
SI MUN DA GAK TECHNIQUES

Turning Attack, Patting Hand

This intercepting method consists of a circular motion of the hands to redirect the attacker's Straight Strike, which is countered with a Piercing Palm.

Turning Attack, Patting Hand

Piercing Palm

Piercing Palm is intended to hit soft body tissues like the throat.

Piercing Palm

Piercing Palm

Knee Hitting, Elbow Strike, Monkey Hand, Hammer Back Strike, Swinging Arm

The exponent executes a knee strike, while at the same time executing elbow strikes and grasping the opponent's neck with Monkey Hand or striking his face with Hammer Back Strike or Swinging Arm to the neck.

Knee Hitting, Monkey Hand

Knee Hitting-Hammer Back Strike

Swing Arm

Raising Knee

The knee can be used offensively and also defensively; for example, intercepting a Horizontal Swing Leg.

Holding Shield Hand to Piercing Palm

This serves two purposes: the upper hand intercepts, which is referred to as Detain Hand, and the lower hand is a Piercing Palm.

Raising Knee

Holding Shield Hand

Holding Shield Hand to Piercing Palm

Seizing Hand

This is designed to intercept an incoming strike and to grasp the opponent's arm to set up a striking or seizing technique.

Seizing Hand

Seizing Hand-Knee Hitting

Seizing Hand

Straight Strike

Resonating Strike-Snug Body Throwing

Resonating Strike is a great strike because it typically takes an opponent off guard; it is usually intended for close-range attacks. However, it provides the capability to execute throwing techniques; for example, a throw referred to as Going Through Leg, Leaning Against Throw.

Resonating Strike

Resonating Strike

Snug Body Throwing

Snug Body Throwing

Snug Body Throwing

Snug Body Throwing

Seizing Hand to Hammer Back Strike

Like Resonating Strike, the Hammer Back Strike is ideal for close-range fighting due to quickness and explosive power.

Seizing Hand to Hammer Back Strike

Seizing Hand to Hammer Back Strike

Thousand Character Arm

Thousand Character Arm can be used to block an incoming strike or actually be used as a strike.

Inward Arm to Slicing Palm

Slicing Palm is intended to strike soft body tissues like the groin and rib cage.

Thousand Character Arm

Inward Arm to Slicing Palm

Inward Arm to Slicing Palm

Holding Shield Hand, Seizing Hand, Straight Strike

These are an example of using the Holding Shield Hand as a guard, which allows the execution of a Seizing Hand and concludes with a Straight Strike.

Holding Shield Hand, Seizing Hand, Straight Strike

Double Spread Arms to Specifying Fingers

The Double Spread Arms are used to intercept, but can be used to break the grasp of an assailant and then striking with Specifying Fingers.

Double Spread Arms to Specifying Fingers

Head Bump

The art of Bumping consist of using certain parts of one's body, e.g., shoulder, hip, back, etc.—in this case the head. The exponents use a Double Slicing Palm to the opponent's rib cage and then grasp the flesh, which is followed up with a Head Bump.

Head Bump

Holding Shield Hand, Spread Arms, to Straight Strike

The Holding Shield Hand is used to ward off a strike, which allows the use of Spread Arm to intercept the incoming strike and then countering with a Straight Strike.

Holding Shield Hand, Spread Arms, to Straight Strike

Bridge Arm to Willow Leaf Palm

The Bridge Arm can be used defensively and offensively. For example, it can intercept an incoming strike and then strike with the edge of the hand or a Willow Leaf Palm.

Bridge Arm to Willow Leaf Palm

Monkey Jump and Thousand Character Arm

The ability to jump is crucial in close-quarter combat, when being pressed by an assailant. For example, the exponent strikes and the assailant intercepts it and starts to counter with hand strikes and a Flicking Leg. The exponent jumps back and uses the Thousand Character Arm to intercept the incoming kick.

Monkey Jump and Thousand Character Arm

CHAPTER 21

BIG KNIFE SKILL
DAI DOU ZUT (大刀朮)

The Dai Dao, or Big Knife, is considered to be a warrior's weapon; for instance, during the Second Sino-Japanese War (July 7, 1937–September 9, 1945) the Dai Dao was the preferred bladed weapon of the Nationalist Army and various militia forces that were fighting against Imperial Japan.

The importance of this particular weapon was forever enshrined in a song: "The Sword March." The song was written by Mai Xin to honor the fearlessness of the Twenty-Ninth Army, which defended the Marco Polo Bridge against the Japanese by wielding the Big Knife.

Big Knife   Big Knife

The design of the Dai Dao is a very versatile three-in-one weapon:

1. The crescent shape for better slashing and cutting.
2. The width from the bottom to the middle of the blade body, which typically measures about three inches and slopes up to the tip of the blade, is usually four to five inches. This assists in parrying projectiles and can be used as a small shield.
3. The ability to create a deep stab wound.

Also, the weight adds effectiveness as a chopping weapon. The typical weight was roughly around three and a half pounds, which was a manageable weight for average individuals to carry and to wield it.

Methods:

1. **Chopping Knife**: Pi Dou (劈刀)
2. **Carry-on Back Knife**: Buê Dou (揹刀)
3. **Stabbing Knife**: Ci Dou (刺刀)

1. Chopping Knife   2. Carry-On Back Knife   3. Stabbing Knife

4. **Lifting Knife**: Tiou Dou (挑刀) or also referred to as Dou Pian Gou Dit Kam (刀片高直砍) or Knife Blade, High Vertical Chop

4a. Lifting Knife

4b. Chopping Knife

5. **Diagonal Chopping Knife**: Kam Dou (砍刀) or also referred to as Dou Pian Kam (刀片砍斜) or Knife Blade, Chopping Slant

5a. Diagonal Chopping Knife

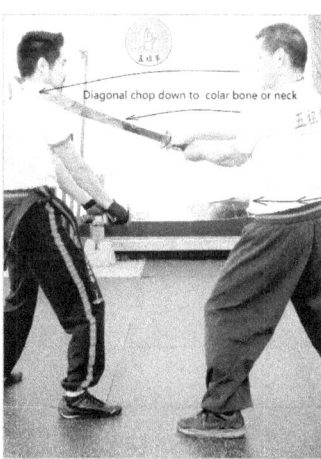

5b. Diagonal Chopping Knife

5c. Diagonal Chopping Knife

Big Knife Skill Dai Dou Zut (大刀朮)

6. **Standing Pushing Knife:** Lip Tui Dou (立推刀)
7. **Horizontal Push Knife:** Hing Tui Dou (橫推刀)

6. Pattern Push Knife

7. Horizontal Push Knife

8. **Shelf Knife:** Gê Dou (架刀)
9. **Shelf Push Knife:** Gê Tui Dou (架推刀)

8. Shelf Knife

9. Shelf Push Knife

DAI DOU ZUT
SECTION ONE:

Side-by-Side Stance, Grasping Knife

Grasping Knife at the side of the body while standing in Side-by-Side Stance.

1. **Covering Stance, Grasping Knife**
   The left leg steps over the right leg, forming a left Covering Stance.

2. **Covering Stance, Covering Pommel**
   The right leg steps over the left leg, forming a right Covering Stance, while the left palm presses upon the pommel.

3. **Horse Stance, Covering Pommel**
   The left leg steps forward to form a Horse Stance.

Side-by-Side Stance, Grasping Knife

1. Covering Stance, Grasping Knife

2. Covering Stance, Covering Pommel

3. Horse Stance, Covering Pommel

SECTION TWO:

1a. Three Battle Stance, Lifting Knife

1b. Three Battle Stance, Lifting Knife

1. **Three Battle Stance, Lifting Knife**
   Grasping Knife forward while legs convert to a right Three Battle Stance, Entwine Knife behind the back and then Lifting Knife.

2. **Three Battle Stance, Chopping Knife**
   Chopping Knife down.

3. **Covering Stance, Shelf Knife**
   The left leg steps over the right leg to form a left Covering Stance, while executing Shelf Knife.

4. **Three Battle Stance, Spread Knife**
   The right leg steps forward to form a right Three Battle Stance while executing a Spread Knife toward the right side.

5. **Covering Stance, Shelf Knife**
   The right leg steps over the left leg to form a right Covering Stance while lifting the knife into Shelf Knife.

2. Three Battle Stance, Chopping Knife

3. Covering Stance, Shelf Knife

4. Three Battle Stance, Spread Knife

6. **Three Battle Stance, Spread Knife**

   The left leg steps forward to form a left Three Battle Stance while executing a Spread Knife toward the left side.

7. **Covering Stance, Shelf Knife**

   The left leg steps over the right leg to form a left Covering Stance while executing Shelf Knife.

8. **Three Battle Stance, Embracing Knife**

   The right leg steps forward to form a right Three Battle Stance, while placing the fuller part of the knife on the dorsal side of the forearm, i.e., Embracing Knife.

5. Covering Stance, Shelf Knife

6a. Three Battle Stance, Spread Knife

6b. Three Battle Stance, Spread Knife

7. Covering Stance, Shelf Knife

8a. Three Battle Stance, Embracing Knife

8b. Three Battle Stance, Embracing Knife

Big Knife Skill Dai Dou Zut (大刀术)

SECTION THREE:

1. Covering Stance, Entwine Back Knife

2. Three Battle Stance, Lifting Knife

1. **Covering Stance, Entwine Back Knife**
   The left leg steps over the right leg, forming a left Covering Stance, while executing Entwine the Back with the Knife.

2. **Three Battle Stance, Lifting Knife**
   Lifting Knife while the right leg steps forward to form a right Three Battle Stance.

3. **Three Battle Stance, Chopping Knife**
   Chopping Knife down.

4. **Single Standing Stance, Diagonal Chopping Knife**
   The left knee lifts to form a left Single Standing Stance, lifting the knife to execute a left Diagonal Chopping Knife, while the left hand is in Detain Hand.

3. Three Battle Stance, Chopping Knife

4a. Single Standing Stance, Diagonal Chopping Knife

4b. Single Standing Stance, Diagonal Chopping Knife

5. **Single Standing Stance, Shelf Knife**
   The left foot steps down, while the right knee lifts to form a right Single Standing Stance, while executing Shelf Knife.

6. **Single Standing Stance, Diagonal Chopping Knife**
   Execute a right Diagonal Chopping Knife.

7. **Three Battle Stance, Stabbing Knife**
   Still maintaining Single Standing Stance, raise Knife and grasp the Knife forward with the left hand in Detain Hand posture; finally the right leg steps down to form a right Three Battle Stance, while Stabbing Knife.

5. Single Standing Stance, Shelf Knife

6. Single Standing Stance, Diagonal Chopping Knife

7a. Three Battle Stance, Stabbing Knife

7b. Three Battle Stance, Stabbing Knife

7c. Three Battle Stance, Stabbing Knife

8. Three Battle Stance, Shelf Knife

8. **Three Battle Stance, Shelf Knife**
   Right leg steps forward to form a left Three Battle Stance, while executing a Shelf Knife.

9. **Single Butterfly Stance, Level Chopping Knife**
   Drop into a right Single Butterfly Stance while executing a Level Chopping Knife toward the left.

10. **Three Battle Stance, Shelf Knife**
    Stand up into a left Three Battle Stance while executing a Shelf Knife.

11. **Single Butterfly Stance, Level Chopping Knife**
    Drop into a right Single Butterfly Stance while executing a Level Chopping Knife toward the right.

9. Single Butterfly Stance, Level Chopping Knife

10. Three Battle Stance, Shelf Knife

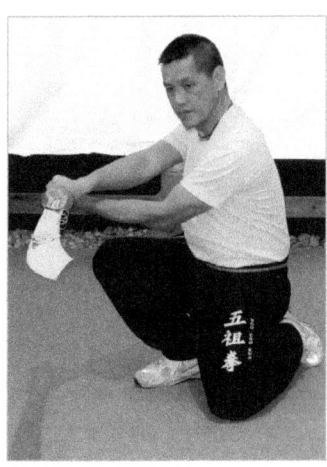

11. Single Butterfly Stance, Level Chopping Knife

SECTION FOUR:

1. **Double Bow Stance, Diagonal Chopping Knife**
   The right leg steps back to right Double Bow Stance while executing a right Diagonal Chopping Knife, while the left hand is in Detain Hand.

2. **Double Bow Stance, Shelf Knife**
   Executing Shelf Knife.

3. **Four Level Stance, Shelf Push Knife**
   The legs shift in Four Level Stance while executing a Shelf Push Knife.

4. **Four Level Stance, Pattern Push Knife**
   The left leg steps back to form a Four Level Stance while executing a Pattern Push Knife.

1a. Double Bow Stance, Diagonal Chopping Knife

1b. Double Bow Stance, Diagonal Chopping Knife

2. Double Bow Stance, Shelf Knife

3. Four Level Stance, Shelf Push Knife

4. Four Level Stance, Pattern Push Knife

5. Covering Stance, Entwine Back Knife

6. Three Battle Stance, Chop Knife

5. **Covering Stance, Entwine Back Knife**
   The left leg steps over the right leg to form a left Covering Stance while executing Entwine Back Knife.

6. **Three Battle Stance, Chop Knife**
   The right leg steps forward to form a right Three Battle Stance while executing a Chop Knife in the center.

7. **Covering Stance, Shelf Knife**
   The left leg steps over the right leg to form a left Covering Stance while lifting the knife into Shelf Knife.

8. **Horse Stance, Shelf Knife**
   The right leg steps forward in a 45° angle while forming a Horse Stance.

9. **Three Battle Stance, Spread Knife**
   Shift the legs to form a right Three Battle Stance, i.e., facing left, while executing Spread Knife toward the right side.

7. Covering Stance, Shelf Knife

8. Horse Stance, Shelf Knife

9. Three Battle Stance, Spread Knife

10. **Covering Stance, Shelf Knife**
    The right leg steps over the left leg to form a right Covering Stance while executing Shelf Knife.

11. **Three Battle Stance, Chopping Knife**
    The left leg steps forward to form left Three Battle Stance while Chopping Knife down.

12. **Covering Stance, Shelf Knife**
    The left leg steps over the right leg to form a left Covering Stance while executing Shelf Knife.

13. **Three Battle Stance, Spread Knife**
    The right leg steps forward to form a right Three Battle Stance while executing Spread Knife.

10. Covering Stance, Shelf Knife

11a. Three Battle Stance, Chopping Knife

11b. Three Battle Stance, Chopping Knife

12. Covering Stance, Shelf Knife

13. Three Battle Stance, Horizontal Chopping Knife

Big Knife Skill Dai Dou Zut (大刀朮)

14. **Covering Stance, Pattern Push Knife**
    The left leg steps over the right leg to form a left Covering Stance while executing a Pattern Push Knife.

15. **Three Battle Stance, Pattern Push Knife**
    Shift into a right Three Battle Stance.

16. **Three Battle Stance, Chopping Knife**
    Raise the knife and Chopping Knife in the center.

14. Covering Stance, Pattern Push Knife

15. Three Battle Stance, Pattern Push Knife

16a. Three Battle Stance, Chopping Knife

16b. Three Battle Stance, Chopping Knife

SECTION FIVE:

1. **Single Standing Stance, Diagonal Chopping Knife**
   The left knee lifts to form a right Single Standing Stance, lifting the knife to execute a left Diagonal Chopping Knife, while the left hand is in Detain Hand.

2. **Three Battle Stance, Shelf Knife**
   The left leg steps down to form a left Three Battle Stance while executing a Shelf Knife.

3. **Single Standing Stance, Shelf**
   The left foot steps down while the right knee lifts to form a right Single Standing Stance, while executing Shelf Knife.

4. **Single Standing Stance, Diagonal Chopping Knife**
   Execute a right Diagonal Chopping Knife.

1a. Single Standing Stance, Diagonal Chopping Knife

1b. Single Standing Stance, Diagonal Chopping Knife

2. Three Battle Stance, Shelf Knife

3. Single Standing Stance, Shelf Knife

4. Single Standing Stance, Diagonal Chopping Knife

Big Knife Skill Dai Dou Zut (大刀朮)

5. Single Standing Stance, Raise Knife

6. Three Battle Stance, Stabbing Knife

5. **Single Standing Stance, Raise Knife**
   Raise Knife and then grasping the Knife forward with the left hand in Detain Hand posture.

6. **Three Battle Stance, Stabbing Knife**
   The right leg steps down to form a right Three Battle Stance while Stabbing.

7. **Rolling, Jumping, Three Battle Stance, Chopping Knife**
   Lift the right knee to form a right Single Standing Stance, while executing a left Diagonal Chopping Knife; however, you continue with the motion, i.e., cartwheel, by lifting the left knee to execute a left Single Standing Stance, while setting up for a chop. Continue with the motion of the left leg stepping down, and quickly lift the right knee to carry the momentum of the cartwheel. Finally, the right leg moves forward to execute a right Three Battle Stance while executing Chopping Knife.

7a. Rolling, Jumping Three Battle Stance, Chopping

7b. Rolling, Jumping Three Battle Stance, Chopping

7c. Rolling, Jumping Three Battle Stance, Chopping

7d. Rolling, Jumping Three Battle Stance, Chopping

7e. Rolling, Jumping Three Battle Stance, Chopping

8. Covering Stance, Shelf Knife

7f. Rolling, Jumping Three Battle Stance, Chopping

9a. Three Battle Stance, Horizontal Chopping Knife

9b. Three Battle Stance, Horizontal Chopping Knife

8. **Covering Stance, Shelf Knife**
   The left foot crosses over the right leg to form a left Covering Stance while executing a Shelf Knife.

9. **Three Battle Stance, Level Chopping Knife**
   The right leg steps forward to form a right Three Battle Stance at a 45° angle while executing a Level Chopping Knife to the right side.

Big Knife Skill Dai Dou Zut (大刀朮)

10. **Covering Stance, Shelf Knife**
    The right leg steps over the left leg to form a right Covering Stance while executing a Shelf Knife.

11. **Single Butterfly Knife, Level Chopping Knife**
    Drop into a left Single Butterfly Knife while executing a Level Chopping Knife toward the left.

12. **Single Butterfly Knife, Level Chopping Knife**
    Drop into a right Single Butterfly Knife while executing a Level Chopping Knife toward the right.

13. **Single Butterfly Knife, Level Chopping Knife**
    Drop into a left Single Butterfly Knife while executing a Level Chopping Knife toward the left.

10. Covering Stance, Shelf Knife

11. Single Butterfly Knife, Level Chopping Knife

12. Single Butterfly Knife, Level Chopping Knife

13. Single Butterfly Knife, Level Chopping Knife

SECTION SIX:

1. **Double Bow Stance, Shelf Knife**
   The right leg steps back to right Double Bow Stance while executing a Shelf Knife.

2. **Four Level Stance, Shelf Push Knife**
   The legs shift in a Four Level Stance while executing a Shelf Push Knife.

3. **Horse Stance, Pattern Push Knife**
   The left leg steps back to form a Horse Stance while executing a Pattern Push Knife.

4. **Covering Stance, Entwine Back Knife**
   The left leg steps over the right leg to form a left Covering Stance while executing Entwine Back Knife.

1a. Double Bow Stance, Shelf Knife

1b. Double Bow Stance, Shelf Knife

2. Four Level Stance, Shelf Push Knife

3. Four Level Stance, Pattern Push Knife

4. Covering Stance, Entwine Back Knife

5. Three Battle Stance, Chop Knife

6. Covering Stance, Shelf Knife

5. **Three Battle Stance, Chop Knife**
   The right leg steps forward to form a right Three Battle Stance while executing a Chop Knife in the center.

6. **Covering Stance, Shelf Knife**
   The left leg steps over the right leg to form a left Covering Stance while lifting the knife into Shelf Knife.

7. **Three Battle Stance, Spread Knife**
   The right leg steps forward at a 45° angle while forming a Horse Stance. Shift the legs to form a right Three Battle Stance, i.e., facing left, while executing Spread Knife toward the right side.

8. **Covering Stance, Shelf Knife**
   The right leg steps over the left leg to form a right Covering Stance while executing Shelf Knife.

7a. Three Battle Stance, Spread Knife

7b. Three Battle Stance, Spread Knife

8. Covering Stance, Shelf Knife

9. **Three Battle Stance, Chopping Knife**
   The left leg steps forward to form left Three Battle Stance while Chopping Knife down.

10. **Covering Stance, Shelf Knife**
    The left leg steps over the right leg to form a left Covering Stance while executing Shelf Knife.

11. **Three Battle Stance, Bring Knife**
    The right leg steps forward to form a right Three Battle Stance while executing Bring Knife is supported by the left forearm.

9a. Three Battle Stance, Chopping Knife

9b. Three Battle Stance, Chopping Knife

10. Covering Stance, Shelf Knife

11a. Three Battle Stance, Bring Knife

11b. Three Battle Stance, Bring Knife

Big Knife Skill Dai Dou Zut (大刀朮)

12. Covering Knife, Entwine Back Knife

12. **Covering Knife, Entwine Back Knife**
    The left leg steps over the right leg to form a left Covering Stance while executing an Entwine the Back with the Knife.

13. **Three Battle Stance, Chopping Knife**
    The right leg steps forward to form a right Three Battle Stance to execute a Chopping Knife.

14. **Single Standing Stance, Diagonal Chopping Knife**
    The left knee lifts to form a right Single Standing Stance while lifting the knife to execute a left Diagonal Chopping Knife.

13a. Three Battle Stance, Chopping Knife

13b. Three Battle Stance, Chopping Knife

15. **Single Standing Stance, Shelf Knife**
    The left foot steps down and the right knee lifts to form a left Single Standing Stance, while executing Shelf Knife.

14a. Single Standing Stance, Diagonal Chopping Knife

14b. Single Standing Stance, Diagonal Chopping Knife

15. Single Standing Stance, Shelf Knife

16. **Single Standing Stance, Diagonal Chopping Knife**
   Execute a right Diagonal Chopping Knife.

17. **Single Standing Stance, Raise Knife**
   Raise knife and then grasp the knife forward with the left hand in Detain Hand posture.

18. **Three Battle Stance, Stabbing Knife**
   The right leg steps down to form a right Three Battle Stance while Stabbing.

19. **Three Battle Stance, Back Knife**
   The knife is swung to one's back, which refers to Back Knife.

16. Single Standing Stance, Diagonal Chopping Knife

17. Single Standing Stance, Raise Knife

18a. Three Battle Stance, Stabbing Knife

18b. Three Battle Stance, Stabbing Knife

19a. Three Battle Stance, Back Knife

19b. Three Battle Stance, Back Knife

19c. Three Battle Stance, Back Knife

Big Knife Skill Dai Dou Zut (大刀朮)

SECTION SEVEN:

1. **Three Battle Stance, Slicing Palm**
   While the knife is poised on the back, the left arm executes a left Slicing Palm.

2. **Going-Up Leg, Holding Knife**
   Lift up the right knee to execute right Going-Up Leg while executing Holding Knife.

3. **Three Battle Stance, Stabbing Knife**
   The right leg steps forward to form a right Three Battle Stance to execute Stabbing Knife.

1. Three Battle Stance, Slicing Palm

2a. Going-Up Leg, Holding Knife

2b. Going-Up Leg, Holding Knife

3a. Three Battle Stance, Stabbing Knife

3b. Three Battle Stance, Stabbing Knife

4. **Covering Stance, Entwine Back Knife**
   The left foot crosses over the right leg to form a left Covering Stance while executing Entwine Back Knife.

5. **Three Battle Stance, Chopping Knife**
   The right leg steps forward to form a right Three Battle Stance while executing a Chopping Knife.

6. **Covering Stance, Shelf Knife**
   The left leg crosses over the right to form a left Covering Stance while executing a Shelf Knife.

7. **Three Battle Stance, Spread Knife**
   The right leg steps forward to form a right Three Battle Stance while executing Spread Knife toward the right side.

4. Covering Stance, Entwine Back Knife

5a. Three Battle Stance, Chopping Knife

5b. Three Battle Stance, Chopping Knife

6. Covering Stance, Shelf Knife

7. Three Battle Stance, Spread Knife

Big Knife Skill Dai Dou Zut (大刀朮)

8a. Turning, Jumping, Three Battle Stance, Chopping Knife

8. **Turning, Jumping, Three Battle Stance, Chopping Knife**

   Lift the right knee up to form a right Single Standing Stance while executing a left Entwine Back Knife; however, you continue with the motion, i.e., spinning, by lifting the left knee to execute a left Single Standing Stance while setting up for a chop. Continue with the motion of the left leg stepping down, and quickly lift the right knee to carry the momentum of the spin. Finally, the right leg moves forward to execute a right Three Battle Stance while executing Chopping Knife.

8b.

8c.

8d.

8e.

8f.

9. **Empty Stance, Chopping Knife**
   Shift weight back to the left le, forming a right Empty Stance, while maintaining Chopping Knife.

10. **Covering Stance, Covering Pommel**
    Shift weight back to form a right Empty Stance, tilting the knife back into Grasping to the side the knife, and then step back out to form a right Three Battle Stance. The left leg steps up to form a Covering Stance, while the left palm is on the pommel, i.e., Covering Pommel.

9. Empty Stance, Chopping Knife

10a. Covering Stance, Covering Pommel

10b. Covering Stance, Covering Pommel

10c. Covering Stance, Covering Pommel

11. **Side-by-Side Stance, Raising Fist**
    Stand upright in a Side-by-Side Stance while executing Raising Fist with the pommel of the knife.

11. Side-by-Side Stance, Raising Fist

Big Knife Skill Dai Dou Zut (大刀朮)

12. Side-by-Side Stance, Double Embracing Fist

12. **Side-by-Side Stance, Double Embracing Fist**
    Bring the arms back to the pectoral muscles.

13. **Side-by-Side Stance, Grasping Knife**
    Lower the arms.

13. Side-by-Side Stance, Grasping Knife

CHAPTER 22

BIG KNIFE PARTNER DRILL
DAI DOU DUI LIAN (大刀對練)

Like the prior hand routines, the Big Knife includes a Partner Drill. However, practitioners must be extremely conscious of distance and timing because there is no room for mistakes. Even though most Big Knives are dull, they are still blunt weapons; hence, someone can get hurt. Therefore, be cautious when practicing and performing.

However, the Big Knife Partner Drill is a great routine due the risk factor, meaning that practitioners learn quickly not to commit mistakes. Therefore, their sense of focus and timing is increased by performing this routine, which enhances eye-to-hand coordination and the ability to move quickly around an opponent. This transfers well back to hand-to-hand combat.

*The author, Daniel Kun, is Exponent **A**; Victor Chow is Exponent **B**.*

SECTION ONE:

1. **Side-by-Side Stance, Grasping Knife**
   Grasping Knife at the side of the body while standing in Side-by-Side Stance.

1. Side-by-Side Stance, Grasping Knife

2. **Empty Stance, Covering Pommel**
   Step out with the right leg to form a right Empty Stance while the left palm presses upon the pommel (this is equivalent to Raising Fist with the hand forms).

SECTION TWO:

1.
   A: **Three Battle Stance, Stabbing Knife**
   B: **Three Battle Stance, Chopping Knife**
   A) The right foot steps forward to form a right Three Battle Stance while Grasping the Knife forward and facing Exponent **B**; finally, Stabbing with Knife.
   B) The right foot steps forward to form a right Three Battle Stance while Raising Knife above one's head; finally, Chopping with Knife blocks the incoming stab.

2. Empty Stance, Covering Pommel

1a. Three Battle Stance, Stabbing Knife-Three Battle Stance, Chopping Knife

1b. Three Battle Stance, Stabbing Knife-Three Battle Stance, Chopping Knife

2.

A: **Three Battle Stance, Chopping Knife**

B: **Covering Stance, Shelf Knife**

A) The left foot steps forward to form a left Three Battle Stance while repositioning the knife to execute a Chop.

B) Seeing the incoming chop, which is blocked with a Shelf Knife, step the left foot over the right leg, i.e., left Covering Stance, to brace the impact of Exponent A's Chop Knife.

2a. Three Battle Stance, Chopping Knife-Three Battle Stance, Shelf Knife

3.

A: **Three Battle Stance, Standing Pushing Knife**

B: **Double Bow Stance, Spread Knife**

A) The knife slices down while the left hand presses on the spine of the knife, converting it into Standing Pushing Knife.

B) The right foot steps forward to form a right Double Bow Stance while executing a Spread Knife on the right side to block the incoming press.

2b. Three Battle Stance, Chopping Knife-Three Battle Stance, Shelf Knife

3. Three Battle Stance, Standing Pushing Knife-Three Battle Stance, Spreading Knife

4.

   A: Three Battle Stance, Chopping Knife

   B: Three Battle Stance, Shelf Knife

   A) Press forward to execute a vertical Chop while stepping forward with the right leg to form a right Three Battle Stance.

   B) Because of the added pressure the knife is lifted, converting to Shelf Knife.

4. Three Battle Stance, Chopping Knife-Three Battle Stance, Shelf Knife

5.

   A: Three Battle Stance, Diagonal Chopping Knife

   B: Three Battle Stance, Diagonal Chopping Knife

   A) The left foot steps forward to form a left Three Battle Stance while executing a Diagonal Chop Knife to intercept an incoming chop.

   B) Shift the body and feet to the left side to form a left Three Battle Stance to execute a Diagonal Chop Knife.

5. Three Battle Stance, Diagonal Chopping Knife-Three Battle Stance, Diagonal Chopping Knife

6.

   A: Three Battle Stance, Chopping Knife

   B: Three Battle Stance, Shelf Knife

   A) The right leg steps forward to form a right Three Battle Stance while executing a Chop.

   B) Quickly respond with a Shelf Knife to block the incoming chop.

6. Three Battle Stance, Chopping Knife-Three Battle Stance, Shelf Knife

7.

A: **Three Battle Stance, Standing Pushing Knife**

B: **Three Battle Stance, Horizontal Push Knife**

A) The left foot steps forward to form a left Three Battle Stance while executing a Standing Pushing Knife.

B) The left foot steps forward to a left Three Battle Stance while executing a Horizontal Push Knife to intercept the incoming strike.

7. Three Battle Stance, Standing Pushing Knife-Three Battle Stance, Horizontal Push Knife

8.

A: **Three Battle Stance, Chopping Knife**

B: **Three Battle Stance, Shelf Knife**

A) Press forward to execute a vertical Chop while stepping forward with the right leg to form a right Three Battle Stance.

B) Because of the added pressure of the body weight, move to the right leg, i.e., converting into a right Three Battle Stance, and the knife is lifted, converting to Shelf Knife.

8. Three Battle Stance, Chopping Knife-Three Battle Stance, Shelf Knife

SECTION THREE:

1.
   A: **Three Battle Stance, Stabbing Knife**
   B: **Three Battle Stance, Chopping Knife**
   C) The left foot slides a bit back while the knife is repositioned to Forward Grasp and then Stabbing with Knife.
   D) The left leg steps back to form a right Three Battle Stance while Raising Knife above the head; finally, Chopping with Knife to block the incoming stab.

2.
   A: **Three Battle Stance, Stabbing Knife**
   B: **Single Standing Stance, Diagonal Chopping Knife**
   A) Stabbing once more.
   B) The left knee lifts to form a left Single Standing Stance, then executing a left Diagonal Chopping Knife.

1a. Three Battle Stance, Stabbing Knife-Three Battle Stance, Chopping Knife

1b. Three Battle Stance, Stabbing Knife-Three Battle Stance, Chopping Knife

2. Three Battle Stance, Stabbing Knife-Single Standing Stance, Diagonal Chopping Knife

3.

A: **Three Battle Stance, Stabbing Knife**
B: **Single Standing Stance, Diagonal Chopping Knife**

A) Grasping the Knife back while stepping back the right leg and forming a left Three Battle Stance, stab once more.
B) The left leg steps down into a Personal Stance, while Raising Knife; then the right knee lifts to form a right Single Standing Stance; then execute a right Diagonal Chopping Knife.

3a. Three Battle Stance, Stabbing Knife-Single Standing Stance, Diagonal Chopping Knife

3b. Three Battle Stance, Stabbing Knife-Single Standing Stance, Diagonal Chopping Knife

4.

A: **Sitting Stance, Grasping Knife**
B: **Empty Stance, Grasping Knife**

A) The right leg steps forward while Grasping Forward Knife.
B) The right foot steps down to form a right Empty Stance while Grasping Forward Knife.

4. Sitting Stance, Grasping Knife-Empty Stance, Grasping Knife

Big Knife Partner Drill Dai Dou Dui Lian (大刀對練)

5.

A: **Three Battle Stance, Pattern Knife**
B: **Three Battle Stance, Stabbing Knife**

A) Execute a Pattern Knife while turning the torso to avoid the stab.
B) The right leg steps forward to form a right Three Battle Stance while Stabbing Knife.

6.

A: **Three Battle Stance, Chopping Knife**
B: **Three Battle Stance, Shelf Knife**

A) Lift the knife to execute a Chop while stepping forward a bit.
B) The left leg steps back to form a 45° and right Three Battle Stance, while executing a Shelf Knife to block the incoming chop.

7.

A: **Kneeling Stance, Diagonal Chopping Knife**
B: **Kneeling Stance, Diagonal Chopping Knife**

A) Drop into a right Kneeling Stance while executing a Diagonal Chopping Knife to intersect an incoming chop.
B) Drop into a left Kneeling Stance while executing a Diagonal Chopping Knife to intersect an incoming chop.

5. Three Battle Stance, Pattern Knife-Three Battle Stance, Stabbing Knife

6. Three Battle Stance, Chopping Knife-Three Battle Stance, Shelf Knife

7. Kneeling Stance, Diagonal Chopping Knife-Kneeling Stance, Diagonal Chopping Knife

8.

A: **Three Battle Stance, Chopping Knife**
B: **Three Battle Stance, Shelf Knife**

A) Stand up into a left Three Battle Stance while executing a Chopping Knife.
B) Stand up into a left Three Battle Stance while executing a Shelf Knife.

8. Three Battle Stance, Chopping Knife-Three Battle Stance, Shelf Knife

9.

A: **Kneeling Stance, Diagonal Chopping Knife**
B: **Kneeling Stance, Diagonal Chopping Knife**

A) Drop into a right Kneeling Stance while executing a Diagonal Chopping Knife to intersect an incoming chop.
B) Drop into a right Kneeling Stance while executing a Diagonal Chopping Knife, at the same time pushing onto the spine of the knife.

9. Kneeling Stance, Diagonal Chopping Knife-Kneeling Stance, Diagonal Chopping Knife

10.

A: **Three Battle Stance, Hiding Knife**
B: **Three Battle Stance, Hiding Knife**

A) Rise up into a right Three Battle Stance while executing Hiding Knife to block incoming chop.
B) Rise up into a right Three Battle Stance while executing Hiding Knife to block the incoming chop.

10. Three Battle Stance, Hiding Knife-Three Battle Stance, Hiding Knife

SECTION FOUR:

1.
   A: **Three Battle Stance, Holding Knife**
   B: **Three Battle Stance, Intercept Knife**

   A) Reversing side is done with the left leg stepping forward; the torso turns into a right Three Battle Stance while executing Holding Knife.
   B) The right leg steps forward to reverse sides, forming a right Three Battle Stance, while executing Intercept Knife.

1. Three Battle Stance, Holding Knife-Three Battle Stance, Intercept Knife

2.
   A: **Three Battle Stance, Chopping Knife**
   B: **Three Battle Stance, Shelf Push Knife**

   A) Step forward to form a left Three Battle Stance while executing a Chop.
   B) Shift torso forward and intercept the incoming chop with a Shelf Push Knife.

2. Three Battle Stance, Chopping Knife-Three Battle Stance, Shelf Push Knife

3.

A: **Three Battle Stance, Stabbing Knife**

B: **Horse Stance, Diagonal Chop Knife**

A) The right leg steps forward to form a right Three Battle Stance while Grasping Knife forward and then Stabbing Knife toward Exponent **B**'s chest.

B) The left leg steps back to form a Horse Stance, which allows the torso to move out of the way and at the same time execute Raising Knife, then a Diagonal Chop Knife to intercept the incoming stab.

4.

A: **Three Battle Stance, Chopping Knife**

B: **Three Battle Stance, Shelf Knife**

A) The left foot steps forward to form a left Three Battle Stance while executing a Chopping Knife.

B) Execute a Shelf Knife to intercept the incoming chop.

3a. Three Battle Stance, Stabbing Knife-Three Battle Stance, Diagonal Chop Knife

3b. Three Battle Stance, Stabbing Knife-Three Battle Stance, Diagonal Chop Knife

4. Three Battle Stance, Chopping Knife-Three Battle Stance, Shelf Knife

Big Knife Partner Drill Dai Dou Dui Lian (大刀對練)

5.

A: Three Battle Stance, Standing Pushing Knife

B: Three Battle Stance, Spread Knife

A) The right leg steps back to angle off a left Three Battle Stance while setting up a Standing Pushing Knife to intercept the incoming chop.

B) The right foot steps out to readjust, right Three Battle Stance to execute Spread Knife.

6.

A: Three Battle Stance, Chopping Knife

B: Three Battle Stance, Shelf Knife

A) The right leg steps forward to form right Three Battle Stance while Raising Knife above head to Chop Knife.

B) Readjust feet while lifting knife into Shelf Knife to intercept the downward chop.

5a. Three Battle Stance, Standing Pushing Knife-Three Battle Stance, Spread Knife

5b. Three Battle Stance, Standing Pushing Knife-Three Battle Stance, Spread Knife

6a. Three Battle Stance, Chopping Knife-Three Battle Stance, Shelf Knife

6b. Three Battle Stance, Chopping Knife-Three Battle Stance, Shelf Knife

7.

A: **Three Battle Stance, Diagonal Chopping Knife**
B: **Three Battle Stance, Diagonal Chopping Knife**

A) The right leg moves back to form a left Three Battle Stance while executing a Diagonal Chopping Knife.
B) The left leg moves back to form a left Three Battle Stance while executing a Diagonal Chopping Knife.

7. Three Battle Stance, Diagonal Chopping Knife-Three Battle Stance, Diagonal Chopping Knife

8.

A: **Three Battle Stance, Chopping Knife**
B: **Three Battle Stance, Shelf Knife**

A) The left foot moves forward into a left Three Battle Stance while pressing forward with the chop.
B) Sustain the pressing knife by shifting interception into Shelf Knife.

8. Three Battle Stance, Chopping Knife-Three Battle Stance, Shelf Knife

9.

A: **Three Battle Stance, Standing Pushing Knife**
B: **Three Battle Stance, Horizontal Push Knife**

A) The right leg steps forward, forming a right Three Battle Stance, while executing a Standing Pushing Knife to intercept an incoming attack.
B) The left leg moves forward, forming a right Three Battle Stance, while executing a Horizontal Push Knife.

9. Three Battle Stance, Standing Pushing Knife-Three Battle Stance, Horizontal Push Knife

Big Knife Partner Drill Dai Dou Dui Lian (大刀對練)

10.

A: **Three Battle Stance, Chopping Knife**
B: **Three Battle Stance, Shelf Knife**

A) The right leg steps forward to form a right Three Battle Stance, while Raising Knife above head to Chop Knife.
B) Readjust feet while lifting the knife into Shelf Knife to intercept a downward chop.

10. Three Battle Stance, Chopping Knife-Three Battle Stance, Shelf Knife

SECTION FIVE:

1.

A: **Three Battle Stance, Stabbing Knife**
B: **Horse Stance, Diagonal Chopping Knife**

A) Shift weight back into the left leg to form a right Empty Stance while Grasping Knife forward; finally, Stabbing Knife toward Exponent **B**'s chest.
B) The left leg steps back to form a Horse Stance, which allows the torso to move out of the way and at the same time execute Raising Knife. Finally, execute a Diagonal Chop to intercept the incoming stab.

1a. Three Battle Stance, Stabbing Knife-Horse Stance, Diagonal Chopping Knife

1b. Three Battle Stance, Stabbing Knife-Horse Stance, Diagonal Chopping Knife

2.

A: **Three Battle Stance, Stabbing Knife**
B: **Single Standing Stance, Diagonal Chopping Knife**

A) Stabbing once more.
B) The left knee lifts to form a left Single Standing Stance, then execute a left Diagonal Chopping Knife.

3.

A: **Three Battle Stance, Stabbing Knife**
B: **Single Standing Stance, Diagonal Chopping Knife**

A) Grasp the knife back while shifting weight back to the rear leg, while the right leg forms into a right Empty Stance and while Stabbing Knife.
B) Quickly the left leg left goes down and the right knee goes up to form a right Single Standing Stance, while executing a Shelf Knife and then executing a right Diagonal Chopping Knife.

2. Three Battle Stance, Stabbing Knife-Single Standing Stance, Diagonal Chopping Knife

3a. Three Battle Stance, Stabbing Knife-Single Standing Stance, Diagonal Chopping Knife

3b. Three Battle Stance, Stabbing Knife-Single Standing Stance, Diagonal Chopping Knife

4.

   A: **Three Battle Stance, Pattern Knife**
   B: **Three Battle Stance, Stabbing Knife**

   A) Execute a Pattern Knife to intercept a stab.

   B) The right leg steps down into a right Three Battle Stance while Stabbing Knife.

5.

   A: **Three Battle Stance, Pattern Knife**
   B: **Three Battle Stance, Diagonal Chopping Knife**

   A) Still maintain the Pattern Knife.

   B) Shift the weight to the left, forming a left Three Battle Stance, while executing a left Diagonal Chopping Knife.

4. Three Battle Stance, Pattern Knife-Three Battle Stance, Stabbing Knife

5. Three Battle Stance, Pattern Knife-Three Battle Stance, Diagonal Chopping Knife

6.

A: Three Battle Stance, Horizontal Push Knife

B: Rolling, Jumping, Three Battle Stance, Chopping Knife

A) The right leg steps back to form a left Sitting Stance, while Grasping Knife forward. Then the body weight moves forward and the left leg steps to form a left Three Battle Stance, while executing a Shelf Push Knife. Finally, the right leg steps forward to a right Three Battle Stance, while executing a Horizontal Push Knife to sustain the attack.

B) The left leg goes across = one's body to form a left Empty Stance, i.e., beginning of the cartwheel motion, while Raising Knife. Quickly raise the right knee to form a right Single Standing Stance, while executing a Chop Knife. Then the right leg comes down quickly, forming a right Three Battle Stance, while Chopping Knife.

6a. Three Battle Stance, Horizontal Push Knife- Rolling, Jumping Three Battle Stance, Chopping Knife

6b. Three Battle Stance, Horizontal Push Knife- Rolling, Jumping Three Battle Stance, Chopping Knife

6c. Three Battle Stance, Horizontal Push Knife- Rolling, Jumping Three Battle Stance, Chopping Knife

7.

A: Three Battle Stance, Shelf Push Knife

B: Three Battle Stance, Chopping Knife

A) The right leg steps back to form a left Sitting Stance while Grasping Knife forward. Then the right leg steps forward to a right Three Battle Stance, while executing a Shelf Push Knife to sustain the attack.

B) The left leg goes across one's body to form a left Empty Stance, i.e., beginning of the cartwheel motion, while Raising Knife. The right leg comes down quickly, forming a right Three Battle Stance, while Chopping Knife.

8.

A: Three Battle Stance, Diagonal Chopping Knife

B: Horse Stance, Diagonal Chopping Knife

A) The right leg moves forward to form a right Three Battle Stance while executing a Diagonal Chop.

B) The torso turns while executing a Diagonal Chop.

7a. Three Battle Stance, Shelf Push Knife-Three Battle Stance, Chopping Knife

7b. Three Battle Stance, Shelf Push Knife-Three Battle Stance, Chopping Knife

8. Three Battle Stance, Diagonal Chopping Knife-Three Battle Stance, Diagonal Chopping Knife

9.

A: **Three Battle Stance, Standing Pushing Knife**
B: **Three Battle Stance, Horizontal Chop Knife**

A) The right leg steps forward, forming a right Three Battle Stance, while executing a Standing Pushing Knife to intercept an incoming attack.
B) The left leg moves forward, forming a right Three Battle Stance, while executing a Horizontal Chop Knife.

9. Three Battle Stance, Standing Pushing Knife-Three Battle Stance, Horizontal Chop Knife

10.

A: **Three Battle Stance, Chopping Knife**
B: **Three Battle Stance, Shelf Knife**

A) The right leg steps forward to form right Three Battle Stance while Raising Knife above head to Chop Knife.
B) Readjust the feet while lifting knife into Shelf Knife to intercept the downward chop.

10. Three Battle Stance, Chopping Knife-Three Battle Stance, Shelf Knife

11.

A: **Kneeling Stance, Diagonal Chopping Knife**
B: **Kneeling Stance, Diagonal Chopping Knife**

A) Drop into a right Kneeling Stance while executing a Diagonal Chopping Knife to intersect an incoming chop.
B) Drop into a left Kneeling Stance while executing a Diagonal Chopping Knife to intersect an incoming chop.

11. Kneeling Stance, Diagonal Chopping Knife-Kneeling Stance, Diagonal Chopping Knife

12.

A: **Three Battle Stance, Chopping Knife**

B: **Three Battle Stance, Shelf Knife**

A) Stand up into a left Three Battle Stance while executing a Chopping Knife.

B) Stand up into a left Three Battle Stance while executing a Shelf Knife.

12. Three Battle Stance, Chopping Knife-Three Battle Stance, Shelf Knife

13.

A: **Kneeling Stance, Diagonal Chopping Knife**

B: **Kneeling Stance, Diagonal Chopping Knife**

A) Drop into a left Kneeling Stance while executing a Diagonal Chopping Knife to intersect an incoming chop.

B) Drop into a right Kneeling Stance while executing a Diagonal Chopping Knife, at the same time pushing onto the spine of the knife.

13. Kneeling Stance, Diagonal Chopping Knife-Kneeling Stance, Diagonal Chopping Knife

14.

A: **Three Battle Stance, Hiding Knife**

B: **Three Battle Stance, Hiding Knife**

A) Rise up into a right Three Battle Stance while executing Hiding Knife to block incoming chop.

B) Rise up into a right Three Battle Stance while executing Hiding Knife to block an incoming chop.

14. Three Battle Stance, Hiding Knife-Three Battle Stance, Hiding Knife

SECTION SIX:

1.

> A: **Three Battle Stance, Chopping Knife**
> B: **Three Battle Stance, Shelf Push Knife**
>
> A) Reversing side is done with the left leg stepping forward; the torso turns into a right Three Battle Stance while executing Raising Knife. Step forward to form a right Three Battle Stance while executing a chop.
> B) The right leg steps forward to the reverse side, forming a right Three Battle Stance, while executing Shelf Knife and then converting to the Shelf Push Knife.

1a. Three Battle Stance, Chopping Knife-Three Battle Stance, Shelf Push Knife

1b. Three Battle Stance, Chopping Knife-Three Battle Stance, Shelf Push Knife

2.

A: Three Battle Stance, Stabbing Knife

B: Three Battle Stance, Diagonal Chopping Knife

A) Shift weight back onto the rear leg to form a right Empty Stance, while Grasping Knife forward. The right leg steps forward to form a right Three Battle Stance, while Stabbing Knife toward Exponent **B**'s chest.

B) Raise knife above the head and shift weight to execute a Diagonal Chop to intercept the incoming stab.

3.

A: Three Battle Stance, Chopping Knife

B: Three Battle Stance, Shelf Knife

A) The left leg steps forward to form left Three Battle Stance while executing Chop Knife.

B) Readjust feet while lifting the knife into Shelf Knife to intercept a downward chop.

2a. Three Battle Stance, Stabbing Knife-Three Battle Stance, Diagonal Chopping Knife

2b. Three Battle Stance, Stabbing Knife-Three Battle Stance, Diagonal Chopping Knife

3. Three Battle Stance, Chopping Knife-Three Battle Stance, Shelf Knife

4.

A: **Three Battle Stance, Standing Pushing Knife**
B: **Three Battle Stance, Spreading Knife**

A) Execute a Standing Pushing Knife to intercept an incoming attack.
B) The left leg moves forward, forming a right Three Battle Stance, while executing Spreading Knife.

5.

A: **Three Battle Stance, Chopping Knife**
B: **Three Battle Stance, Shelf Knife**

A) The right leg steps forward to form right Three Battle Stance while Raising Knife above head to Chop Knife.
B) Readjust feet while lifting knife into Shelf Knife to intercept a downward chop.

6.

A: **Covering Stance, Diagonal Chopping Knife**
B: **Covering Stance, Shelf Knife**

A) The right leg steps over the left leg to form a right Covering Stance while executing Diagonal Chop Knife.
B) The right leg steps over the left leg to form a right Covering Stance while executing Shelf Knife.

4. Three Battle Stance, Standing Pushing Knife-Three Battle Stance, Spreading Knife

5. Three Battle Stance, Chopping Knife-Three Battle Stance, Shelf Knife

6. Covering Stance, Diagonal Chopping Knife-Covering Stance, Shelf Knife

Big Knife Partner Drill Dai Dou Dui Lian (大刀對練)

7.

A: **Three Battle Stance, Diagonal Chopping Knife**
B: **Three Battle Stance, Diagonal Chopping Knife**
   A) The left leg steps forward to form a left Three Battle Stance while executing Diagonal Chop Knife.
   B) The left leg steps forward to form a left Three Battle Stance while executing Diagonal Chop Knife.

7. Three Battle Stance, Diagonal Chopping Knife-Three Battle Stance, Diagonal Chopping Knife

8.

A: **Three Battle Stance, Chopping Knife**
B: **Three Battle Stance, Shelf Knife**
   A) The right leg steps forward to form right Three Battle Stance while executing Chop Knife.
   B) Readjust feet while lifting knife into Shelf Knife to intercept a downward chop.

8. Three Battle Stance, Chopping Knife-Three Battle Stance, Shelf Knife

9.

A: **Three Battle Stance, Standing Pushing Knife**
B: **Covering Stance, Shelf Knife**
   A) The left foot moves forward to execute a left Three Battle Stance while executing a Standing Pushing Knife.
   B) The right leg steps over the left leg to form a right Covering Stance while executing a Shelf Knife.

9. Three Battle Stance, Standing Pushing Knife-Covering Stance, Shelf Knife

10.

A: **Three Battle Stance, Standing Pushing Knife**
B: **Three Battle Stance, Horizontal Push Knife**

A) Execute a Standing Pushing Knife to intercept an incoming attack.
B) The right leg is quickly shifting back to a right Three Battle Stance while executing a Horizontal Push Knife.

10. Three Battle Stance, Standing Pushing Knife-Three Battle Stance, Horizontal Push Knife

11.

A: **Three Battle Stance, Chopping Knife**
B: **Three Battle Stance, Shelf Knife**

A) The right leg steps forward to form a right Three Battle Stance while Raising Knife above head to Chop Knife.
B) Readjust feet while lifting the knife into Shelf Knife to intercept a downward chop.

11. Three Battle Stance, Chopping Knife-Three Battle Stance, Shelf Knife

SECTION SEVEN:

1.
   A: **Three Battle Stance, Stabbing Knife**
   B: **Horse Stance, Diagonal Chopping Knife**

   A) Shift weight back into the left leg to form a right Empty Stance while Grasping Knife forward; then step forward with the right leg to form a right Three Battle Stance, while Stabbing Knife toward Exponent **B**'s chest.
   B) The left leg steps back to form a Horse Stance, which allows the torso to move out of the way and at the same time execute Raising Knife; finally, using a Diagonal Chop to intercept the incoming stab.

2.
   A: **Three Battle Stance, Standing Pushing Knife**
   B: **Covering Stance, Shelf Knife**

   A) The left leg steps forward to form a left Three Battle Stance while executing a Standing Pushing Knife.
   B) The right leg steps over the left leg to form a left Covering Stance while executing a Shelf Knife.

1a. Three Battle Stance, Stabbing Knife-Three Battle Stance, Diagonal Chopping Knife

1b. Three Battle Stance, Stabbing Knife-Three Battle Stance, Diagonal Chopping Knife

2. Three Battle Stance, Standing Pushing Knife-Covering Stance, Shelf Knife

3.

A: **Three Battle Stance, Stabbing Knife**

B: **Single Standing Stance, Diagonal Chop Knife**

A) The right leg steps forward to form a right Three Battle Stance while executing a Stabbing Knife.

B) The right leg steps down quickly, which allows the left knee to raise to form a left Single Standing Stance, while executing a Diagonal Chop Knife.

3. Three Battle Stance, Stabbing Knife-Single Standing Stance, Diagonal Chopping Knife

4.

A: **Three Battle Stance, Stabbing Knife**

B: **Single Standing Stance, Diagonal Chop Knife**

A) The right leg steps forward to form a right Three Battle Stance while executing a Stabbing Knife.

B) The right leg steps down quickly, which allows the right knee to raise to form a right Single Standing Stance, while executing a Diagonal Chop Knife.

4. Three Battle Stance, Stabbing Knife-Single Standing Stance, Diagonal Chopping Knife

5.

A: **Three Battle Stance, Pattern Knife**

B: **Three Battle Stance, Stabbing Knife**

A) The right leg steps forward to form a right Three Battle Stance while executing a Pattern Knife to intercept an incoming stab.

B) The right leg steps down to form a right Three Battle Stance while Stabbing Knife.

5. Three Battle Stance, Pattern Knife-Three Battle Stance, Stabbing Knife

6.

   A: **Horse Stance, Diagonal Chop Knife**
   B: **Horse Stance, Diagonal Chop Knife**
   A) Turn waist to execute a Diagonal Chop Knife.
   B) Turn waist to execute a Diagonal Chop Knife.

7.

   A: **Three Battle Stance, Hiding Knife**
   B: **Empty Stance, Hiding Knife**
   A) The right leg steps across, still maintaining a right Three Battle Stance, while executing Hiding Knife to block incoming chop.
   B) The right leg steps back in an arc, while executing a right Empty Stance, and utilizing Hiding Knife to block an incoming chop.

6. Kneeling Stance, Diagonal Chopping Knife-Kneeling Stance, Diagonal Chopping Knife

7. Three Battle Stance, Hiding Knife-Three Battle Stance, Hiding Knife

SECTION EIGHT:

1.

A: Three Battle Stance, Shelf Push Knife

B: Three Battle Stance, Chopping Knife

A) The left foot steps forward to form a left Three Battle Stance while holding Horizontal Push Knife. Lift up the knife while to executing a Shelf Push Knife.

B) The right foot steps around to form a Horse Stance, while Raising Knife, then the feet shift to form a right Three Battle Stance while executing a Chop Knife.

1a. Three Battle Stance, Shelf Push Knife-Three Battle Stance, Chopping Knife

1b. Three Battle Stance, Shelf Push Knife-Three Battle Stance, Chopping Knife

2.

A: **Three Battle Stance, Pattern Knife**
B: **Three Battle Stance, Stabbing Knife**

A) The right leg steps forward to form a right Three Battle Stance while maintaining Shelf Push Knife; then execute a Pattern Knife. The right leg steps back to form a left Three Battle Stance while holding Horizontal Push Knife and finally executing Pattern Push Knife.

B) The left leg stars to move forward to form a right Three Battle Stance while Grasping Knife forward to execute to Stab Knife. Lift the right leg while Grasping Knife Forward, and forward to form a right Three Battle Stance while executing Stabbing Knife.

2a. Three Battle Stance, Pattern Knife-Three Battle Stance, Stabbing Knife

2b. Three Battle Stance, Pattern Knife-Three Battle Stance, Stabbing Knife

3.

A: **Three Battle Stance, Pattern Push Knife**

B: **Three Battle Stance, Stabbing Knife**

A) The right leg steps back to form a left Three Battle Stance while holding Horizontal Push Knife and executing Pattern Push Knife.

B) Lift the right leg while Grasping Knife Forward and go forward to form a right Three Battle Stance while executing Stabbing Knife.

3a. Three Battle Stance, Pattern Push Knife-Three Battle Stance, Stabbing Knife

3b. Three Battle Stance, Pattern Push Knife-Three Battle Stance, Stabbing Knife

4.

A: **Three Battle Stance, Diagonal Chopping Knife**
B: **Three Battle Stance, Stabbing Knife**

A) The right leg steps forward to form a right Three Battle Stance while Raising Knife and then executing a Diagonal Chopping Knife.
B) Shift weight to the rear leg and execute a right Empty Stance while Grasping Knife forward, which is followed by a right Three Battle Stance and Stabbing Knife.

4a. Three Battle Stance, Diagonal Chopping Knife-Three Battle Stance, Stabbing Knife

5.

A: **Horse Stance, Diagonal Chopping Knife**
B: **Horse Stance, Diagonal Chopping Knife**

C) Use Raising Knife to execute a Diagonal Chopping Knife.
D) Use Raising Knife to execute a Diagonal Chopping Knife.

4b. Three Battle Stance, Diagonal Chopping Knife-Three Battle Stance, Stabbing Knife

5a. Three Battle Stance, Diagonal Chopping Knife-Three Battle Stance, Diagonal Chopping Knife

5b. Three Battle Stance, Diagonal Chopping Knife-Three Battle Stance, Diagonal Chopping Knife

6. **Empty Stance, Covering Pommel**
   Shift the weight back to form a right Empty Stance, tilting the knife back into Grasping Knife to the side of the arm, and execute a Raising Fist with the pommel of the knife.

7. **Side-by-Side Stance, Grasping Knife**
   Bring the arms back to the pectoral muscles and lower arms down to the waist.

6a. Empty Stance, Covering Pommel

6b. Empty Stance, Covering Pommel

7. Side-by-Side Stance, Grasping Knife

CHAPTER 23

FIVE FOOT STAFF SKILL
NGO CIAK GUA (五 尺棍)

At the dawn of time, humanity employed various implements for its survival and one of these was a stick. Even though the Bronze Age and Iron Age altered the landscape, the mere stick continued to strive and its apex was the Shàolín Temple.

In the sixteenth century, a Yú, Dàyóu (1503–1579), a renowned Ming dynasty general, invigorated the Shàolín Temple by introducing them to his staff—or stick knowledge—that the monks could utilize against the Wōkòu or Japanese pirates that raided the eastern coastline of China. The monks were commissioned to fight against the pirates; therefore, an elite warrior monk participated in at least four battles. This proved the value of the staff in the battlefield in the age of muskets.

Five Ancestor Fist staff heritage stems from this rich legacy that is still vibrant to this day, which can be seen throughout its various staff routines:

- **Five Foot Staff**: Ngo Ciak Gua (五 尺棍)
- **Seven Foot Staff**: Cit Ciak Gua (七 尺棍)
- **Level Eye Brow Staff**: Zê Mai Gua (齊眉棍)
- **Meteor Staff**: Lau Xing Gua (流星棍)

The tradition of Kong Han is to teach the Five Foot Staff first; it introduces practitioners to a single-ended staff, which focuses on direct strikes and quick interceptions.

NGO CIAK GUA

SECTION ONE:

1. **Side-by-Side Stance, Grasping Staff**
   Grasping Staff on the side of the body while standing in Side-by-Side Stance.

2. **Single Standing Stance, Double Hand, Upright Grasping Staff**
   Lift up the right knee to form a right Single Standing Stance while lifting the staff. This particular posture is referred to as Double Hand, Upright Grasping Staff.

3. **Single Standing Stance, Pulling Staff**
   The right leg steps down, allowing the torso to turn to the left side, i.e., west. At the same time, lift the left knee to form a left Single Standing Stance. The right hand starts to descend to Pulling Staff down to the right side.

4. **Single Standing Stance, Double Hand, Upright Grasping Staff**
   The left foot descends down, allowing the right knee to lift, forming a right Single Standing Stance. The right hand rises in the process, forming Double Hand, Upright Grasping Staff.

1. Side-by-Side Stance, Grasping Staff

2. Single Standing Stance, Double Hand, Upright Grasping Staff

3. Single Standing Stance, Pulling Staff

4. Single Standing Stance, Double Hand, Upright Grasping Staff

5. **Single Standing Stance, Slanting, Embracing Staff**

   The right leg descends, allowing the torso to turn to the left side, i.e., west, and allowing the left knee to rise to form a left Single Standing Stance. The raising the staff in the posture referred to as Slanting, Embracing Staff.

6. **Three Battle Stance, Chopping Staff**

   The right leg descends to form a right Three Battle Stance while Chopping Staff down.

7. **Three Battle Stance, Stabbing Staff**

   The next movement refers to Roll Staff, which means bringing back the center of the staff to the hip. This is followed with Stabbing Staff.

5. Single Standing Stance, Slanting, Embracing Staff

6. Three Battle Stance, Chopping Staff

7. Three Battle Stance, Stabbing Staff

8. Three Battle Stance, Stabbing Staff

SECTION TWO:

1. Covering Stance, Double Hand, Upright Grasping Stick

1. **Covering Stance, Double Hand, Upright Grasping Stick**
   The right leg steps over the left leg, going toward the left, i.e., west, while executing a right Covering Stance. At the same time perform Double Hand, Upright Grasping Stick.

2. **Three Battle Stance, Diagonal Chopping Stick**
   The left leg steps out to form a 45º angle Three Battle Stance while executing a Diagonal Chopping Stick.

3. **Three Battle Stance, Pulling Staff**
   The left leg steps over the right leg, forming a right Covering Stance and then forming a right Three Battle Stance, i.e., 45º angle, while maintaining a Pulling Staff posture.

2a.. Three Battle Stance, Diagonal Chopping Stick

2b. Three Battle Stance, Diagonal Chopping Stick

3a. Three Battle Stance, Pulling Staff

3b. Three Battle Stance, Pulling Staff

4. **Four Level Stance, Line Staff**
   Right leg steps forward to form a Four Level Stance while executing Line Staff.

5. **Three Battle Stance, Chopping Staff**
   The right leg steps forward to form a right Three Battle Stance. First execute Embracing Staff and then Chopping Staff.

6. **Three Battle Stance, Stabbing Staff**
   The next movement refers to Roll Staff, which means bringing back the center of the staff to one's hip. This is followed with Stabbing Staff.

4. Four Level Stance, Line Staff

5a. Three Battle Stance, Chopping Staff

5b. Three Battle Stance, Chopping Staff

6a. Three Battle Stance, Stabbing Staff

6b. Three Battle Stance, Stabbing Staff

Five Foot Staff Skill Ngo Ciak Gua (五尺棍)

SECTION THREE:

1. Single Standing Stance, Pulling Staff

1. **Single Standing Stance, Pulling Staff**
   Lift up the right knee to form a right Single Standing Stance, i.e., west; at the same time execute Pulling Staff toward the right side.

2. **Single Standing Stance, Shelf Staff**
   The right leg steps down, quickly jumping back, while lifting the left knee to form a left Single Standing Stance, while executing a Shelf Staff.

3. **Three Battle Stance, Chopping Staff**
   The left leg steps down to form a right Three Battle Stance, while executing Embracing Staff to Chopping Staff.

4. **Three Battle Stance, Stabbing Staff**
   Followed by Roll Staff and Stabbing Staff.

2. Single Standing Stance, Shelf Staff

3a. Three Battle Stance, Chopping Staff

3b. Three Battle Stance, Chopping Staff

4a. Three Battle Stance, Stabbing Staff

4b. Three Battle Stance, Stabbing Staff

SECTION FOUR:

1. **Covering Stance, Double Hand, Upright Grasping Stick**

   The right leg steps over the left leg, going toward the left, i.e., west, while executing a right Covering Stance. At the same time perform Double Hand, Upright Grasping Stick.

2. **Three Battle Stance, Collapse Staff**

   The left leg steps out to form a 45°-angle Three Battle Stance, while executing a Diagonal Chopping Stick, which is followed with a motion referred to as Collapse Staff.

3. **Covering Stance, Double Hand, Upright Grasping Stick**

   The left leg steps over the right leg, going toward the left, i.e., east, while executing a left Covering Stance. At the same time perform Double Hand, Upright Grasping Stick.

1. Covering Stance, Double Hand, Upright Grasping Stick

2a. Three Battle Stance, Collapse Staff

2b. Three Battle Stance, Collapse Staff

3. Covering Stance, Double Hand, Upright Grasping Stick

4. **Three Battle Stance, Collapse Staff**
   The left leg steps out to form a 45° angle Three Battle Stance, while executing a Diagonal Chopping Stick, followed with a motion referred to Collapse Staff.

5. **Four Level Stance, Line Staff**
   The right leg steps back to form a Four Level Stance while executing Line Staff facing the right side, i.e., east.

4a. Three Battle Stance, Collapse Staff

4b. Three Battle Stance, Collapse Staff

5. Four Level Stance, Line Staff

6. **Three Battle Stance, Chopping Staff**
   The right leg steps forward to form a right Three Battle Stance. The Staff first executes Embracing Staff and shifts to Shelf Staff and finally Chopping Staff.

7. **Three Battle Stance, Stabbing Staff**
   The next movement is Roll Staff, followed with Stabbing Staff.

6a. Three Battle Stance, Chopping Staff

6b. Three Battle Stance, Chopping Staff

6c. Three Battle Stance, Chopping Staff

7a. Three Battle Stance, Stabbing Staff

7b. Three Battle Stance, Stabbing Staff

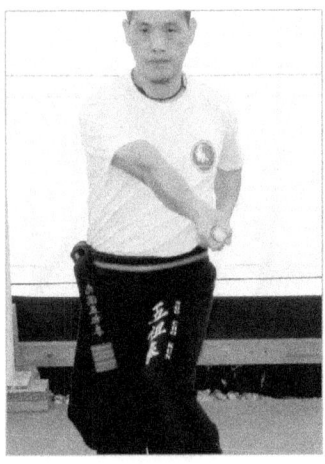

1. Three Battle Stance, Stabbing Staff

SECTION FIVE:

1. **Three Battle Stance, Stabbing Staff**
   The left leg steps forward to form a left Three Battle Stance while Stabbing Staff.

2. **Four Level Stance, Opposing Roll Staff**
   Shift stance, i.e., Four Level Stance, with torso facing right, i.e., east, while Opposing Roll Staff, meaning the edge of the hand faces out.

3. **Three Battle Stance, Chopping Staff**
   Shift into a right Three Battle Stance while lifting the staff to Shelf Staff and then Chopping Staff.

2. Four Level Stance, Opposing Roll Staff

3a. Three Battle Stance, Chopping Staff

3b. Three Battle Stance, Chopping Staff

3c. Three Battle Stance, Chopping Staff

4. **Three Battle Stance, Stabbing Staff**
   Roll Staff and follow by Stabbing Staff.

5. **Horse Stance, Opposing Grasp Stabbing Staff**
   The next posture is referred to as Monkey Descends, which consists of the left leg positioning itself beside the right foot's arc, called the Personal Stance, and Roll Staff, which is when the left leg steps out to form a Horse Stance, while executing an Opposing Grasp Stabbing Staff to the back, i.e., south.

4a. Three Battle Stance, Stabbing Staff

4b. Three Battle Stance, Stabbing Staff

5a. Horse Stance, Opposing Grasp Stabbing Staff

5b. Horse Stance, Opposing Grasp Stabbing Staff

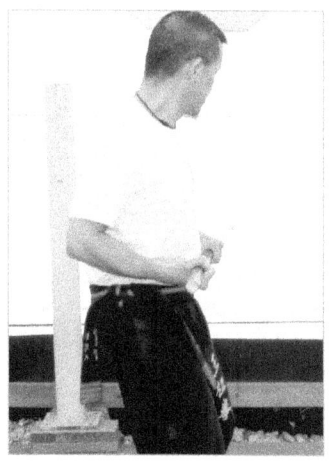

5c. Horse Stance, Opposing Grasp Stabbing Staff

Five Foot Staff Skill Ngo Ciak Gua (五尺棍)

SECTION SIX:

1. Empty Stance, Opposing Grasp Pull Staff

1. **Empty Stance, Opposing Grasp Pull Staff**
   The left leg moves in to form a left Empty Stance, while executing an Opposing Grasp Pull Staff to the left. This is poetically referred to as Monkey Low Guard.

2. **Single Standing Stance, Opposing Grasp Pull Staff**
   The left leg arcs to jump and turn clockwise, landing in a right Single Standing Stance, while still maintaining Opposing Grasp Pull Staff.

3. **Horse Stance, Shelf Staff**
   The right leg steps down to form a Horse Stance while executing a Shelf Staff.

2a. Single Standing Stance, Opposing Grasp Pull Staff

2b. Single Standing Stance, Opposing Grasp Pull Staff

2c. Single Standing Stance, Opposing Grasp Pull Staff

3. Horse Stance, Shelf Staff

4. **Three Battle Stance, Chopping Staff**
   The right leg steps forward to form a right Three Battle Stance. The Staff first executes Shelf Staff, then shifts to Embracing Staff and finally Chopping Staff.

5. **Three Battle Stance, Stabbing Staff**
   The next movement is to Roll Staff, followed with Stabbing Staff.

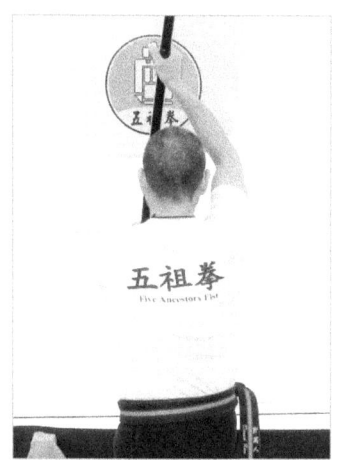

4a. Three Battle Stance, Chopping Staff

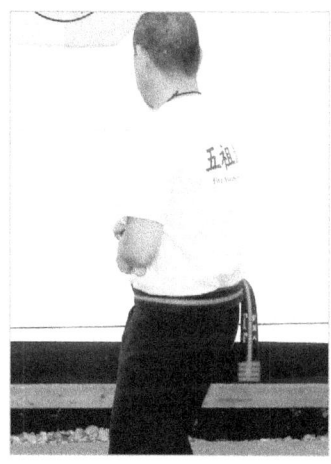

4b. Three Battle Stance, Chopping Staff

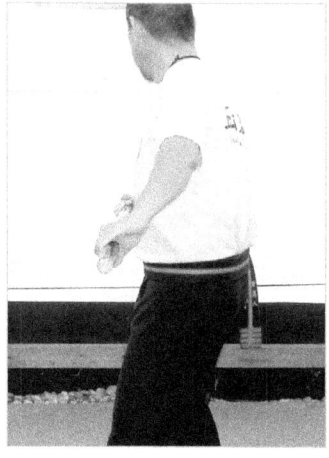

5a. Three Battle Stance, Stabbing Staff

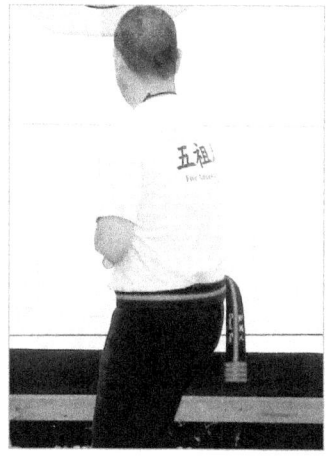

5b. Three Battle Stance, Stabbing Staff

SECTION SEVEN:

1. **Covering Stance, Collapsing Staff**
   The right leg steps over the left leg, going toward the left, i.e., west, while executing a right Covering Stance. At the same time perform Pull Staff toward the right and then Collapsing Staff.

2. **Three Battle Stance, Diagonal Chopping Stick**
   The left leg steps out to form a 45° angle Three Battle Stance while executing a Diagonal Chopping Stick.

3. **Covering Stance, Collapsing Staff**
   The left leg steps over the right leg, forming a right Covering Stance, while performing a Pulling Staff posture to Collapsing Staff.

1a. Three Battle Stance, Diagonal Chopping Stick

1b. Covering Stance, Collapsing Staff

2. Covering Stance, Collapsing Staff

3a. Covering Stance, Collapsing Staff

3b. Covering Stance, Collapsing Staff

4. **Three Battle Stance, Point Staff**

   The right leg goes forward to form a right Three Battle Stance, while Roll Staff to Point Staff.

5. **Four Level Stance, Line Staff**

   The left leg steps back to form a Four Level Stance, while executing Line Staff facing the left side, i.e., west.

6. **Three Battle Stance, Chopping Staff**

   The right leg steps forward to form a right Three Battle Stance. The Staff first executes Embracing Staff and then Chopping Staff.

4a. Three Battle Stance, Point Staff

4b. Three Battle Stance, Point Staff

5. Four Level Stance, Line Staff

6a. Three Battle Stance, Chopping Staff

6b. Three Battle Stance, Chopping Staff

7a. Three Battle Stance, Stabbing Staff

7. **Three Battle Stance, Stabbing Staff**
   The next movement is to Roll Staff, followed with Stabbing Staff.

8. **Single Standing Stance, Pulling Staff**
   Lift up right knee to form a right Single Standing Stance, i.e., west, at the same time executing Pulling Staff toward the right side.

9. **Single Standing Stance, Pulling Staff**
   The right leg steps down; quickly jump back while lifting the left knee to form a left Single Standing Stance, while maintaining Pulling Staff.

7b. Three Battle Stance, Stabbing Staff

8. Single Standing Stance, Pulling Staff

9. Single Standing Stance, Pulling Staff

10. **Three Battle Stance, Chopping Staff**

    The right leg steps forward to form a right Three Battle Stance. The Staff first executes Shelf Staff, then shifts to Embracing Staff and finally Chopping Staff.

11. **Three Battle Stance, Stabbing Staff**

    The left leg steps down to form a right Three Battle Stance while executing Chopping Staff, followed by Roll Staff and finally Stabbing Staff.

10a. Three Battle Stance, Chopping Staff

10b. Three Battle Stance, Chopping Staff

11a. Three Battle Stance, Stabbing Staff

11b. Three Battle Stance, Stabbing Staff

Five Foot Staff Skill Ngo Ciak Gua (五尺棍)

1. Covering Stance, Pulling Staff

SECTION EIGHT:

1. **Covering Stance, Pulling Staff**
   The right leg steps over the left leg, while executing a right Covering Stance, at the same time performing Pulling Staff.

2. **Three Battle Stance, Collapse Staff**
   The left leg steps out to form a 45° angle Three Battle Stance while maintaining Pulling Staff, and then executing a Collapse Staff.

3. **Covering Stance, Collapse Staff**
   The left leg steps over the right leg while executing a left Covering Stance, at the same time performing Pulling Staff and then executing a Collapse Staff.

4. **Three Battle Stance, Collapse Staff**
   The right leg steps forward to form a right Three Battle Stance while Pulling Staff and then executing a Collapse Staff.

5. **Four Level Stance, Line Staff**
   The right leg steps back to form a Four Level Stance while executing Line Staff facing the right side, i.e., west.

2a. Three Battle Stance, Collapse Staff

2b. Three Battle Stance, Collapse Staff

3a. Covering Stance, Collapse Staff

3b. Covering Stance, Collapse Staff

4a. Three Battle Stance, Collapse Staff

4b. Three Battle Stance, Collapse Staff

5. Four Level Stance, Line Staff

6. **Three Battle Stance, Chopping Staff**
   The right leg steps forward to form a right Three Battle Stance. The Staff first executes Shelf Staff and then Chopping Staff.

7. **Three Battle Stance, Stabbing Staff**
   The next movement is to Roll Staff, followed with Stabbing Staff.

6a. Three Battle Stance, Chopping Staff

6b. Three Battle Stance, Chopping Staff

7a. Three Battle Stance, Stabbing Staff

7b. Three Battle Stance, Stabbing Staff

1a. Horse Stance, Opposing Grasp Stabbing Staff

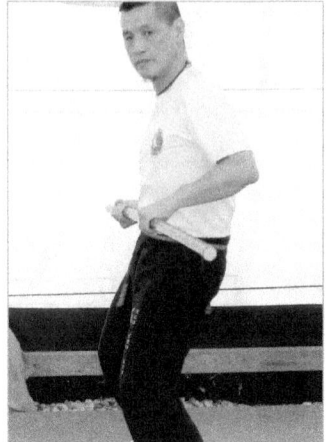

1b. Horse Stance, Opposing Grasp Stabbing Staff

SECTION NINE:

1. **Horse Stance, Opposing Grasp Stabbing Staff**
   The next posture is referred to as Monkey Descends, which consist of the left leg positioning itself beside the right foot's arc, called the Personal Stance, while executing Roll Staff, which is when the left leg steps out to form a Horse Stance while executing an Opposing Grasp Stabbing Staff to the back, i.e., south.

2. **Empty Stance, Opposing Grasp Pull Staff**
   The left leg moves in to form a left Empty Stance while executing an Opposing Grasp Pull Staff to the left. This is poetically referred to as Monkey Low Guard.

3. **Empty Stance, Opposing Grasp Pull Staff**
   The left leg steps back to allow the right leg to move across to form a right Empty Stance while executing an Opposing Grasp Pull Staff to the left. This is poetically referred to as Monkey Low Guard.

1c. Horse Stance, Opposing Grasp Stabbing Staff

2. Empty Stance, Opposing Grasp Pull Staff

3. Empty Stance, Opposing Grasp Pull Staff

4. **Single Standing Stance, Shelf Staff**
   The left leg arcs to jump and turn clockwise, landing in a right Single Standing Stance, while still maintaining Shelf Staff.

5. **Three Battle Stance, Chopping Staff**
   The right leg steps forward to form a right Three Battle Stance. The Staff first executes Shelf Staff, then shifts to Embracing Staff and then Chopping Staff.

6. **Empty Stance, Chopping Staff**
   The next movement consists of the right leg forming a right Empty Stance while maintaining Chopping Staff posture.

4a. Single Standing Stance, Shelf Staff

4b. Single Standing Stance, Shelf Staff

5a. Three Battle Stance, Chopping Staff

5b. Three Battle Stance, Chopping Staff

6. Empty Stance, Chopping Staff

7. **Empty Stance, Shelf Staff**
   Execute Shelf Staff.

8. **Four Level Stance, Line Staff**
   The right leg steps back to form a Four Level Stance while executing Line Staff.

9. **Four Level Stance, Hanging-Up Staff**
   The right leg steps back to form a Four Level Stance while executing Line Staff, and then turn staff into Embracing Staff, followed by executing Hanging-Up Staff.

7. Empty Stance, Shelf Staff

8. Four Level Stance, Line Staff

9a. Four Level Stance, Hanging-Up Staff

9b. Four Level Stance, Hanging-Up Staff

9c. Four Level Stance, Hanging-Up Staff

9d. Four Level Stance, Hanging-Up Staff

10. **Empty Stance, Willow Leaf Palm**

    The right foot steps forward to execute a right Empty Stance while Embracing Staff and executing a left Willow Leaf Palm.

11. **Four Level Stance, Embracing Fist**

    The right leg steps back to form a Four Level Stance and the left hand converts to Embracing Fist.

12. **Side-by-Side Stance, Grasping Staff**

    The right leg moves in to form a Side-by-Side Stance while maintaining the Embracing Fist, and finally lowering fist and Staff to the side.

10. Empty Stance, Willow Leaf Palm

11. Four Level Stance, Embracing Fist

12a. Side-by-Side Stance, Grasping Staff

12b. Side-by-Side Stance, Grasping Staff

CHAPTER 24

FIVE FOOT STAFF PARTNER DRILL
NGO CIAK GUA DUI LIAN (五尺棍)

As with the prior routines, the Five Foot Staff also possesses a partner drill, which adds more depth to the practitioners' learning experience. The partner drill strongly stresses the notion of distances, which is crucial within combat, especially close-quarter combat. Also it works on the coordination of the upper body with the lower body. Five Foot Staff Partner Drill stresses this strongly compared to other routines because the motion of the staff is interconnected with the footwork and stances.

*The author, Daniel Kun, is Exponent **A**; Devan Kraushar is Exponent **B**.*

SECTION ONE:

1. **Side-by-Side Stance, Grasping Staff**
   Grasping Staff on the side of the body while standing in Side-by-Side Stance.

1. Side-by-Side Stance, Grasping Staff

2. **Side-by-Side Stance, Grasping Staff**
   Face one another while maintaining the same posture as before.

3.
   A: **Three Battle Stance, Turn Staff**
   B: **Three Battle Stance, Turn Staff**
   A) The left foot steps back, in the process forming a right Three Battle Stance, while executing a strike referred to as Turn Staff.
   B) The left foot steps back, in the process forming a right Three Battle Stance, while executing a strike referred to as Turn Staff.

4.
   A: **Three Battle Stance, Pointing Staff**
   B: **Single Standing Stance, Pull Staff**
   A) Pointing Staff toward Exponent **B**'s legs.
   B) Lift the right knee while hopping back to form a right Single Standing Stance, and executing Pull Staff.

2. Side-by-Side Stance, Grasping Staff

3. Three Battle Stance, Turn Staff-Three Battle Stance, Turn Staff

4. Three Battle Stance, Pointing Staff-Single Standing Stance, Pull Staff

5.

A: **Three Battle Stance, Stabbing Staff**
B: **Single Standing Stance, Double Hand, Upright Grasping Staff**

A) Execute a Stabbing Staff toward exponent **B**'s face.
B) Hop onto the right foot while descending, which allow the left knee to lift, forming a left Single Standing Stance. At the same time intercept the incoming stab with Double Hand, Upright Grasping Staff.

5. Three Battle Stance, Stabbing Staff-Single Standing Stance, Double Hand, Upright Grasping Staff

6.

A: **Three Battle Stance, Stabbing Staff**
B: **Three Battle Stance, Roll Staff**

A) Maintain the Stabbing Staff posture.
B) The left leg steps down to form a right Three Battle Stance, while executing Roll Staff with the intent to press down on the opponent's staff.

6. Three Battle Stance, Stabbing Staff-Three Battle Stance, Roll Staff

7.

A: **Three Battle Stance, Roll Staff**
B: **Three Battle Stance, Stabbing Staff**

A) The left leg steps out into an angle while executing Roll Staff with the incoming stab.
B) Stabbing Staff toward Exponent **A**'s chest.

7. Three Battle Stance, Rolling Staff-Three Battle Stance, Stabbing Staff

Five Foot Staff Partner Drill Ngo Ciak Gua Dui Lian (五尺棍)

SECTION TWO:

1.
   A: **Three Battle Stance, Slanting Strike Staff**
   B: **Covering Stance, Slanting Strike Staff**
   A) Execute a Slanting Strike Staff.
   B) The right leg steps over the left leg while forming a right Covering Stance and executing a Slanting Strike Staff.

8. Three Battle Stance, Slanting Strike Staff-Covering Stance, Slanting Strike Staff

2.
   A: **Three Battle Stance, Pull Staff**
   B: **Three Battle Stance, Pull Staff**
   A) The left leg steps forward to form a left Three Battle Stance while executing a Pull Staff.
   B) The right leg steps forward to form a left Three Battle Stance while executing a Pull Staff.

9. Three Battle Stance, Pull Staff-Three Battle Stance, Pull Staff

3.
   A: **Covering Stance, Slanting Strike Staff**
   B: **Covering Stance, Slanting Strike Staff**
   A) The right leg steps over left leg while forming a right Covering Stance and executing a Slanting Strike Staff.
   B) The left leg steps over right leg while forming a left Covering Stance and executing a Slanting Strike Staff.

10. Covering Stance, Slanting Strike Staff-Covering Stance, Slanting Strike Staff

4.

A: **Three Battle Stance, Slanting Strike Staff**
B: **Three Battle Stance, Slanting Strike Staff**

A) The left leg steps forward to form a left Three Battle Stance while maintaining the Slanting Strike Staff posture.
B) The right leg steps forward to form a right Three Battle Stance while maintaining the Slanting Strike Staff posture.

11. Three Battle Stance, Slanting Strike Staff-Three Battle Stance, Slanting Strike Staff

5.

A: **Single Standing Stance, Pull Staff**
B: **Three Battle Stance, Pointing Staff**

A) Lift the right knee while hopping back to form a right Single Standing Stance and executing a Pull Staff.
B) Pointing Staff toward Exponent **A**'s legs.

6.

A: **Three Battle Stance, Pushing Staff**
B: **Four Level Stance, Line Staff**

A) The right leg steps down to form a left Three Battle Stance while executing a Pushing Staff.
B) Shift into a Four Level Stance while executing Line Staff to intercept the incoming strike.

12. Single Standing Stance, Pull Staff-Three Battle Stance, Pointing Staff

13. Three Battle Stance, Pushing Staff-Four Level Stance, Line Staff

7.
   A: **Three Battle Stance, Shelf Push Staff**
   B: **Three Battle Stance, Chop Staff**
   A) Adjust stance to embrace the incoming strike, which is intercepted with Shelf Push Staff.
   B) The right leg steps forward to form a right Three Battle Stance while executing a Chop Staff.

8.
   A: **Three Battle Stance, Turn Staff**
   B: **Three Battle Stance, Stabbing Staff**
   A) Adjust staff to Embracing Staff and then execute Turn Staff.
   B) Stabbing Staff toward the torso of Exponent **A**.

14. Three Battle Stance, Shelf Push Staff-Three Battle Stance, Chop Staff

15a. Three Battle Stance, Turn Staff-Three Battle Stance, Stabbing Staff

16b. Three Battle Stance, Turn Staff-Three Battle Stance, Stabbing Staff

9.

A: **Three Battle Stance, Pointing Staff**
B: **Single Standing Stance, Pull Staff**

A) The right leg steps forward to form a right Three Battle Stance while Pointing Staff toward Exponent **B**'s legs.

B) Lift the right knee while hopping back to form a right Single Standing Stance and execute Pull Staff.

16. Three Battle Stance, Pointing Staff-Single Standing Stance, Pull Staff

10.

A: **Three Battle Stance, Stabbing Staff**
B: **Single Standing Stance, Double Hand, Upright Grasping Staff**

A) Execute a Stabbing Staff toward exponent **B**'s face.

B) Hop onto the right foot while descending, which allow the left knee to lift, forming a left Single Standing Stance. At the same time intercept the incoming stab with Double Hand, Upright Grasping Staff.

17. Three Battle Stance, Stabbing Staff-Single Standing Stance, Double Hand, Upright Grasping Staff

11.

A: **Three Battle Stance, Stabbing Staff**
B: **Three Battle Stance, Roll Staff**

A) Maintain the Stabbing Staff posture.

B) The left leg steps down to form a right Three Battle Stance while executing Roll Staff with the intent of pressing down on the other's staff.

18. Three Battle Stance, Stabbing Staff-Three Battle Stance, Roll Staff

Five Foot Staff Partner Drill Ngo Ciak Gua Dui Lian (五尺棍)

SECTION THREE:

1.
   - A: **Three Battle Stance, Roll Staff**
   - B: **Three Battle Stance, Roll Staff**
   - A) Roll Staff position.
   - B) Roll Staff position.

2.
   - A: **Three Battle Stance, Roll Staff**
   - B: **Three Battle Stance, Stabbing Staff**
   - A) The left leg steps out into an angle while executing Roll Staff with the incoming stab.
   - B) Stabbing Staff toward Exponent **A**'s chest.

3.
   - A: **Covering Stance, Slanting Strike Staff**
   - B: **Covering Stance, Slanting Strike Staff**
   - A) The right leg steps over left leg, while forming a right Covering Stance, while executing a Slanting Strike Staff.
   - B) The left leg steps over right leg, while forming a left Covering Stance, while executing a Slanting Strike Staff.

1. Three Battle Stance, Roll Staff-Three Battle Stance, Roll Staff

2. Three Battle Stance, Roll Staff-Three Battle Stance, Stabbing Staff

3. Covering Stance, Slanting Strike Staff-Covering Stance, Slanting Strike Staff

4.
   A: **Three Battle Stance, Pull Staff**
   B: **Three Battle Stance, Pull Staff**
   A) The left leg steps forward to form a left Three Battle Stance, while executing a Pull Staff.
   B) The right leg steps forward to form a left Three Battle Stance, while executing a Pull Staff.

5.
   A: **Covering Stance, Slanting Strike Staff**
   B: **Three Battle Stance, Slanting Strike Staff**
   A) The right leg steps over left leg, while forming a right Covering Stance, while executing a Slanting Strike Staff.
   B) Execute a Slanting Strike Staff.

6.
   A: **Covering Stance, Pull Staff**
   B: **Covering Stance, Pull Staff**
   A) The right leg steps over left leg while forming a right Covering Stance and executing a Pull Staff.
   B) The left leg steps over right leg while forming a left Covering Stance and executing a Pull Staff.

4. Three Battle Stance, Pull Staff-Three Battle Stance, Pull Staff

5. Covering Stance, Slanting Strike Staff-Three Battle Stance, Slanting Strike Staff

6. Covering Stance, Pull Staff-Covering Stance, Pull Staff

7.
A: **Three Battle Stance, Slanting Strike Staff**
B: **Three Battle Stance, Slanting Strike Staff**
A) The left leg steps forward to form a left Three Battle Stance while executing a Slanting Strike Staff.
B) The right leg steps forward to form a left Three Battle Stance while executing a Slanting Strike Staff.

7. Three Battle Stance, Slanting Strike Staff-Three Battle Stance, Slanting Strike Staff

8.
A: **Empty Stance, Pull Staff**
B: **Three Battle Stance, Pull Staff**
A) The right leg steps forward while forming a right Empty Stance and executing a Pull Staff.
B) Execute a Pull Staff.

8. Empty Stance, Pull Staff-Three Battle Stance, Pull Staff

9.
A: **Empty Stance, Slanting Strike Staff**
B: **Three Battle Stance, Slanting Strike Staff**
A) The left leg steps forward while forming a left Empty Stance, with the objective to move around Exponent **B**, and executing a Slanting Strike Staff.
B) Execute a Slanting Strike Staff.

9. Empty Stance, Slanting Strike Staff-Three Battle Stance, Slanting Strike Staff

10.
A: **Three Battle Stance, Pushing Staff**
B: **Four Level Stance, Line Staff**
A) The left leg steps down to form a left Three Battle Stance while executing a Pushing Staff.
B) Shift into a Four Level Stance while executing Line Staff to intercept the incoming strike.

11.
A: **Three Battle Stance, Shelf Push Staff**
B: **Three Battle Stance, Chopping Staff**
A) Adjust stance to embrace incoming strike, which is intercepted with Shelf Push Staff.
B) The right leg steps forward to form a right Three Battle Stance while executing a Chop Staff.

10. Three Battle Stance, Pushing Staff-Four Level Stance, Line Staff

11. Three Battle Stance, Shelf Push Staff-Three Battle Stance, Chop Staff

SECTION FOUR:

1.

> A: **Empty Stance, Roll Staff**
> B: **Three Battle Stance, Roll Staff**
> A) The right leg crosses the left leg to form a right Empty Stance while executing Roll Staff position.
> B) Roll Staff position.

2.

> A: **Three Battle Stance, Turn Staff**
> B: **Three Battle Stance, Stabbing Staff**
> A) Step back into a left Three Battle Stance while first executing Roll Staff and then Turn Staff.
> B) Stab Staff toward Exponent A's Torso.

3.

> A: **Three Battle Stance, Line Staff**
> B: **Four Level Stance, Push Staff**
> A) Adjust the feet into right Three Battle Stance while adjusting staff into Line Staff to intercept the incoming strike.
> B) The left leg steps forward, forming a Four Level Stance, while executing a Push Staff.

1. Empty Stance, Roll Staff-Three Battle Stance, Roll Staff

2. Three Battle Stance, Turn Staff-Three Battle Stance, Stabbing Staff

3a. Three Battle Stance, Line Staff-Four Level Stance, Push Staff

3b. Three Battle Stance, Line Staff-Four Level Stance, Push Staff

4.

A: Three Battle Stance, Chopping Staff

B: Three Battle Stance, Shelf Push Staff

A) The left leg steps forward in a left Three Battle Stance while executing Chopping Staff.

B) Adjust the staff to execute Shelf Push Staff and intercept the incoming chop.

5.

A: Three Battle Stance, Shelf Push Staff

B: Three Battle Stance, Chopping Staff

A) Adjust the staff to execute Shelf Push Staff and intercept the incoming chop.

B) Right leg steps forward executing a right Three Battle Stance, while executing Chopping Staff.

4. Three Battle Stance, Chopping Staff-Three Battle Stance, Shelf Push Staff

5. Three Battle Stance, Shelf Push Staff-Three Battle Stance, Chopping Staff

6.
   A: **Empty Stance, Chopping Staff**
   B: **Three Battle Stance, Stabbing Staff**
   A) Shift weight onto the left leg while forming a right Empty Stance and executing Upright Grasping Staff and then quickly Chopping Staff.
   B) Roll Staff to Stabbing Staff at Exponent A's torso.

7.
   A: **Empty Stance, Embracing Staff**
   B: **Personal Stance, Roll Staff**
   A) The right leg steps forward to form a right Three Battle Stance while executing a Push Staff; however, after missing, the right leg steps forward to allow the torso to turn around into a left Empty Stance while Embracing Staff.
   B) While doing Embracing Staff, quickly duck under the swinging staff, forming a left Personal Stance while executing Roll Staff.

6a. Empty Stance, Chopping Staff-Three Battle Stance, Stabbing Staff

6b. Empty Stance, Chopping Staff-Three Battle Stance, Stabbing Staff

7a. Empty Stance, Embracing Staff-Personal Stance, Roll Staff

7b. Empty Stance, Embracing Staff-Personal Stance, Roll Staff

8.
A: **Three Battle Stance, Embracing Staff**
B: **Four Level Stance, Stabbing Staff**
A) The left leg steps back to form a left Three Battle Stance while executing Embracing Staff to intercept the incoming strike.
B) The left foot steps out to form a Four Level Stance while executing Stabbing Staff.

8. Three Battle Stance, Embracing Staff-Four Level Stance, Stabbing Staff

9.
A: **Three Battle Stance, Pointing Staff**
B: **Empty Stance, Pull Staff**
A) Readjust the stance to execute Point Staff at Exponent **B**'s legs.
B) The left leg moves forward to form a left Empty Stance while executing a Pull Staff to intercept the incoming strike.

9. Three Battle Stance, Pointing Staff-Empty Stance, Pull Staff

10.
A: **Three Battle Stance, Pointing Staff**
B: **Empty Stance, Pull Staff**
A) The right leg steps forward to form a right Three Battle Stance while executing Point Staff at Exponent **B**'s legs.
B) The left leg moves backward, allowing the torso to turn; at which time the right leg goes forward to form a right Empty Stance while executing a Pull Staff to intercept the incoming strike.

10. Three Battle Stance, Pointing Staff-Empty Stance, Pull Staff

11.

A: **Three Battle Stance, Line Staff**
B: **Single Standing Stance, Embracing Staff**

A) Execute quickly a Line Staff to strike Exponent **B**'s head.
B) Lift the right knee quickly in right Single Standing Stance while executing Embracing Staff to intercept the strike.

11. Three Battle Stance, Line Staff-Single Standing Stance, Embracing Staff

SECTION FIVE:

1.

A: **Three Battle Stance, Turn Staff**
B: **Three Battle Stance, Turn Staff**

A) Readjust the stance to execute a Turn Staff.
B) The right leg steps down to form a right Three Battle Stance while executing a Turn Staff.

1. Three Battle Stance, Turn Staff-Three Battle Stance, Turn Staff

2.

A: **Empty Stance, Roll Staff**
B: **Three Battle Stance, Roll Staff**

A) Shift weight to the left leg to form a right Empty Stance while executing Roll Staff.
B) Roll Staff.

2. Empty Stance, Roll Staff-Three Battle Stance, Roll Staff

3.

A: **Three Battle Stance, Turn Staff**
B: **Three Battle Stance, Stabbing Staff**
A) Step forward to form a right Three Battle Stance while executing a Turn Staff.
B) Execute a Stabbing Staff.

4.

A: **Covering Stance, Slanting Strike Staff**
B: **Covering Stance, Slanting Strike Staff**
A) The right leg steps over the left leg to form a right Covering Stance while executing a Slanting Strike Staff.
B) The right leg steps over the left leg to form a right Covering Stance while executing a Slanting Strike Staff.

5.

A: **Three Battle Stance, Pull Staff**
B: **Three Battle Stance, Pull Staff**
A) The left leg steps forward to form a left Three Battle Stance while executing a Pull Staff.
B) The left leg steps forward to form a left Three Battle Stance while executing a Pull Staff.

3. Three Battle Stance, Turn Staff-Three Battle Stance, Stabbing Staff

4. Covering Stance, Slanting Strike Staff-Covering Stance, Slanting Strike Staff

5. Three Battle Stance, Pull Staff-Three Battle Stance, Pull Staff

6.

A: **Covering Stance, Slanting Strike Staff**

B: **Covering Stance, Slanting Strike Staff**

A) The right leg steps over the left leg to form a right Covering Stance while executing a Slanting Strike Staff.

B) The left leg steps over the right leg to form a left Covering Stance while executing a Slanting Strike Staff.

6. Covering Stance, Slanting Strike Staff-Covering Stance, Slanting Strike Staff

7.

A: **Empty Stance, Pull Staff**

B: **Three Battle Stance, Pointing Staff**

A) The left leg steps forward to form a right Empty Stance while executing a Roll Staff and then intercepting a strike with Pull Staff.

B) The right leg steps back to form a left Three Battle Stance while executing a Roll Staff and then a Pointing Staff.

7a. Empty Stance, Pull Staff-Three Battle Stance, Pointing Staff

7b. Empty Stance, Pull Staff-Three Battle Stance, Pointing Staff

8.

A: **Three Battle Stance, Pushing Staff**
B: **Four Level Stance, Line Staff**
A) The right leg steps down to form a left Three Battle Stance while executing a Pushing Staff.
B) Shift into a Four Level Stance while executing Line Staff to intercept the incoming strike.

9.

A: **Three Battle Stance, Shelf Push Staff**
B: **Three Battle Stance, Chopping Staff**
A) Adjust the stance to embrace the incoming strike, which is intercepted with Shelf Push Staff.
B) The right leg steps forward to form a right Three Battle Stance while executing a Chopping Staff.

8. Three Battle Stance, Pushing Staff-Four Level Stance, Line Staff

9. Three Battle Stance, Shelf Push Staff-Three Battle Stance, Chopping Staff

10.

A: **Three Battle Stance, Turn Staff**
B: **Three Battle Stance, Stabbing Staff**

A) The right leg steps forward to form a right Empty Stance; adjust staff to Embracing Staff. The right foot steps down to form a right Three Battle Stance while executing Turn Staff.

B) Roll Staff and then Stabbing Staff toward the torso of Exponent **A**

11.

A: **Empty Stance, Pointing Staff**
B: **Single Standing Stance, Pull Staff**

A) The right leg cross the left leg to form a right Empty Stance while executing a Pointing Staff.

B) The right knee goes up to form a right Single Standing Stance while executing a Pull Staff.

10a. Three Battle Stance, Turn Staff-Three Battle Stance, Stabbing Staff

10b. Three Battle Stance, Turn Staff-Three Battle Stance, Stabbing Staff

11. Empty Stance, Pointing Staff-

12.

A: **Three Battle Stance, Chopping Staff**

B: **Single Standing Stance, Embracing Staff**

A) The right leg steps forward to form a right Three Battle Stance while executing Chopping Staff.

B) Hop back, the right foot steps down and the left knee goes up to form a left Single Standing Stance while executing Embracing Staff.

12. Three Battle Stance, Chopping Staff-Single Standing Stance, Embracing Staff

SECTION SIX:

1.

A: **Three Battle Stance, Turn Staff**

B: **Three Battle Stance, Turn Staff**

A) Readjust the stance to execute a Turn Staff.

B) The left leg steps down to form a right Three Battle Stance while executing a Turn Staff.

2.

A: **Empty Stance, Roll Staff**

B: **Three Battle Stance, Roll Staff**

A) Shift weight back to form a right Empty Stance while executing Roll Staff.

B) Roll Staff.

1. Three Battle Stance, Turn Staff-Three Battle Stance, Turn Staff

2. Empty Stance, Roll Staff-Three Battle Stance, Roll Staff

Five Foot Staff Partner Drill Ngo Ciak Gua Dui Lian (五尺棍)

3.
   A: **Three Battle Stance, Turn Staff**
   B: **Three Battle Stance, Turn Staff**
   A) The right leg steps forward to form a right Three Battle Stance while executing Turn Staff.
   B) Execute Turn Staff.

4.
   A: **Covering Stance, Slanting Strike Staff**
   B: **Covering Stance, Slanting Strike Staff**
   A) The right leg steps over the left leg, forming a right Covering Stance, while executing a Slanting Strike Staff.
   B) The left leg steps over the right leg, forming a left Covering Stance, while executing a Slanting Strike Staff.

5.
   A: **Three Battle Stance, Pull Staff**
   B: **Three Battle Stance, Pull Staff**
   A) The left leg steps forward to form a left Three Battle Stance while executing a Pull Staff.
   B) The right leg steps forward to form a left Three Battle Stance while executing a Pull Staff.

3. Three Battle Stance, Turn Staff-Three Battle Stance, Turn Staff

4. Covering Stance, Slanting Strike Staff-Covering Stance, Slanting Strike Staff

5. Three Battle Stance, Pull Staff-Three Battle Stance, Pull Staff

6.

A: **Empty Stance, Slanting Strike Staff**
B: **Three Battle Stance, Slanting Strike Staff**

A) The right leg steps cross the left leg to form a right Empty Stance while executing Slanting Strike Staff.
B) Execute Slanting Strike Staff.

7.

A: **Covering Stance, Pull Staff**
B: **Covering Stance, Pull Staff**

A) The right leg steps over the left leg, forming a right Covering Stance, while executing Pull Staff.
B) The left leg steps over the right leg, forming a left Covering Stance, while executing Pull Staff.

8.

A: **Three Battle Stance, Slanting Strike Staff**
B: **Three Battle Stance, Slanting Strike Staff**

A) The left leg steps forward to form a left Three Battle Stance while executing Slanting Strike Staff.
B) The left leg steps forward to form a left Three Battle Stance while executing Slanting Strike Staff.

6. Empty Stance, Slanting Strike Staff-Three Battle Stance, Slanting Strike Staff

7. Covering Stance, Pull Staff-Covering Stance, Pull Staff

8. Three Battle Stance, Slanting Strike Staff-Three Battle Stance, Slanting Strike Staff

9.

A: **Empty Stance, Pull Staff**
B: **Empty Stance, Pull Staff**
A) The right leg goes across the left leg to form a right Empty Stance while executing Pull Staff.
B) The right leg goes across the left leg to form a right Empty Stance while executing Pull Staff.

10.

A: **Three Battle Stance, Slanting Strike Staff**
B: **Three Battle Stance, Slanting Strike Staff**
A) The right leg steps back to form a left Three Battle Stance while executing a Slanting Strike Staff.
B) The right leg steps back to form a left Three Battle Stance while executing a Slanting Strike Staff.

11.

A: **Three Battle Stance, Pushing Staff**
B: **Four Level Stance, Line Staff**
A) The right leg steps down to form a left Three Battle Stance while executing a Pushing Staff.
B) Shift into a Four Level Stance while executing Line Staff to intercept the incoming strike.

9. Empty Stance, Pull Staff-Empty Stance, Pointing Staff

10. Three Battle Stance, Slanting Strike Staff-Three Battle Stance, Slanting Strike Staff

11. Three Battle Stance, Pushing Staff-Four Level Stance, Line Staff

12.

A: **Three Battle Stance, Shelf Push Staff**
B: **Three Battle Stance, Chopping Staff**

A) Adjust stance to embrace the incoming strike, which is intercepted with Shelf Push Staff.
B) The right leg steps forward to form a right Three Battle Stance while executing a Chopping Staff.

12. Three Battle Stance, Shelf Push Staff-Three Battle Stance, Chopping Staff

SECTION SEVEN:

1.

A: **Three Battle Stance, Turn Staff**
B: **Three Battle Stance, Stabbing Staff**

A) Form a right Empty Stance and step back into a left Three Battle Stance, first Roll Staff and then Turn Staff.
B) First Roll Staff and then Stab Staff toward Exponent **A**'s Torso.

1a. Three Battle Stance, Turn Staff-Three Battle Stance, Stabbing Staff

1b. Three Battle Stance, Turn Staff-Three Battle Stance, Stabbing Staff

Five Foot Staff Partner Drill Ngo Ciak Gua Dui Lian (五尺棍)

2.

A: **Three Battle Stance, Slanting Strike Staff**
B: **Three Battle Stance, Push Staff**
A) Execute Slanting Strike Staff.
B) The left leg steps forward to left Three Battle Stance while executing Push Staff.

3.

A: **Three Battle Stance, Chopping Staff**
B: **Three Battle Stance, Shelf Push Staff**
A) The right leg steps forward to form a right Three Battle Stance while executing a Chopping Staff.
B) Adjust stance to embrace the incoming strike, which is intercepted with Shelf Push Staff.

4.

A: **Three Battle Stance, Shelf Push Staff**
B: **Three Battle Stance, Chopping Staff**
A) The right leg steps back to form a left Three Battle Stance to embrace the incoming strike, which is intercepted with Shelf Push Staff.
B) The right leg steps forward to form a right Three Battle Stance while executing a Chopping Staff.

2. Three Battle Stance, Slanting Strike Staff-Three Battle Stance, Push Staff

3. Three Battle Stance, Chopping Staff-Three Battle Stance, Shelf Push Staff

4. Three Battle Stance, Shelf Push Staff-Three Battle Stance, Chopping Staff

5.

A: **Three Battle Stance, Turn Staff**
B: **Three Battle Stance, Stabbing Staff**

A) The right leg steps forward to form a right Empty Stance while executing Embrace Staff. Then the right leg steps back to form a left Three Battle Stance and execute Turn Staff.
B) Roll Staff, followed with Stabbing Staff.

5a. Three Battle Stance, Turn Staff-Three Battle Stance, Stabbing Staff

5b. Three Battle Stance, Turn Staff-Three Battle Stance, Stabbing Staff

6.

A: **Three Battle Stance, Embracing Staff**

B: **Four Level Stance, Stabbing Staff**

A) The right leg steps forward to form a right Empty Stance while executing a Slanting Strike Staff. After missing, the right leg steps forward to allow the torso to turn around into a left Empty Stance while Embracing Staff. The left leg steps back to form a right Three Battle Stance while executing Embracing Staff to intercept the incoming strike.

B) While executing Embracing Staff, quickly duck under the swinging staff, forming a left Personal Stance, while executing Roll Staff. Then the left foot steps out to form a Four Level Stance while executing Stabbing Staff.

6a. Three Battle Stance, Embracing Staff-Four Level Stance, Stabbing Staff

6b. Three Battle Stance, Embracing Staff-Four Level Stance, Stabbing Staff

6c. Three Battle Stance, Embracing Staff-Four Level Stance, Stabbing Staff

7.

A: **Three Battle Stance, Pointing Staff**
B: **Empty Stance, Pull Staff**
A) The left leg steps forward to form left Three Battle Stance to execute Pointing Staff at Exponent **B**'s legs.
B) The left leg moves forward to form a left Empty Stance while executing a Pull Staff to intercept the incoming strike.

7. Three Battle Stance, Pointing Staff-Empty Stance, Pull Staff

8.

A: **Three Battle Stance, Pointing Staff**
B: **Empty Stance, Pull Staff**
A) The right leg steps forward to form a right Three Battle Stance while executing Pointing Staff at Exponent **B**'s legs once more.
B) The left leg moves backward, allowing the torso to turn, at which time the right leg goes forward to form a right Empty Stance while executing a Pull Staff to intercept the incoming strike.

8. Three Battle Stance, Pointing Staff-Empty Stance, Pull Staff

9.

A: **Empty Stance, Ascending Line Staff**
B: **Single Standing Stance, Embracing Staff**
A) Execute quickly an Ascending Line Staff; the objective is to strike Exponent **B**'s head in a right Empty Stance.
B) Lift the right knee quickly in right Single Standing Stance while executing Embracing Staff to intercept the strike.

9. Empty Stance, Ascending Line Staff-Single Standing Stance, Embracing Staff

Five Foot Staff Partner Drill Ngo Ciak Gua Dui Lian (五尺棍)

SECTION EIGHT:

1.
   - **A: Three Battle Stance, Turn Staff**
   - **B: Three Battle Stance, Turn Staff**
   - A) The right foot steps forward, in the process forming a right Three Battle Stance, while executing Turn Staff.
   - B) The right foot steps down, in the process forming a right Three Battle Stance, while executing Turn Staff.

1. Three Battle Stance, Turn Staff-Three Battle Stance, Turn Staff

2.
   - **A: Three Battle Stance, Turn Staff**
   - **B: Three Battle Stance, Stabbing Staff**
   - A) Lean back to form a right Empty Stance while executing Rolling Staff; then the right foot steps down to form a right Three Battle Stance while executing Turn Staff.
   - B) Rolling Staff followed with Stabbing Staff

2a. Three Battle Stance, Turn Staff-Three Battle Stance, Stabbing Staff

2b. Three Battle Stance, Turn Staff-Three Battle Stance, Stabbing Staff

3.
   A: **Empty Stance, Shelf Staff**
   B: **Empty Stance, Shelf Staff**
   A) Lean back to form a right Empty Stance while executing Shelf Staff.
   B) Lean back to form a right Empty Stance while executing Shelf Staff.

4.
   A: **Three Battle Stance, Descending Turning Staff**
   B: **Three Battle Stance, Descending Turning Staff**
   A) The right leg steps back to form a left Three Battle Stance while executing Descending Turning Staff toward the left side.
   B) The right leg steps back to form a right Three Battle Stance while executing Descending Turning Staff toward the left side.

5. **Three Battle Stance, Hanging-Up Staff**
   Shift feet to form a right Three Battle Stance while executing Hanging-Up Staff.

3. Empty Stance, Shelf Staff-Empty Stance, Shelf Staff

4. Three Battle Stance, Descending Turning Staff-Three Battle Stance, Descending Turning Staff

5. Three Battle Stance, Hanging-Up Staff-Three Battle Stance, Hanging-Up Staff

Five Foot Staff Partner Drill Ngo Ciak Gua Dui Lian (五尺棍)

6. **Empty Stance, Willow Leaf Palm**
   The left foot steps forward to execute a left Empty Stance while Embracing Staff and executing a left Willow Leaf Palm.

7. **Side-by-Side Stance, Grasping Staff**
   The left leg moves in to form a Side-by-Side Stance, while maintaining the Embracing Fist, and finally lowering the fists and Staff to the side.

6. Empty Stance, Willow Leaf Palm

7a. Side-by-Side Stance, Grasping Staff

7b. Side-by-Side Stance, Grasping Staff

CHAPTER 25

FIVE FOOT STAFF TECHNIQUES
NGO CIAK GUA TECHNIQUES

Hold, Block, Collapse, Roll, Stab

1. Grasping Staff.
2. The author twists to execute Hold Staff, which is torqued to intercept to one's left.

1. Grasping Staff

2. Hold Staff

3. The objective of Collapse Staff is to vibrate the staff, creating a small burst of energy, which correlates to the notion of Issuing Energy from the Five Powers.
4. The notion of the Roll Staff consists of cuing the staff, which is sliding up and down the staff.
5. Demonstrating Hold, Roll, Stab

3. Collapse Staff

4. Roll Staff

5a. Hold, Roll, Stab

5b. Hold, Roll, Stab

5c. Hold, Roll, Stab

Block, Collapse, Roll, Stab

1. Grasping Staff.
2. The author twists to execute Block Staff, which is torqued to intercept to one's left.
3. Executing Collapse Staff.
4. Roll Staff.
5. Stab Staff.

1. Grasping Staff

2. Block Staff

3. Collapse Staff

4. Roll Staff

5. Stab Staff

Monkey Hop Back, Pull, Chopping

1. The author raises his knee to move his leg out of an incoming strike, but at the same time intercepts with a motion referred to as Pull Staff, whose objective is to move to the side from an incoming strike.

2. The lifted right leg hops back, which allows the author to execute Chop Staff. Chops are forceful strikes that use vertical momentum to generate striking power.

1. Pull Staff

Line, Push

1. The opponent executes a technique called Line Staff that, as the name implies, is a vertical posture to block an incoming strike. The author executes a technique called Push Staff. The objective is to literally push forward horizontally with the staff, be it to block or strike; in this case, using the end of the staff to strike.

2. Chop Staff

1a. Line-Push

1b. Line-Push

Block, Point, Slanting Strike

1. The author executes Block Staff, whose objective is to move the incoming weapon toward one's right or clockwise.
2. The author executes Point Staff, which is similar to piercing staff, but focused toward the lower half of an opponent's body, i.e., legs.
3. The author executes a Slanting Strike Staff, which is diagonal strike.

1. Block Staff

2. Point Staff

3. Slanting Strike Staff

Point, Collapse

1. The author executes Point Staff to the opponent's knee.
2. The author executes a Collapse Staff toward the opponent's face.

Monkey Bow, Stab

1. The author ducks and executes a Stab Staff.

1. Point Staff

2. Collapse Stick

1a. Monkey Bow, Stab

1b. Monkey Bow, Stab

Slice Palm, Seizing Hand, Controlling-Seizing

1. The author and exponent Grasp Staff.
2. The author executes a Slice Palm.
3. The author executes Seizing Hand.

1. Grasp Staff

2a. Slice Palm

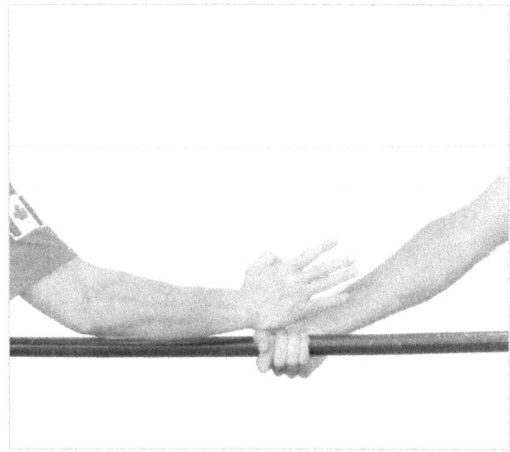

2b. Slice Palm

3a. Seizing Hand

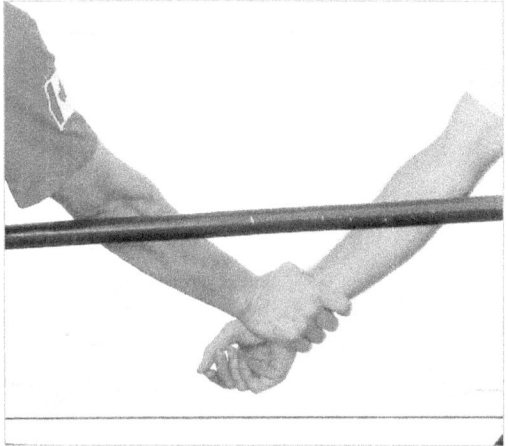

3b. Seizing Hand

4. The author demonstrates Controlling-Seizing techniques on the opponent's elbow and arm.

Whipping Arm

1. The author demonstrates Whipping Arm.

4a. Controlling-Seizing

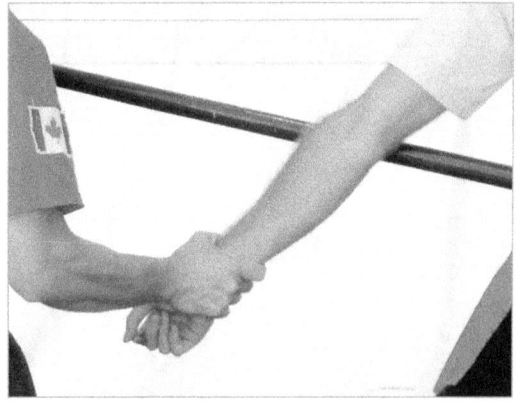

4b. Controlling-Seizing

4c. Controlling-Seizing

4d. Controlling-Seizing

1a. Whipping Arm

1b. Whipping Arm

CHAPTER 26

NGO CHO KUN MU SUT LUI DAI (LÉITÁI) ARENA SPORTS FIGHTING
五祖拳武術擂臺比賽

Kong Han participates in full-contact bouts, which are referred to as Sǎnshǒu, which originally took place on a Léitái or an open platform stage. Typically, Sǎnshǒu matches are divided into two categories: No Facial Contact, and Facial Contact.

Sparring has always been part of Kong Han's curriculum. Sparring grants the students the opportunity to experience combat in a control and safe environment. In the old days, due to the social or political circumstance, physical confrontation was the norm; therefore, a practitioner quickly gained through actual participation be it in defending the neighborhood or the village against bandits or acting as security escort for merchants or government officials.

In fact, most Ngo Cho Kun schools during that particular period were members of the local militia; they assisted the government forces in providing peace and order. The absence of modern firearms at that time has made the training in Ngo Cho Kun very important and one way to identify an excellent fighter was through the staging of Léitái matches.

Today's Léitái matches has evolved to become less violent; safer and geared towards the promotion of a good martial spirit without giving up the core essence and concept of Ngo Cho Kun.

Equipment

Equipment in no headshot consists of:
- Open finger gloves or bare hand
- Body armor
- Groin guard
- Shin and instep guard (optional)
- Mouthpiece (optional)
- Knee pad (optional)
- Elbow pad (optional)

The second format includes a head shot; therefore, fighters wear head gear consisting of a face guard and an open finger glove with more padding on the first portion (see photo). Again, because of the nature of Ngo Cho Kun explosive power striking the head protector with face mask is to provide some form of protection against hear injuries such as skull and jaw fractures the extra padded fist glove serve the same purpose.

- Body armor
- Mouthpiece
- Groin protector
- Shin and instep guard
- Knee pad
- Elbow pad

Rules and Techniques:

Techniques that are allowed:
- Straight punch (major)
- Hook punch (major)
- Hammer fist strike (major)
- Uppercut (major)
- Chop hand (major)

- Palm strike (major)
- Elbow strike (major to body area only)
- Knee strike (major to body area only)
- Front kick (major)
- Sidekick (major)
- Roundhouse kick (major)
- Sweeping kick (major)
- Scissor kick (major)
- Ax kick (minor)

Takedowns:

- Stand up twin hand sweeping (major)
- Hip sweep takedown (major)
- Shoulder lift (major)
- Scissor kicks take down (major)
- Sweeping (major)
- Grabbing kicks takedown (major)
- Leg trip (major)
- Double leg takedown (minor)

Divisions:

- Male and Female 120 below Jr. Lightweight
- 121 – 134 lbs. = Lightweight
- 135 – 145 lbs. = Light Middleweight
- 146 – 160 lbs. = Middleweight
- 161 – 175 lbs. = Light Heavyweight
- 176 lbs. + = Heavyweight

Rules: No Head I and with Headshot II

No Head Shot format

Techniques	Head	Body	Legs/thigh	Points	Penalty	Details
Punches	No	Yes	No	1	Warning for accidental hitting the head	Disqualification for intentional striking the head
Chop hand, palm strike	No	Yes	No	1	Warning for accidental hitting the head	Disqualification for intentional striking the head
Elbow	No	Yes	No	1	Warning for accidental elbowing the head	Disqualification for intentional striking the head
Kneeing	No	Yes	No	1	Warning for accidental kneeing the head	Disqualification for intentional striking the head
Front kick and side kick	No	Yes	No	1	Warning for accidental kicking the head	Disqualification for intentional kicking the head
Roundhouse kick	No	Yes	Yes	1 to body area only	Warning for accidental kicking the head	Kicking side and upper thigh only and side of shin area no points. Intentionally kicking the head = disqualification.
Successful takedowns or sweeping while remaining in standing position	0	0	0	2		Disqualification for unsportsmanlike conduct
Takedowns while going down staying on top	0	0	0	1		
Forcing an opponent to step out or thrown out of the arena				3		
Groin, neck and back	x	x	x	x	Warning for accidental hitting	Disqualification for intentional striking the back, groin and neck

Format II with Head shot

Techniques	Head	Body	Legs/thigh	Points	Penalty	Details
Punches	Yes	Yes	No	1		Disqualification for unsportsmanlike conduct striking foul areas
Chop hand, palm strike	Yes	Yes	No	1		Disqualification for unsportsmanlike conduct striking foul areas
Elbow	No	Yes	No	1	Warning for elbowing the head	Disqualification for intentional elbowing the head or ignoring warnings
Kneeing	No	Yes	No	1	Warning for kneeing the head	Disqualification for intentional kneeing the head and ignoring warnings
Front kick and side kick	Yes	Yes	No	1		Disqualification for unsportsmanlike conduct striking foul areas
Roundhouse kick	Yes	Yes	Yes	1		Kicking side and upper thigh only and side of shin area no points
Successful takedowns or sweeping while remaining	0	0	0	2		Disqualification for unsportsmanlike conduct striking foul areas
Standing position						
Forcing an opponent to step out or thrown out of the arena				3		
Takedowns while going down staying on top	0	0	0	1		Disqualification for unsportsmanlike conduct striking foul areas

1. Rounds 3 minutes / round for 3 rounds.
2. Use of full power is allowed on both formats the no head and with a headshot.
3. Referee reserved the right to stop or discontinued a fight if one fighter proves to be too dominant against the other fighter such stoppage is = Referee stop rule the dominant fighter is declared the winner.
4. A fighter that scores more points than the other wins the bout after three rounds.
5. A Fighter that scores a TKO wins fight
6. One fighter cannot continue because of low stamina or legitimate fight injuries is ruled as TKO or Referee stop fight.
7. A Fighters must engage each other within five seconds the fighter that kept backing away or refusing to engage will received a warning and 1 point deduction continuous to avoid to engage result in disqualification.
8. Takedowns must be executed within 3 seconds.
9. Both fighters' loose balance and goes down no point.
10. Both fighters go down due to takedown execution the fighter that lands on top of the other get 1 point.
11. Takedown execution one fighter remains standing the other goes down the fighter that remain standing get 2 points.
12. Fighting arena 24 feet x 24 feet either on a flat surface or raised platform x one foot.
13. A Fighter who fell off due to their own action = + 3 points to the other fighter.
14. Pushed or forced out of the arena = 3 points
15. No striking when one fighter is down on the ground fights are re-set
16. Thrown, punch or kicked out of the arena is allowed = 3 points to the fighter who successfully throws, punch or kicked the other fighter out of the arena.
17. For no head shot format all strikes, kicks, elbows and knees must target the body armor area only.
18. Foul area: No striking the back, neck, and groin for both no head shot and with headshot format.

Judges and officials
1. There will be at least four corner judges to score points
2. One time keeper to keep time of rounds and bouts
3. Score calculators there will at least be two
4. One referee in the arena to act as an arena official in making sure fighters engages each other according to the rules of engagement.
5. One medical or certified health official
6. In case of a tie the referee act as the tie breaker
7. If there is a dispute of the decision the official awarding of the winner will be put on hold until the dispute is settled.
8. All disputes will be reviewed through video replay for final determination.
9. All disputes will have to be settled within 24 hours or less.

Uniforms:
1. Judges will be wearing official tournament blazers or jackets
2. Timekeeper and score calculators will be wearing official vest
3. The referee will be wearing official polo T-shirt
4. Fighters must wear their official school, region or country colors or uniforms.
5. T-shirt with fighters school logo
6. Martial Art pants
7. Fighting shorts just above the knee.

Rules:

Illegal or foul unacceptable techniques and behaviors that will result in immediate disqualification:
1. Eye gouges
2. Striking the throat
3. Joint breaking
4. Striking the groin
5. Spitting
6. Biting
7. And all other forms of unsportsmanlike conduct as may be deemed by officials as unacceptable such as threatening other athletes and officials, use of foul language.
8. Display of political, social, racial and religious intolerance and violence and promoting hate.

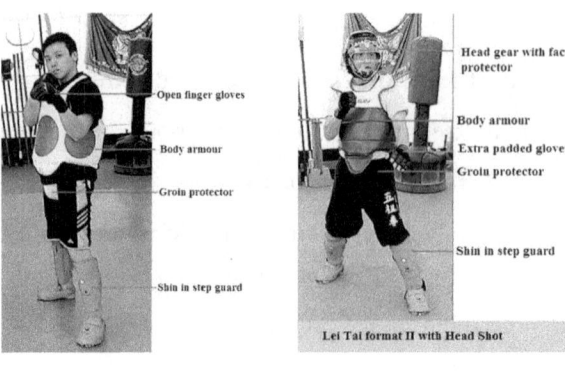

No Head Shot format   With Headshot format

Drills and Training

Drills help develop the natural instinct to react and improve muscle-body, mind and spirit concentration and coordination, help in improving stamina, speed, power, timing and distancing that will develop into actual applicable techniques. Drills are carried out in a repetitious manner spread out by sets example; 100x punching bag / 3 or 5 sets in between sets do stretching, weights and forms.

1. 1-2-3 straight Strike (Reverse punch)
2. Block and counter with 1-2-3 punch
3. Charge punch 1-2-3
4. Foot shuffling+ punching
5. Launch punch 1-2 + round house step back side kick
6. Front kick + follow through with 1-2 straight punch. Front snap kick or push kick.
7. X-punch combination for with head shot format
8. X-punch + two straight punch for with headshot format
9. Front kick + 1-2 punch sweep or trip
10. Front kick + 1-2 punch step back, then side kick
11. Front kick drills continuous
12. Front kick power kick drills
13. Roundhouse kick with instep
14. Roundhouse kicks with the ball of the foot
15. Side kick drills

16. Side kick speed drills
17. Front kick + roundhouse kick
18. Front kick + reverse kick
19. Sweep + side kick
20. Front kick + round house kick+ side kick _ reverse kick
21. Sweep or tripping + punch 1-2
22. Power punching
23. Machine gun punching
24. Chop sweep + punch
25. Knee strike
26. Knee+ elbow strike
27. Elbow strike
28. Elbow strike + chop hand strike + punch
29. Sang sau (twin sweeping or tripping di tzat style)
30. Side step, hip throw takedown
31. Grab a roundhouse takedown drill
32. Grab a front kick takedown drill
33. Grab a side kick takedown drill
34. Block a roundhouse + punch-punch
35. Block a side kick + punch-punch
36. Block a front kick + punch-punch
37. Scissor kicks takedown
38. Low reverse sweep
39. Knee strike, block + takedown
40. Di sip Kun fighting form and drill
41. Si Mun Pah Kat fighting form and drill
42. Song Sui fighting form and drill
43. Di Tzat figting form
44. Weights do not use heavy weights use for strength and speed 45. Stretching, all sorts of conventional stretching 46. Chin ups, pushups, running, sit ups etc.

45. Kah Ngo Ki = forearm conditioning to strengthen the ability to block kicks and improve striking technique.

46. Léitái training rounds to apply if not all as much as the drill applications and techniques with a Léitái partner that include testing stamina, focusing, reaction, concentration. Training rounds normally go for 3 minutes; a round rest is 1 minute and then another 3 minute round stage I light contact. Stage II full contact.

Ngo Cho Kun empty hand forms that are ideal in improving concentration, stamina, foot work, hand techniques and mobility are:

1. Di Sip Kun
2. Di Sip Kun fighting drill
3. Si Mun Pah Kat
4. Si Mun Pah Kat
5. Song Sui
6. Song Sui fighting drill
7. 7. Di Tzat

The forms must be executed in full concentration and in combat mindset, full energy, power, technique, and speed.

Si Peng Beh "45 degree fighting stance"

The Four Level Stance it allows you better mobility to move side to side, forward or backward it makes you a smaller target and allows you to execute offensive or defensive techniques more effectively.

The Embracing Tile hand guard position allows you to stay on guard to protect your upper, middle and lower body. The upper hand to protect against strike to the head, the lower hand against kicks to the body.

High Guard

Center Guard

Low guard

LÉITÁI BASIC TECHNIQUES:

Stand up side hip takedown (側髖扔)

Stand up side hip takedown (側髖扔)

Knee strike, block (罷膝打)

Low kick, block (低踢停止)

Charge punch "ramming the gates" (突拳打)

Charge punch "ramming the gates" (突拳打)

Controlling the opponent's lead arm "bridging and destroy" (过渡毁)

Chop sweep "pincer sweep" (砍扫)

Inside horizontal elbow strike (内横手肘打)

Inside low kick "chop roots" (低内踢)

Leg spin takedown (拿脚转摔)

Leg spin takedown (拿脚转摔)

Leg spin takedown (拿脚转摔)

Outside low kick (外低团踢)

Overhand dive punch (抢手拳打)

Straight leg takedown (直踢过摔)

Straight leg takedown (直踢过摔)

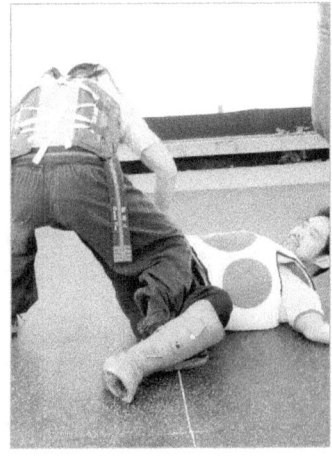
Straight leg takedown (直踢过摔)

Grab knee strike (抓手膝打)

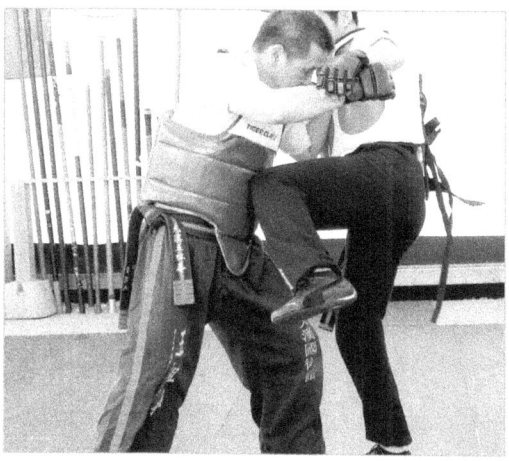

Grab knee strike (抓手膝打)

Horse kick (尥蹶子)

Side kick leg trap, pull down (邊踢圈套)

Side kick leg trap, pull down (邊踢圈套)

Side kick leg trap, pull down (邊踢圈套)

Stand up sweeping, two hands, take down (雙手足掃)

Front snap kick straight punch (踢拳打)

Front snap kick straight punch (踢拳打)

Punching combination upper cut-rear hand straight punch-lead hand straight punch (拳打連轉)

Head punch straight (拳打頭)

Hook Punch (鉤拳打)

Hook kick (鉤踹)

Overhand punch to face (抢手拳打頭)

Underneath leg sweep (后扫腿)

Ngo Cho Kun Mu Sut Lui Dai (léitái) Arena Sports Fighting 五祖拳武術擂臺比賽

Scissors kick takedown (剪掃)

Scissors kick takedown (剪掃)

Scissors kick takedown (剪掃)

CONCLUSION

This book is meant as an introduction to one of China's most formidable styles of combat, envisioned for an urban setting where confrontations are head on.

The rich legacy of this art stems from the foundation of China's illustrious martial history all the way to its last apex at the closing end of the Qīng dynasty. At the same time the second epoch, began in the Philippines, has been introduced, which now extends to the Western Hemisphere.

We were introduced to the roots of this formidable discipline, which consists of the physiology that is crucial in developing the style's explosive energy, and various methodologies to guarantee success in a confrontation.

Finally, we were introduced to the fundamental routines that make this discipline one of China's greatest treasures, now taking root across the globe.

The authors would like to thank our developmental editor, Arnaldo Ty Nunez, for his scholarly knowledge in book writing, history in Chinese martial arts and his professionalism in editing my manuscript to my satisfaction and appreciation, thank you very much. And to the manuscripts copy editor, Jody Amato, for cleaning up the grammar and finding all the inconsistencies in the presentation to help us unify the material.

With great appreciation to our publisher, Dr. Mark Wiley, for accepting our manuscript for publication and distribution to readers worldwide, thank you for your time and efforts.

Special acknowledgment to Grandmaster Alexander Co for opening the doors of Ngo Cho Kun to the world with his first English-Chinese language book, *Way of Ngo Cho Kun*, first published and distributed in 1987; it was a very informative book that has greatly enhanced our knowledge of Ngo Cho Kun.

APPENDIX 1

GREEN LION

The discipline of Ngó Chó Kûn consists of many traditions, including the Ki Gun, which represents the fallen Míng dynasty. However, there are other that are rare, for example, Ci Sai or Green Lion (青獅), which originated from the art of Lam Tai Zo Gun (南太祖拳).

Unlike all other lion dances, the Ci Sai is neither a dance nor a ceremonial lion. It is actually a symbol. The Ci Sai, with its fierce face and sharp Fangs, denotes the Qīng dynasty for its brutality and harsh rule. The color green represents the word green; in the Fújiàn dialect of Mǐnnányǔ (閩南語), green is pronounced "Ci," which is Qīng in Mǐnnányǔ and sounds similar to Cing. Therefore, the green also symbolizes the Qīng Green Standard Army, or Lùyíng (綠營), that are deployed in local civilian populations and act as constabulary to enforce Qīng laws.

Finally, the shaven forehead of the lion and its wavy black hair represent the Manchu hairstyle, or queue, which was a shaved forehead and the back of the hair braided. This particular hairstyle was forced upon the Hàn as a sign of submission by a conquered people. Also, it was used to quickly identify radicals. Therefore, whoever refused to have their forehead shaved was at risk of being arrested and beheaded. There was brutal saying: "Shave your forehead or lose your head."

The Ci Sai routine consists of exponents fighting the Ci Sai with various weapons to symbolize the struggles of the Hàn against the Manchu for their freedom. Finally, the ritual ends with the Ci Sai being subdued.

The tradition no longer represents political aggression or social rebellion, but hope, peace, and unity. However, it is very rare to see the Ci Sai performed today; hopefully, a new generation will uphold this unique tradition in the coming years. If not, it will fade away.

APPENDIX 2

THE ELDERS

Ngo Cho Kun's is a reality in due to countless of individuals, who unselfishly satisfied their time to practice, develop, and share their beloved art to others and for them we greatly indebted. This is a short biography of some of the crucial exponents, who were instrumental in the development of Ngo Cho Kun.

Hou, Iu (何阳, 1795-1880)
Originally from Yǒngdìng County, which is located at the border of Fújiàn and Guǎngdōng. He was a proprietor of a small inn within Yǐngzhōu District, which is located in Ānhuī province. It is assumed that he was an exponent of Tai Zo Deng Gun (太祖长拳). He operated the Hou Iu Dong (何阳堂) or the Positive Hall, which was located in Zhāngzhōushì, Fújiàn province. There he taught a style referred to as Hou Iu Kun or Positive Fist. His martial arts prowess were renowned for his diamond power energy often described as: Ging Zeng Zi (劲钻精).

One of his outstanding students was Chua, Giok-Beng (蔡玉鸣); he would be instrumental in expanding upon his teacher's art by developing Ho Yang Pai Ngo Cho Kun.

Chua, Giok-Beng (蔡玉鸣 1853 -1910)

Was born in the year of Qīng in the reign of Xiánfēng (1850-1861) on December 30th; he grew up in the city of Zhāngzhōu, Fújiàn provinces. His father was

Chua, Giok-Beng

a successful entrepreneur, which granted him the ability to indulge his son in his interest, which was martial arts. Numerous instructors were hired to instruct him in various styles of Mu Sut (martial arts) in particular the disciplines of Ming Tai Zo Kun and Tai Zo Diou Kun. One of his instructors was Ou, Iu (河阳).

Giok-Beng was an avid student, who was a quick learned and most of all diligent, which is crucial to be a proficient martial artist. When Ou passed away Giok-Beng by tradition took the remains of his late teacher back to his homeland to Hénán province. Afterward Giok-Beng decided to take a sojourn to research and learn other disciplines of Mu Sut. For instance, he would be introduced to the art of Ing Cun Biak Hok Kun (永春白鶴拳), Hiao Kun (猴拳), and other disciplines.

After his ten years sojourn he return home back to Quánzhōu, where he started to teach the Mu Sut he acquire and started to nurture the art of Ngo Cho Kun, which consist of the disciples of: Tai Zo Diou Kun (太祖长拳), Hiao Kun (猴拳), Lou Han Kun (羅漢拳), Biak Hok Kun (白鶴拳), and Dat Mo Kun (達摩拳); it would be referred to as Ngo Cho Kun Hou Iu Pai. In short Ngo Cho Kun was chosen to give honor to five styles that would be the core of his discipline. The Hou Iu was in reference to his first major instructor, Hou, Iu.

Chua's influence in the Quánzhōu area would be notable that he would open two Mu Guan: Sia Gong (聖公) or Sacred Hall, and Ling E or Dragon Association (龍會).

His skills were so exceptional he mastered the light body technique the ability to leap, jump, hurdle through obstacles effortless today it can be express or compare to Parkour he was also very deadly with his iron palm technique because of his special abilities he gain the nickname Pan Be Ho "Crane of Pan Beh Village". He is also a practicing herbal doctor providing medical services to the community.

In later years, Chua Giok-Beng will shun materialism he will devote his time to society with charitable ways, giving away his wealth to the people understanding the harsh reality of those who are less fortunate at the same time continue to further his martial arts skills taking it into new heights not only in combat but though charity and living a life of asceticism. His devoted disciples will provide for him protecting him from harm and making sure that he is not forgotten.

Li, Zun-Lin (李俊仁, 1849 -1933)

Li Zun-Lin started training in martial art at the Dōngchán Temple of Quánzhōu. Zun-Lin would excel in his training and after a few years of training, he decided to return to his hometown, Yǒngchūn, Fújiàn provinces. Upon arriving home he started to formalize his own style based upon the arts he have learned:

- Ming [dynasty] Grand Ancestor Fist: Ming Tai Cho Kun (明太祖拳)
- Monkey Fist: Kao Kun (猴拳)
- Ing Cun Pe Hao Kun (永春白鶴拳)
- Arhat Boxing: Lohan Kun (羅漢拳)
- Bodhidharma Fist: Tat Chun (Dat-Mo) Kun (達摩拳)

Li would referred to his art as Ing Cun Ngo Cho Kun or Yǒngchūn Five Ancestor Fist. Li Zun-Lin will pass his knowledge to his nephew Ken, Teck-Guan and in the mid-1900s Kan will establish schools in Singapore and Malaysia.

Gan, Diak-Nguan

Gan, Diak-Nguan (1884-1946干德源)

Gan was born in Yǒngchūn; He was well respected for his knowledge of martial arts and medicine. His martial arts tutelage was under the supervision of his uncle, Li Zun-Lin.

In the early 1900's Gan relocated to Singapore and established a medicial clinic and a martial hall (school). By 1918 he established another martial hall in Kuala Lumpur and nine years later in Malacca. His legacy still continues to this day in Singapore.

Lim, Kui-Lu (林九如, 1862-1937)

A prominent master of Tai Cho Kun in Quánzhōu, after being bested by Chua, Giok-Beng, he would eventually become one of Chua's top disclipes. He would eventually become a great disciple of Sijo Chua Giok Beng, he would later be instrumental in adding more materials to the advancement of Ngo Cho Kun Ho Yang Pai in combination to Taizuquan. He had many students, including his son Lim Tian'en (taught in Quanzhou city), Lo Ban Teng (taught in Zhangzhou, Shima, Xiamen and settle in Indonesia), Miao Yue (Chongfu Temple, Quanzhou) and Lu Pengqi (Head of the Martial arts association in Quanzhou), Gong PO Cham amongst many others.

Lim, Kui-Lu

Tan Kiong Beng (陈京铭)

One of the Ten Tigers of Chua Giok Beng, Master Tan Kiong Beng is famous for his iron palm technique in 1918 he will visit Manila as a healer and in 1935 he will assign his son the young Master Tan Ka Hong to open and operate an Ngo Cho Kun training center in Manila, Philippines. Master Tan Ka Hong (1914 -1990) and associates will name their school Beng Kiam Athletic Club in memory of their Grandmaster Chua Giok Beng. Tan Kiong Beng was also once a martial classmate of Lo Yan Chiu both trained under Master Kong Po Chiam before Tan Kiong Beng join Chua Giok Beng and became his disciple.

Tan Kiong Beng

Lo Yan Chiu

Lo Yan Chiu (盧言秋, 1878-1944)

Was born in Quanzhou he started at age 14 studying martial arts with Master Zhuang Dan (庄胆), and then he became a disciple of Kong Po Chiam (公婆詹) a Tai Cho -Ngo Cho Kun master and disciple of the famous Master Lim Kui Lu (林九如). He also met and interacted with the famous Master Chua Giok Beng and his disciples Chen Qingming, Tan Kiong Beng and others thus expanding his skills, abilities and knowledge of Tai Cho-Ngo Cho Kun. After only 5 years of intense training, Lo Yan Chiu opened his school in 1897 at Wei Tou village, instructing in Tai Cho-Goh Cho Kun and offering medical services.

In 1899, he traveled overseas over nine years to countries including Burma (Myanmar), Malaysia, Indonesia, Hong Kong, Vietnam and Singapore. He gained great experience and in 1909 returned to Quanzhou. During the turbulent years of 1910-1912, Lo Yan Chiu was involved in the nationalist movement having served as combat instructor and medical officer of the 183rd Div. 19th Route Nationalist Army.

In 1936, the Sino-Japanese war commenced and by urging of his students given his advanced age and his involvement against Japan he relocated to Manila. In 1937, Lo Yan Chiu setup the **Kong Han Athletic Club** and taught there.

Sim Yong Tik (1881-1964 沈揚德,)

Master Sim was the last indoor disciple of Sijo Chua Giok Beng. Master Sim in the 1930s expanded Ngo Cho Kun to Singapore, Indonesia, Myanmar (Burma), Quanzhou and Xiamen His Wuzuquan will have a strong emphasis on the Peak Hok (White Crane) of Yong Chun system.

Sim Yong Tik

Lo Ban Teng (盧萬定 1886 -1958)

Was originally from Zhangzhou, Fujian whose family ran a Liquor business and was born with a natural talent for martial arts. When he was 23 years old he commenced the study of Wuzuquan with a store owner, Yu Chiok Sam (尤俊岸) who was a disciple of Chua Giok Beng (Cai Yuming). Lo Ban Teng helped with the running of his family Liquor business and had to travel frequently to neighboring areas such as Xiamen and Quanzhou. At the introduction of his teacher, he studied with martial uncles Wei Yinnan (魏隐南), Weng Chaoyan (翁朝言) in Xiamen and with Lin Jiuru (林九如 Lim Kui Lu) in Quanzhou. In 1927 Lo Ban Teng moved to Indonesia, where he practiced medicine and taught martial arts. He was known not only for his medical skills, but for his martial physical strength and his direct, honest and hard to everyone utilitarian character.

Lo Ban Teng

Lo Ban Teng was the most influential figure in establishing Chua Giok Beng-Wuzuquan in Indonesia. One prime emphasis of his lineage is to breathe right to develop a hard blow as well as the ability to bear the hard blow of an opponent. During his whole life Lo deepened his martial arts by watching attack and defense behaviors of domestic animals, such as roosters, in fights. The adapted movements include shouting, shuddering of the body in delivering blows, and tensing the body in receiving blows. In fact, one of his favorite techniques was "Hen Flapping Her Wing (Kee Bo Ceng Sit)" in which an incoming punch is simultaneously countered by disjointing the attacker's elbow. Lo Ban Teng will pass his skills and legacy to Lim Tjoei Kang (林粹刚 1896-1966 fk Lin Cuigang) and Kwik Tjong Thay (郭种泰 1916 -2001, Guo Zhongtai) Lim Tjoie Kang was a student and a nephew of Lo Ban Teng and an adopted son of Sim Yong Tik.

At present the Lo Ban Teng Wuzuquan is still being taught in Indonesia by several disciples and has branched out to Germany and USA.

Bai Yufeng (白玉峰) the Northern Wuzuquan

Bai Yufeng was a 14th century famous northern Shaolin martial art master according to an article written by Dr Yang, Jwing-Ming is that based on northern Shaolin records, Bai Yufeng was a Shaolin master who adapted the Shaolin name Qiu Yue Chan Shi he will combine the Five Animal system into one (1) Tiger (2) Crane (3) Snake (4) leopard and (5) Dragon they will be called Wu Xing Quan 五形拳. According to the book Shaolin Temple Record, he developed the then existing 18 Buddha Hands techniques into 173 techniques. Not only that, he compiled the existing techniques contained within Shaolin and wrote the book, The Essence of Five Fist 無極五拳. This book included and discussed the practice methods and applications of the Five Fist (Animal) Patterns also known as Wu Quan 五拳.

It is believed that after the fall of the Ming dynasty several followers of Bai Yu Feng fled, and migrated to south China following the path of many former Ming loyalists soon their martial art will integrate, blend and start getting influence with the southern martial art system evolving and adapting into Five Ancestors Fist incorporating Yong Chun White Crane, Ming Tai Cho and Southern Lo Han boxing.

In the early 1960s the late Grandmaster Chee Kim Thong from Malaysia, after his good friend and disciple Grandmaster Yap Ching Hai convince him to publicly reveal his Ngo Cho Kun system that is descended from the Bai Yufeng lineage GM Chee will agree and start to teach it to the general public. Presently the Chee Kim Thong Pugilistic Society with headquarters' in Malaysia is the only known descendant of the Bai Yufeng-Ngo Cho Kun. Just like there exist the Northern Shaolin and Southern Shaolin, a northern Martial Art and southern Martial Art each distinctly having their own history in Ngo Cho Kun it will be the same the existence of a northern and southern Ngo Cho Kun.

The Bai Yufeng-Goh Cho Kun existence in Fujian was so secretive that the only known existing grandmaster was Grandmaster Lin Xian who according to the writings of the CKT Society, was that GM Lin Xian taught the late GM Chee Kim Thong sometime in the 1930s their system of Wuzuquan; in fact GM Chee Kim Thong would be his only known student and inheritor of what is to be Bai Yufeng-Wuzuquan.

From 1880 – 1960 the Goh Cho Kun Ho Yang, Tai Cho-Goh Cho Kun and Yong Chun-Goh Cho Kun were the only known Goh Cho Kun in the Fujian Martial Art community, in the early 1960s the Bai Yufeng-Wuzuquan lineage that was revealed through the efforts of the late GM Chee Kim Thong of Malaysia who has kept their lineage secret for decades it will be accepted as another part of the Ngo Cho Kun history.

What made Wuzuquan such an outstanding martial art system is that it is able to adapt to the martial art environment and keep up with the ever changing times.

Wuzuquan can now be express and identify base on the following:

Tai Cho-Goh Cho Kun
Ho Yang Pai- Goh Cho Kun
Yong Chun-Goh Cho Kun
Bai Yufeng-Goh Cho Kun

All these four are express as Ngo (Goh) Cho Kun 五祖拳.

Goh Cho Kun will have a significant influence also in the development of Japanese martial arts most notably Okinawan karate.

The legacy of Ngo Cho Kun has now expanded worldwide with schools in Europe, North America, South America and Asia, epitomized and unified under the International South Shaolin Wuzuquan Federation headquarters in Quanzhou, Fujian China.

APPENDIX 3

FORMS AND WEAPONS

Hand Forms - Kun Toh (Quan Tao) 拳套

There are a total of 44 hand forms, the hand forms noted below are the most common and standard hand forms

1. Di sip kun	二十拳	Twenty Punches
2. Si Mun Pah Kat	四門打角	Four Doors Hitting Corner
3. Sam Chien	三戰	Three Battles
4. Tien Te Lin Chien	天地靈戰	Heaven, Earth, Spirit, War
5. Sam Chien Sip Di	三戰十字	Three Battles Cross Pattern
6. Song Sui	雙綏	Double Banner
7. Di Tzat	二札	Second Degree
8. Sa Tzat	三札	Third Degree
9. Si Tzat	四札	Fourth Degree
10. Ngo Tzat	五札	Fifth Degree
11. Ngo Toh Tim Taoh	五肚胜頭	Five Times Hitting Head
12. Lien Shia Wat	連城法	Lotus Way
13. Te Suat	地搖	Earth Shakes
14. Tien Kwan Chien	天綰戰	Heaven, War
15. Pak Kwa Chiong	八卦	Eight Pentagon Palm
16. Hi Li Po	孩兒抱	Cradling shield
17. Chong Hap Kun	綜合拳	United Fist form of The International South Shaolin Wuzuquan Union

18. Sang Liao	雙龍	Twin Dragon
19. Chieng Hung Kun	清風拳	Ramming Fist
20. Pieng Beh Chien	平馬戰	Even Horse Battle
21. Lien Kwan Chien	連綰戰	Round Ring Battle
22. Ngo Cho Chien	五虎戰	Five Ancestors Battle

Empty Hand and Weapons Fighting drills (對練) **"dui lian"**

1. Sam Chien Stage I fighting drill
2. Sam Chien Stage II fighting drill
3. Di Sip Kun two person fighting drill
4. Si Mun Pah Kat two person fighting drill
5. Song Sui two person fighting drill
6. Sam Chien Sip Di two person fighting drill
7. Ngo Toh Tim Taoh two person fighting drill
8. Lo Han Chiu two person fighting drill
9. Da Dao vs Da Dao fighting drill
10. Knife vs. empty hand
11. Sam Hap, 1 vs. 2 empty hand fighting drill
12. Pole vs. Pole fighting drill
13. Tan Toh (single aber) vs. pole staff
14. Sang Pi (sai) vs. pole staff or horse cutting knife
15. Sang Te Kwai (tonfa) vs. pole or horse cutting knife
16. Tso Kwai u toh; right hand kwai- left hand knife vs. pole and stick weapons.
17. Trident vs. 7 foot pole and horse cutting knife.
18. Sai vs sai fighting drill
19. Spear vs Dao fighting drill
20. Sang Dao vs. three person arm with tan dao

Weapons 器械 Keh Si "Qi Xie"

These are a total of 18 long and 15 short weapons the list below are the common and standard weapons.

1. Ngo Chiet Khun	五尺棍	5 ft. staff (short pole)
2. Chit Chio Khun	七尺棍	7 foot staff
3. Chi Beh Khun	齊眉棍	Level Eye brow staff
3. Liu Xing Khun	流星棍	Meteor staff
4. Kwan Toh	關刀	Gen. Kwan's blade or crescent pole-arm
5. Swah Peh	開山鉤	Mountain Trident
6. Tsiun	矛	Spear
7. Chiem Beh Toh	斬馬刀	Horse cutting knife
8. Kaw Tsiun	鉤矛	Hook spear
9. Tan Toh	單刃	Single blade
10. Sang Toh	雙刀	Twin blade
11. Da Dao	大刀	Big blade
12. Sang Te Kwai	雙短拐	Twin short crutches 'tonfa"
13. Sang Te Pi	雙短鞭	Twin short flog "sai"
14. Sang Ho Kaw	雙虎鉤	Twin tiger hook
15. Sang Chiet Toh	雙彎刀	Twin cutlass blade
16. Kiam	劍	Sword
17. Kaw tsat Neng Pi	九鐵截鞭	Nine sectional whip
18. Sa Tsat Kun	三節桿	Three sectional staff
19. Sang Po Toh	雙斧頭	Twin axe
20 Pin Tah	扁擔	Peddler's staff
21. Sang Te Tsiun	雙短矛	Twin short spear
22. Tim Pai chiet dao	盾牌彎刀	Shield with cutlass
23. Teng Di Khun	16 英尺長杆	Long lance staff
24. Dao Zhe San	鋼刀折扇	Steel bladed fan
25. Ho San	傘武器	Umbrella

APPENDIX 4

LEVEL AND RANKING

Instructor I black Duan	Have at least absorb 4 hand forms and 1 weapon form and understood and able to apply the techniques and principle.
Instructor II black Duan	Have at least understood and absorb 5 hand forms and 2 weapons.
Instructor III black Duan	Have at least understood and absorb 7 hand forms and 2 weapons.
Chief Instructor IV black Duan	Have at least understood and absorb 8 hand forms, 3 weapons and able to formulate fighting principle.
Chief Instructor V black Duan	Have at least understood and absorb 9 hand forms, 4 weapons and formulate fighting principle.
Chief Instructor VI black Duan	Have at least understood and absorb 10 hand forms and 4 weapons forms and formulate fighting principle.
Master "Sifu" VII black-red Duan	10 + hands and 4+ weapon forms and its applications, formulate theories and applications.
Master "Sifu" VIII black-red Duan	12 + hands and 6+ weapon forms and applications, formulate and apply new theories.
Grandmaster Chong Sifu" IX black-red Duan	
Grandmaster "Chong Sifu" X black-red Duan	

Certificate Color Code

Green	Blue
Student	Asst. Instructor
Black	Red
Instructor	Chief Instructor

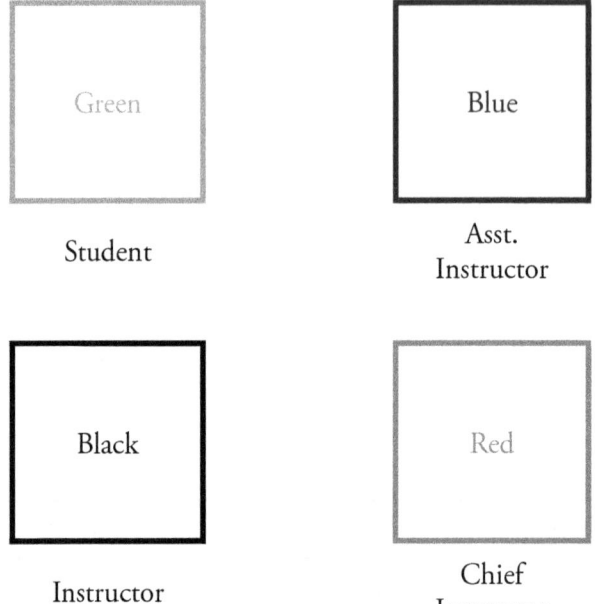

[Photo: 29.1]

Canada Kong Han Ngo Cho Kun Kung Fu Association

加拿大光漢五祖拳武術會

[Photo: 29.2]

O Duan "Black Belt" 黑段

Instructor I	4 hand forms	2 weapon
	fighting drills, concept, application and principle	fighting drills, concept, application and principle
Instructor II	5 hand forms	2 weapons
	fighting drills, concept, application and principle	fighting drills, concept, application and principle
Instructor III	7 hand forms	3 weapons
	fighting drills, concept, application and principle	fighting drills, concept, application and principle
Chief Instructor IV	8 hand form	4 weapons
	fighting drills, concept, application and principle	fighting drills, concept, application and principle
Chief Instructor V	10 hand forms	4 weapons
	fighting drills, concept, application and principle	fighting drills, concept, application and principle
Chief Instructor VI	10 hand forms	6 weapons
	fighting drills, concept, application and principle	fighting drills, concept, application and principle
Master "Sifu" VII	11 - 13 hand forms	6 or + weapons
	fighting drills, concept, application and principle	fighting drills, concept, application and principle
	Thesis, advance theories	Thesis, advance theories
Master "Sifu" VIII	15+ hand forms	7 or + weapons
	fighting drills, concept, application and principle	fighting drills, concept, application and principle
	Thesis, advance theories	Thesis, advance theories
Grand Master "Sifu" IX	16 or + hand forms	8 or + weapons
	fighting drills, concept, application and principle	fighting drills, concept, application and principle
	Thesis, advance theories	Thesis, advance theories
Chief Grand Master "Ta Sifu" X		

Level and Ranking

The KH NCK O-Duan (black belt) 黑段

The O-Duan 黑段 is a black belt or sash that symbolizes the technical skills and competitive abilities of the wearer, the black color symbolizes the degree of experience and training, the hard work, dedication, courage and devotion and the red stripe is the color code of arms of KH GCK. The O-Duan is awarded to successful students who have train in KH GCK extensively, have understood, and absorb the principle and techniques that comes with experience, discipline, dedication and character. It marks the beginning of their journey and history in training, progressing and development to become Master of the art of Kong Han Ngo Cho Kun Kung Fu.

The journey begins and graduated as follows:

1st Duan Instructor

2nd Duan Instructor

3rd Duan Instructor

4th Duan Chief Instructor or Sifu

5th Duan Chief Instructor or Sifu

6th Duan Chief Instructor or Sifu

7th Duan Sifu Master

8th Duan Sifu Master

9th Duan Sifu Grand Master

10th Duan Ta Sifu Chief Grand Master

The five materials required to be awarded the O Duan I as covered in this book are: 1. Sam Chien, 2. Di Sip Kun, 3. Si Mun Pah Kat empty hand and 4. Weapons Da Dao and 5. Goh Tsio Kuhn including their corresponding fighting drills technique applications and concept.

APPENDIX 5

TERMINOLOGY BY CHAPTER

INTRODUCTION:

English	Táiyǔ (Taiwanese Hokkien)	Mǐnnányǔ (Southern Min)	Pīnyīn (Mandarin)	Traditional Chinese logograms	Simplified Chinese logograms
Shāndōng (Eastern Mountain) Province	Soa-Tong Séng	San-Dong Sing	Shāndōngshěng	山東省	山东省
Flowery Fist	Hôa Kûn	Hua Gun	Huáquán	華拳	华拳
Plum (Prune) Blossom Fist	Mûi Hoe Kûn	Mui Hua Gun	Méihuāquán	梅花拳	梅花拳
Praying (Mantis) Mantis Fist	Tông Lông Kûn	Dong Long Gun	Tánglángquán	螳螂拳	螳螂拳
Establish Good Fortune	Hok-Kiàn	Hok-Gian	Fújiàn	福建	福建
Short Boxing	Té Kûn	De Gun	Duǎnquán	短拳	短拳
White Crane Fist	Pe̍k Ho̍k Kûn	Bê Hok Gun	Báihèquán	白鶴拳	白鹤拳
Cantonese (Broad East Language)	Kóng Tong Ōe	Gong-Dong Uê	Guǎngdōnghuà	廣東話	广东话
Sing Spring Fist	Ēng Chhun Kûn	Ing Cun Kun	Yǒngchūnquán	詠春拳	咏春拳
Five Ancestors Fist	Ngó Chó Kûn	Ngo Zo Gun	Wǔzǔquán	五祖拳	五祖拳

Quánzhōu (Spring Province) City	Chôaⁿ-Chiu Chhī	Zuan-Ziu Ci	Quánzhōushì	泉州市	泉州市
Qīng (Pure) dynasty	Chheng Tiau	Cing Diao	Qīngcháo	清朝	清朝

CHAPTER 1: HERITAGE OF SOUTHERN FIST

English	Táiyǔ (Taiwanese Hokkien)	Mǐnnányǔ (Southern Min)	Pīnyīn (Mandarin)	Traditional Chinese logograms	Simplified Chinese logograms
Hokkien	Hok-Kiàn Ōe	Hok-Gian Hua	Fújiànhuà	福建話	福建话
Míng (Bright) dynasty	Bêng Tiau	Min Diao	Míngcháo	明朝	明朝
Zhu, Primary Ornament	Chu, Gôan-Chiong	Zu, Nguan-Ziong	Zhū, Yuánzhāng	朱元璋	朱元璋
Yuán (Primary) dynasty	Gôan Tiau	Nguan Diao	Yuáncháo	元朝	元朝
Great Military Emperor	Hông Bú Tè	Hong Mu Dê	Hóngwǔdì	洪武帝	洪武帝
Yángzǐ (Raising) River	Iông Chí Kang	Iong Zy Gang	Yángzǐjiāng	揚子江	扬子江
Mandarin (Official Language)	Koaⁿ Ōe	Guan Hua	Guānhuà	官話	官话
Grand Ancestor Fist	Thài Chó Kûn	Tai Zo Gun	Tàizǔquán	太祖拳	太祖拳
Sòng dynasty	Sòng Tiau	Song Diao	Sòngcháo	宋朝	宋朝
Zhao, Correct Heir	Tiō, Khong-Ĭn	Diao, Kung-In	Zhào, Kuāngyìn	趙匡胤	赵匡胤
Ming Great Fist	Bêng Hông Kûn	Min Hong Gun	Mínghóngquán	明洪拳	明洪拳
Jurchen	Lí Chin	Ly Zin	Nǚzhēn	女真	女真
Manchuria	Móa-Chiu	Maun-Ziu	Mǎnzhōu	滿洲	满洲
Jīn (Gold) dynasty	Kim Tiâu	Gim Diao	Jīncháo	金朝	金朝
Grand Ancestor Long Fist	Thài Chó Chhiâng Kûn	Tai Zo Deng Gun	Tàizǔchángquán	太祖長拳	太祖长拳

Chinese Ethnicity	Hàn Chók	Han Zok	Hànzú	漢族	汉族
Manchu (Manchurian Ethnicity)	Má Chók	Maun Zok	Mǎnzú	滿族	满族
Oppose the Qīng, Restore the Míng	Hóan Chheng Hók Bêng	Huan Cing Hok Min	Fǎnqīngfùmíng	反清復明	反清复明
Shàolín (Young Forest) Monastery	Siàu Nâ Sī	Siao Lim Si	Shàolínsì	少林寺	少林寺
Hénán (Southern River) Province	Hô-Lâm Séng	Hou-Lam Sing	Hénánshěng	河南省	河南省
Shàolín (Young Forest) Fist	Siàu Nâ Kûn	Siao Lim Gun	Shàolínquán	少林拳	少林拳
Zhèng, The Success	Tēⁿ, Sêng-Kong	Ding, Sing-Gong	Zhèng, Chéng-gōng	鄭成功	郑成功
Koxinga	Kok, Sìⁿ–Iâ	Gok, Si-Ia	Guóxìngyé	國姓爺	国姓爷
Taiwan (Stage Bay)	Tâi-Ôan	Tai-Uan	Táiwān	臺灣	台灣
Xiàmén (Gate Way of Tall Buildings) City	Hā-Mńg Chhī	Ha-Mun Ci	Xiàménshì	廈門市	厦门市
Heaven, Earth Society	Thiⁿ Tē Hōe	Tian Dê Huê	Tiāndìhuì	天地會	天地会
Great Gate	Hông Mńg	Hong Mun	Hóngmén	洪門	洪门
Dr. Sun, Yat-Sen	Sun, Ėk-Sian	Sun, Iak-Sian	Sūn, Yìxiān	孫逸仙	孙逸仙

CHAPTER 2: ROOTS OF GRAND ANCESTOR-FIVE ANCESTOR FIST

English	Táiyǔ (Taiwanese Hokkien)	Mǐnnányǔ (Southern Min)	Pīnyīn (Mandarin)	Traditional Chinese logograms	Simplified Chinese logograms
Zhāngzhōu City	Chiang-Chiu Chhī	Ziong-Ziu Ci	Zhāngzhōushì	漳州市	漳州市
Wu, Heart	Ngō, Sim	Ngo, Sim	Wù, Xīn	悟心	悟心
Eastern Pagoda (Meditation)	Tong-Siân	Dong Dang	Dōngchán	東禪	东禅
Chua, Giok Beng	Chhòa, Giȯk-Bêng	Cai, Ngiok-Min	Cài, Yùmíng	蔡玉明	蔡玉明
Lǐ, The Eminent Humane	Lí, Chùn-Jîn	Li, Zun-Lin	Lǐ, Jùnrén	李俊仁	李俊仁
Grand Ancestor Fist	Thài Chó͘ Kûn	Tai Zo Gun	Tàizǔquán	太祖拳	太祖拳
Monkey Fist	Kâu Kûn	Gao Gun	Hóuquán	猴拳	
Arhat Fist	Lô-Hàn Kûn	Lou-Han Gun	Luóhànquán	羅漢拳	罗汉拳
White Crane Fist	Pe̍h Ho̍h Kûn	Biak Hok Gun	Báihèquán	白鶴拳	白鹤拳
Bodhidharma Fist	Ta̍t-Mô Kûn	Dat Mo Gun	Dámóquán	達摩拳	达摩拳
Five Ancestor Fist He Yang School	Ngó͘ Chó͘ Kûn Ôa Iúⁿ Phài	Ngo Zo Gun Hou Iu Pai	Wǔzǔquán-héyángpài	五祖拳何陽派	五祖拳何阳派
Míng [dynasty] Grand Ancestor Fist	Bêng Thài Chó͘ Kûn	Min Tai Zo Gun	Míngtàizǔquán	明太祖拳	明太祖拳
Forever Spring White Crane Boxing	Éng Chhun Pe̍h Ho̍h Kûn	Ing Cun Biak Hok Gun	Yǒngchūnbáihèquán	永春白鶴拳	永春白鹤拳
Field	Hú Tiân	Hu Dian	Pútián	莆田	莆田
Míng Great Fist	Bêng Hông Kûn	Min Hong Gun	Mínghóngquán	明 洪拳	明 洪拳
Sun, Comprehending Emptiness (Monkey King)	Sun, Ngō-Khnag	Sun, Ngo-Kong	Sūn, Wùkōng	孫悟空	孙悟

CHAPTER 3: LEGACY BEGINS

English	Táiyǔ (Taiwanese Hokkien)	Mǐnnányǔ (Southern Min)	Pīnyīn (Mandarin)	Traditional Chinese logograms	Simplified Chinese logograms
Lo, Yan-Chu	Lô, Gân-Chhiu	Lo, Ngian-Ciu	Lú, Yánqiū	盧言秋	卢言秋
Lo, Yung-Sheng	Lô, Sian-Seⁿ	Lo, Sian Seng	Lú, Xiānshēng	盧先生	卢先生
Fong, Sai Yuk	Hong, Sè-Gio̍k	Hng, Se-Ngiok	Fāng, Shìyù	方世玉	方世玉
Confucius	Khang Chí	Kong Zi	Kǒngzǐ	孔子	孔子
Green-Dragon Halberd [Moon Falling Knife]	Chheng Lêng Ián Ge̍h To	Ci Liang Ian Nge Dou	Qīng lóngyǎnyuèdāo	青龍偃月刀	青龙偃月刀
Guan Yu (Mountain Pass Feather)	Koan-Ú	Guan-U	Guānyǔ	關羽	关羽
Zong, Courage	Chng Tám	Zong, Dam	Zhuāng, Dǎn	莊膽	庄胆
Southern Young Forest Temple	Lâm Siàu Nâ Sī	Lam Siao Lim Si	Nánshàolínsì	南少林寺	南少林寺
Kong, Po-Chiam	Kong, Pô-Chiam	Gong, Bou-Ziam	Gōng, Pózhān	公婆詹	公婆詹
Lim, Kui-Lu	Nâ, Kiú-Jî	Lim, Giu-Ly	Lín, Jiǔrú	林九如	林九如
Tan, Kiong-Beng	Tân, Kiong-Bêng	Dan, Ging-Ming	Chén, Jīngmíng	陳京銘	陈京铭
Ten Tiger of Five Ancestors Fist	Si̍p Hó͘ Ngó͘ Chó͘ Kûn	Sip Ho Ngo Zo Gun	Shíhǔwǔzǔquán	十虎五祖拳	十虎五祖拳
Enclosed Head (town)	Ûi-Thâu	Ui-Tao	Wéitóu	圍頭	围头
Falling, Striking Doctor	Tia̍t Táⁿ Tōa	Diat Da Dai	Diēdǎdài	跌打大	跌打大
Daoism (Teaching the Road)	Tō Kah	Dou Gao	Dàojiào	道教	道教
Éméi Mountain	Gô-Bî Soaⁿ	Ngo-Mi San	Éméishān	峨嵋山	峨嵋山

Sìchuān Province	Sì-Chhoan Séng	Si-Ceng Sing	Sìchuānshěng	四川省	四川省
Short Iron Flogger	Té Thih Pian	De Ti Bi	Duǎntiěbiān	短鐵鞭	短铁鞭
Nine Section Steel Whip	Káu Thih Chiát Pian	Giu Ti Zuê Bi	Jiǔtiějiébiān	九鐵截鞭	九铁截鞭
Lo, The True Tiger	Hó͘ Bú Lô͘	Ho Miou Lo	Hǔmǔqiū	虎母秋	虎母秋
Kong Han Mu Guan (Clear Chinese Martial School)	Kong Hàn Bú Kóan	Gong Han Mu Guan	Guānghàn-wǔguǎn	光漢武館	光汉武馆
Benevolent, Righteousness, Courtesy, Wisdom, and Faith	Lîn, Gī, Lé, Tì, Sìn	Lin, Ngi, Le, Di, Sin	Rén, Yì, Lǐ, Zhì, Xìn	仁, 義, 禮, 智, 信	仁, 义, 礼, 智, 信

CHAPTER 4: THE KONG HAN ATHLETIC CLUB

English	Táiyǔ (Taiwanese Hokkien)	Mǐnnányǔ (Southern Min)	Pīnyīn (Mandarin)	Traditional Chinese logograms	Simplified Chinese logograms
Lo, King-Hui	Lô͘, Khèng-Hui	Lo, King-Hui	Lú, Qìnghuī	盧慶輝	卢庆辉
Heng Han Athletic Club	Heng Hàn Kok Su̍t Kóan	Hing Han Gok Sut Guan	Xīnghànguó shùguǎn	興漢國術館	兴汉国术馆
Taipei City	Tâi-Pak Chhī	Dai-Bak Ci	Táiběishì	臺北市	台北市
Tainan City	Tâi-Lâm Chhī	Dai-Lam Ci	Táinánshì	臺南市	台南市

CHAPTER 5: 2ND GENERATION- LO, KING-HUI

English	Táiyǔ (Taiwanese Hokkien)	Mǐnnányǔ (Southern Min)	Pīnyīn (Mandarin)	Traditional Chinese logograms	Simplified Chinese logograms
Hong Kong	Hiuⁿ-Káng	Hiu-Gang	Xiānggǎng	香港	香港
Military Art	Bú Su̍t	Mu Sut	Wǔshù	武術	武术

| International South Shàolín Wǔzǔquán Research Union | Kok Chè Lâm Siàu Nâ Ngó Chó Kûn Géng Kiù Hōe | Gok Zê Lam Siao Lim Ngo Zo Gun Ngian Giu Huê | Guójìnánshàolínwǔzǔquányánjiūhuì | 國際南少林五祖拳研究會 | 国际南少林五祖拳研究会 |

CHAPTER 6: THE PRESENT- LO, ZU-MING

English	Táiyǔ (Taiwanese Hokkien)	Mǐnnányǔ (Southern Min)	Pīnyīn (Mandarin)	Traditional Chinese logograms	Simplified Chinese logograms
Lo, Zu-Ming (Henry)	Lô, Su-Bêng	Lo, Sy-Min	Lú, Sīmíng	盧思明	卢思明
Zhèngzhōu City	Tēⁿ-Chiu Chhī	Di Ziu Ci	Zhèngzhōushì	鄭州市	郑州市
Set Way	Thò Lō͘	Tou Lo	Tàolù	套路	套路
Scatter Hand	Sàn Siu	Sua Ciu	Sànshǒu	散手	散手
Striking Platform	Lûi Tâi	Lui Dai	Lèitái	擂臺	擂台
Duan (Selection)	Tōaⁿ	Duan	Duàn	段	段
Brazil Fei Lung (Flying Dragon) Kong Han Kung Fu (Martial Art) Academy	Pa Sai Pe Lêng Kong Hàn Bú Su̍t Óh Īⁿ	Ba Sai Be Ling Gong Han Mu Sut Ou I	Bāxīfēilóngguāng hànwǔshùxué yuàn	巴西飛龍光漢武術學院	巴西飛龍光汉武术学

CHAPTER 7: GUIDING PRINCIPLE

English	Táiyǔ (Taiwanese Hokkien)	Mǐnnányǔ (Southern Min)	Pīnyīn (Mandarin)	Traditional Chinese logograms	Simplified Chinese logograms
Five Attacks	Ngó͘ Kek	Ngo Giak	Wǔjī	五擊	五击
Striking	Táⁿ	Da	Dǎ	打	打
Kicking	That	Tiak	Tī	踢	踢
Seizing	Ná	La	Ná	拿	拿
Throwing	Sut	Sut	Shuāi	摔	摔
Bumping	Tōng	Dong	Zhuàng	撞	撞
Strength	La̍t	Zi	Lì	力	力
Energy	Kèng	Ging	Jìn	勁	劲

Three Battle/ San Chien	Saⁿ Chiàn	Sam Zian	Sānzhàn	三戰	三战
Steam (Vital Energy)	Khì	Ki	Qì	氣	气
Heaven, Earth Effective Battle	Thiⁿ Tē Lêng Chiàn	Tian Dê Liang Zian	Tiāndìlíngzhàn	天地靈戰	天地灵战
Three Battle, Twenty Fist	Saⁿ Chiàn Lī Sip Kûn	Sam Zian Li-Sip Gun	Sānzhànèr shíquán	三戰二十拳	三战二十拳
Five Limb (Parts) Strength/ Ngo Ki Lat	Ngó Chi La̍t	Ngo Zi Liak	Wǔzhīlì	五肢力	五肢力
Ten Character	Sip Jī	Sip Li	Shízì	十字	十字
Way/Form	Lō͘	Lo	Lù	路	路
Battle Way	Chiàn Lō͘	Zian Lo	Zhànlù	戰路	战路
Leg	Thúi	Tui	Tuǐ	腿	腿
Hips	Tūn Pō͘	Dun Bo	Túnbù	臀部	臀部
Shoulder	Pok	Pok	Bó	膊	膊
Arm/Hand	Siu	Ciu	Shǒu	手	手
Steam Achievement/ Working Vital Energy	Khì Kong	Ki Gong	Qìgōng	氣功	气功
Meridian system	Keng Lo̍k	Ging Lok	Jīngluò	經絡	经络
Issuing Energy	Hoat Kèng	Huat Ging	Fājìn	發勁	发
Four Method	Sì Hoat	Si Huat	Sìfǎ	四法	四法
Sink	Tiâm	Dim	Chén	沈	沈
Swallow	Thun	Tun	Tūn	吞	吞
Float	Phû	Pu	Fú	浮	浮
Spit	Thó͘	To	Tǔ	吐	吐
Hundred Gathering	Pah Hōe	Ba Huê	Bǎihuì	百會	百会
Gathering Overcast (Perineum)	Hōe Im	Huê Im	Huìyīn	會陰	会阴
Cinnabar Field	Tan Tiân	Dan Dian	Dāntián	丹田	丹田
Bridging	Kiô	Giao	Qiáo	橋	桥
Internal	Lāi	Lai	Nèi	內	內
External	Gōa	Ngua	Wài	外	外
Insubstantial	Im	Im	Yīn	陰	阴

Substantial	Iong	Iong	Yáng	陽	阳
Dragon	Lêng	Ling	Lóng	飛	飛
Tiger	Hó͘	Ho	Hǔ	虎	虎
Relaxed	Song	Song	Sōng	鬆	松
Extreme Extremities	Thài Kėk	Tai Giak	Tàijí	太極	太极
Density	Bit	Me	Mì	密	密
Intensity	Kiūⁿ	Giu	Qiáng	強	强
Tension	Kín	Gin	Jǐn	緊	紧
Tàishān Mountain	Thài Soaⁿ	Tai San	Tàishān	泰山	泰山
Conception Vessel	Līm Mėh	Lim Mê	Rènmài	任脈	任脉
Governing Vessel	Mėh Tok	Mê Dok	Dūmài	督脈	督脉
Three Battle Stance	Saⁿ Chiàn Pō͘	Sam Zian Bo	Sānzhàn	三戰步	三战步
Intent	Ì	I	Yì	意	意
Light Movement	Khin Tōng	Kin Dang	Qīng Dòng	輕動	轻动
Escaping Swiftly	Pháu Khok	Pak Kok	Pǎokù	跑酷	跑酷
Four Doors Striking Corner	Sì Mn̂g Táⁿ Kak	Si Mun Da Gak	Sìméndǎjiǎo	四門打角	四门打角
Double Pacifying Fist	Siang Sui Kûn	Sang Sui Gun	Shuāngsuíquán	雙綏拳	双绥拳
Standing Strike	Lip Tûi	Lip Dui	Lìchuí	立捶	立捶
Linking Fist	Chong Hȧh Kûn	Zong Hap Gun	Zōnghéquán	綜合拳	综合拳
Set Fist	Thò͘ Kûn	Tou Gun	Tàoquán	套拳	套拳
Hand Model	Siu Hêng	Ciu Hing	Shǒuxíng	手型	手型
Weapon Skill	Hâi Sut	Hai Sut	Xièshú	械術	械术
Partner Drill	Tùi Liān	Dui Lian	Duìliàn	對練	对练
Bridge Method	Kiô Hoat	Qiao Huat	Qiáofǎ	橋法	桥法
Weapons	Hâi	Hai	Xiè	械	械
Armed Escort	Pio Kiȯk	Biao Giak	Biāojú	鏢局	镖局
Single Knife	Tan To	Dan Dou	Dāndāo	單刀	单刀
Big Knife	Tōa To	Dai Dou	Dàdāo	大刀	大刀
Sword	Kiàm	Giam	Jiàn	劍	剑

English	Táiyǔ (Taiwanese Hokkien)	Mǐnnányǔ (Southern Min)	Pīnyīn (Mandarin)	Traditional Chinese logograms	Simplified Chinese logograms
Double Short Iron Floggers	Siang Té Thih Pian	Sang De Ti Bi	Shuāngduǎn-tiěbiān	雙短鐵鞭	双短铁鞭
Double Short Crutch	Siang Té Kóai	Sang De Guai	Shuāngduǎn	雙短拐	双短
Staff	Kùn	Gun	Gùn	棍	棍
General Guan's Knife	Koan Tōa	Guan Dou	Guāndāo	關刀	关刀
Cutting Mountain Hook or Trident	Khai Soaⁿ Kau	Kai San Gao	Kāishāngōu	開山鈎	开山钩
Nine Section Steel Whip	Káu Thih Chiát Pian	Giu Ti Zuê Bi	Jiǔtiějiébiān	九鐵截鞭	九铁截鞭
Slap and Hit	Phah Táⁿ	Piak Da	Pāidǎ	拍打	拍打
Iron Body Achievement	Thih Sin Kong	Ti Sin Gong	Tiěshēngōng	铁身功	铁身功
Iron Palm Achievement	Thih Chiúⁿ Kong	Ti Ziu Gong	Tiězhǎnggōng	铁掌功	铁掌功
Martial Virtue	Bú Tek	Mu Diak	Wǔdé	武德	武德

CHAPTER 8: KI GONG

English	Táiyǔ (Taiwanese Hokkien)	Mǐnnányǔ (Southern Min)	Pīnyīn (Mandarin)	Traditional Chinese logograms	Simplified Chinese logograms
Steam (Vital Energy)	Khì	Ki	Qì	氣	气
Steam Achievement/ Working Vital Energy	Khì Kong	Ki Gong	Qìgōng	氣功	气功
Cinnabar Field	Tan Tiân	Dan Dian	Dāntián	丹田	丹田
Essence/Spirit	Sîn	Sin	Shén	神	神

CHAPTER 9: THE MODELS

English	Táiyǔ (Taiwanese Hokkien)	Mǐnnányǔ (Southern Min)	Pīnyīn (Mandarin)	Traditional Chinese logograms	Simplified Chinese logograms
Method	Hoat	Huat	Fǎ	法	法
Capturing and Seizing	Khîm Ná	Kim La	Qínná	擒拿	擒拿
Throwing	Sut	Sut	Shuāi	摔	摔
Striking	Tá^n	Da	Dǎ	打	打
Battle Stance	Chiàn Pō͘	Zian Bo	Zhànbù	戰步	战步
Asking, Guarding Hand	Mn̄g Hō͘ Siu	Mun Ho Ciu	Wènhùshǒu	問護手	问护手
Twenty Fist	Lī Sip Kûn	Li-Sip Gun	Èrhíquán	二十拳	二十拳
Fist Method	Kûn Hoat	Gun Huat	Quán	拳法	拳法
Straight Strike	Tit Tûi	Dit Dui	Zhíchuí	直搥	直捶
Level Strike	Pê͘n Tûi	Bing Dui	Píngchuí	平搥	平捶
Hammer Back Fist	Thûi Pè Kûn	Dui Be Gun	Chuíbèiquán	鎚背拳	锤背拳
Hanging-Up Strike	Kòa Tûi	Gua Dui	Guàchuí	掛搥	挂捶
Double Resonating Strike	Siang Tín Tûi	Sang Zin Dui	Shuāngzhènchuí	雙振搥	双振捶
Double Colliding Fist	Siang Chōng Tûi	Sang Dong Dui	Shuāngzhuàngchuí	雙撞搥	双撞捶
Hooking Strike	Kau Tûi	Gao Dui	Gōuchuí	鉤搥	钩捶
Passing-Through Strike	Kǹg Tûi	Guan Dui	Guànchuí	貫搥	贯捶
Double Planting Strike	Siang Chai Tûi	Sang Zai Dui	Shuāngzāichuí	雙栽搥	双栽捶
Double Rock Strike	Siang Chio̍h Tûi	Sang Sia Dui	Shuāngshíchuí	雙石搥	双石捶
Baiting Strike	Kau Tûi	Siong Gao Dui	Shànggōuchuí	上鉤搥	上钩捶
Seizing Hand	Ná Siu	La Ciu	Náshǒu	拿手	拿手
Resonating Strike	Tín Tûi	Zin Dui	Zhuàngchuí	振搥	振捶
Embracing Fist	Pau Kûn	Bao Gun	Bāoquán	包拳	包拳
Pulling Locking Fist	Lah Só Kûn	La Sou Gun	Lāsuǒquán	拉鎖拳	拉锁拳

Giving Respect Fist	Mñg Hāu Kûn	Meng Hiou Kun	Wènhòuquán	問候拳	问候拳
Hand/Arm Method	Siu Hoat	Ciu Huat	Shǒufǎ	手法	手法
Piercing Finger Hand	Chhēng Cháiⁿ Siu	Cuan Zi Ciu	Chuānzhǐshǒu	穿指手	穿指手
Poking Eye Socket	Thóng Khong	Tong Kong	Tǒngkuàng	捅眶	捅眶
Double Finger Hand	Siang Cháiⁿ Siu	Sang Zi Ciu	Shuāngzhǐshǒu	雙指手	双指手
Slicing Palm	Chhiat Chiúⁿ	Ciat Ziu	Qiēzhǎng	切掌	切掌
Tiger Claw Hand	Hó͘ Jiáu Siu	Ho Zao Ciu	Hǔzhuǎshǒu	虎爪手	虎爪手
Double Flank Defense	Siang Hiáp Pó Hō͘	Sang Hiap Bou Ho	Shuāngxiébǎohù	雙脅保護	双胁保护
Double Covering Hand	Siang Kài Siu	Sang Gai Ciu	Shuānggàishǒu	雙蓋手	双盖手
Double Downward Defense	Siang Kē Pó Hō͘	Sang Ge Bou Ho	Shuāngdībǎohù	雙低保護	双低保护
Holding Shield Hand	Phō Pâi Siu	Pou Bai Ciu	Bàopáishǒu	抱牌手	抱牌手
Butterflies Palm	Ô͘ Tiáp Chiúⁿ	O Diap Ziu	Húdiézhǎng	蝴蝶掌	蝴蝶掌
Inward Arm	Lāi Hān Siu	Lap Han Ciu	Nèihànshǒu	內捍手	內捍手
Obstruction Arm	Keh Siu	Ge Ciu	Géshǒu	格手	格手
Whipping Arm	Pian Siu	Bi Ciu	Biānshǒu	鞭手	鞭手
Chopping Arm	Khám Siu	Kam Ciu	Kǎnshǒu	砍手	砍手
Thousand Character Arm	Chhian Jī Siu	Cui Li Ciu	Qiānzìshǒu	千字手	千字手
Striking Chop Arm	Táⁿ Phek Siu	Da Pi Ciu	Dǎpīshǒu	打劈手	打劈手
Double Epiphysis Poke	Siang Hiou Thóng	Sang Hiou Tong	Shuānghóutǒng	雙骺捅	双骺捅
Double Sweeping Hand	Siang Sàu Siu	Sang Sou Ciu	Shuāngsǎoshǒu	雙掃手	双扫手
Bridge Method	Kiô Hoat	Giao Huat	Qiáofǎ	橋法	桥法

Double Spreading Arm	Siang Thoaⁿ Siu	Sang Lua Ciu	Shuāngtānshǒu	雙攤手	双摊手
Double Opening Arm	Siang Khái Siu	Sang Hai Ciu	Shuāngkǎishǒu	雙闓手	双闿手
Joining Arm	Piàⁿ Siu	Ping Ciu	Pīnshǒu	拼手	拼手
Sinking Bridge	Tiàm Kiô	Dim Giao	Chénqiáo	沉橋	沉桥
Double Piercing Bridge	Siang Chhēng Kiô	Sang Cuan Giao	Shuāngchuānqiáo	雙穿橋	双穿桥
Elbow Method	Tiú Hoat	Diu Huat	Zhǒufǎ	肘法	肘法
Vertical Elbow	Chhiòng Tiú	Ziong Diu	Zòngzhǒu	縱肘	纵肘
Lifting Elbow	Tàⁿ Tiú	Dam Diu	Dānzhǒu	擔肘	担肘
Level Elbow	Pêⁿ Tiú	Bing Diu	Píngzhǒu	平肘	平肘
Propping-Up Elbow	Thèⁿ Tiú	Teng Diu	Chēngzhǒu	撐肘	撑肘
Crushing Elbow	Chap Tiú	Zap Diu	Zázhǒu	砸肘	砸肘
Leg Method	Thúi Hoat	Tui Huat	Tuǐfǎ	腿法	腿法
White Crane Jumping Kick	Péh Hóh Bà Tê	Biak Hok Bao Di	Báihèbàodì	白鶴趵踶	白鹤趵踶
Golden Scissors Leg	Kim Chián To Thúi	Gim Zian Dou Tui	Jīnjiǎndāotuǐ	金剪刀腿	金剪刀腿
Front Kick	Chêng Tê	Zui Tat	Qiántī	前踢	前踢
In-Front Going-Up Leg	Chêng Têⁿ Thúi	Zui Ding Tui	Qiándēngtuǐ	前蹬腿	前蹬腿
Turning Side Kick	Ǹg Chhek Tê	Hiong Ciak Tat	Xiàngcètī	向側踢	向侧踢
Across Swing Leg	Hôaiⁿ Pái Thúi	Hui Bai Tui	Héngbǎituǐ	橫擺腿	横摆腿
Side-Of Thread Leg	Chhek Sōan Thúi	Ciak Suan Tui	Cèchuàituǐ	側踹腿	侧踹腿
Sweeping Leg	Sàu Thúi	Sao Tui	Sàotuǐ	掃腿	扫腿

CHAPTER 10: RAISING FIST

English	Táiyǔ (Taiwanese Hokkien)	Mǐnnányǔ (Southern Min)	Pīnyīn (Mandarin)	Traditional Chinese logograms	Simplified Chinese logograms
Embracing Seal	Phō Ìn	Pou In	Bàoyìn	抱印	抱印
Raising Fist	Khí Kûn	Ki Gun	Qǐquán	起拳	起拳
Giving Respect Fist	Mn̄g Hāu Kûn	Mun Hiou Gun	Wènhòuquán	問候拳	问候拳
Side-by-Side Stance	Pèng Pō͘	Bing Bu	Bìngbù	並步	并步
Both Side Fist	Lióng Kûn	Leng Gun	Liǎngquán	兩拳	两拳
Lifting Knee	Thê Sit	Si Siak	Tíxī	提膝	提膝
Embracing Fist	Pau Kûn	Bao Gun	Bāoquán	包拳	包拳
Detain Fist	Khàu Kûn	Kiou Gun	Kòuquán	扣拳	扣拳
Four Level Stance	Sì Pêⁿ Pō͘	Si Bing Bu	Sìpíngbù	四平步	四平步
Double Flank Defense	Siang Hiáp Pó Hō͘	Sang Hiap Bou Ho	Shuāngxiébǎohù	雙脅保護	双胁保护
Double Planting Strike	Siang Chai Tûi	Sang Zai Dui	Shuāngzāichuí	雙栽搥	双栽捶
Double Covering Hand	Siang Kài Siu	Sang Gai Ciu	Shuānggàishǒu	雙蓋手	双盖手
Ten Character Arm	Sip Jī Siu	Sip Li Ciu	Shízìshǒu	十字手	十字手
Double Spreading Arm	Siang Thoaⁿ Siu	Sang Lua Ciu	Shuāngtānshǒu	雙攤手	双摊手
Double Capturing Until Eyebrow	Siang Khîm Chì Bâi	Sang Kim Zi Mai	Shuāngqínzhìméi	雙擒至眉	双擒至眉
Double Seizing Hand	Siang Lo Siu	Sang Liou Ciu	Shuānglōu	雙摟手	双搂手
Double Embracing Fist	Siang Pau Kûn	Sang Bao Gun	Shuāngbāoquán	雙包拳	双包拳
Double Joining Arm	Siang Piàⁿ Siu	Sang Ping Ciu	Shuāngpīnshǒu	雙拼手	双拼手

CHAPTER 11: GUARDING SKILL

English	Táiyǔ (Taiwanese Hokkien)	Mǐnnányǔ (Southern Min)	Pīnyīn (Mandarin)	Traditional Chinese logograms	Simplified Chinese logograms
Guarding Skills	Hông Siú Ki Sut	Hong Siu Gi Sut	Fángshǒujìshù	防守技術	防守技术
Grasping Hand, Double Guard	Chip Siu Siang Ōe	Zip Ciu Sang Ue	Zhíshǒushuāngwèi	執手雙衛	执手双卫
Embracing Tile	Phō Pâi	Pou Bai	Bàopái	抱牌	抱牌
Empty Stance	Hi Pō	Hy Bu	Xūbù	虛步	虚步
Protecting Center Body	Pó Tèng Thé	Bou Tê Diong	Bǎozhōngtǐ	保中體	保中体

CHAPTER 12: THREE BATTLE WAY

English	Táiyǔ (Taiwanese Hokkien)	Mǐnnányǔ (Southern Min)	Pīnyīn (Mandarin)	Traditional Chinese logograms	Simplified Chinese logograms
Three Battle (San Chien) Way	Saⁿ Chiàn Lō͘	Sam Zian Lo	Sānzhànlù	三戰路	三战路
Ascending Footstep	Siōng Pō͘	Siong Bu	Shàngbù	上步	上步
Double Piercing Palm	Siang Ch-hēng Chiúⁿ	Sang Cuan Ziu	Chuānchuānzhǎng	雙穿掌	双穿掌
Descending Footstep	Hā Pō͘	Ha Bu	Xiàbù	下步	下步
Double Downward Guard	Siang Kē Pó Hō͘	Sang Ge Bou Ho	Shuāngdībǎohù	雙低保護	双低保护

CHAPTER 13: THREE BATTLE PARTNER DRILL

English	Táiyǔ (Taiwanese Hokkien)	Mǐnnányǔ (Southern Min)	Pīnyīn (Mandarin)	Traditional Chinese logograms	Simplified Chinese logograms
Three Battle (San Chien) Partner Drill	Saⁿ Chiàn Tùi Liān	Sam Zian Dui Lian	Sānzhànduìliàn	三戰對練	三战对练
Double Hooking Strike	Siang Kau Tùi	Sang Gao Dui	Shuānggōuchuí	雙鉤搥	双钩捶
Double Hand Protecting the Gate	Siang Siu Pó Mn̂g	Sang Ciu Bou Mun	Shuāngshǒubǎomén	雙手保門	双手保门

English	Táiyǔ (Taiwanese Hokkien)	Mǐnnányǔ (Southern Min)	Pīnyīn (Mandarin)	Traditional Chinese logograms	Simplified Chinese logograms
Tray Elbow	Pôaⁿ Tiú	Bua Diu	Pánzhǒu	盤肘	盘肘
Specifying Fingers	Pio Cháiⁿ	Biao Zi	Biāozhǐ	鏢指	镖指
Lifting Palm	Liâu Chiúⁿ	Liao Ziu	Liāozhǎng	撩掌	撩掌
Flicking Leg	Tân Thúi	Dan Tui	Tántuǐ	彈腿	弹腿
Chopping Arm	Phek Siu	Pi Ciu	Pīshǒu	劈手	劈手

CHAPTER 15: DI SIP KUN

English	Táiyǔ (Taiwanese Hokkien)	Mǐnnányǔ (Southern Min)	Pīnyīn (Mandarin)	Traditional Chinese logograms	Simplified Chinese logograms
Twenty Fist (Di Sip Kun)	Lī Sip Kûn	Li-Sip Gun	Èrhíquán	二十拳	二十拳
Iron Arm	Thih Siu	Ti Ciu	Tiěshǒu	鐵手	铁手
Falling, Beating Wine (Dit Da Jáu)	Tiȧt Táⁿ Chiú	Diat Da Ziu	Diēdǎjiǔ	跌打酒	跌打酒
Three Star Striking	Sam San Piān	Sam Sing Bian	Sānxīngbiàn	三星抃	三星抃
Bridging Arm	Kiô Siu	Giao Ciu	Qiáoshǒu	橋手	桥手
Cutting-Off Bridge	Chiȧt Kiô	Ziat Giao	Jiéqiáo	截橋	截桥
Double Hanging-Up Hand	Siang Kòa Siu	Sang Gua Ciu	Shuāngguàshǒu	雙掛手	双挂手

CHAPTER 16: DI SIP DUI LIAN

English	Táiyǔ (Taiwanese Hokkien)	Mǐnnányǔ (Southern Min)	Pīnyīn (Mandarin)	Traditional Chinese logograms	Simplified Chinese logograms
Twenty Fist (Di Sip Kun) Partner Drill	Lī Sip Kûn Tùi Liān	Li-Sip Gun Dui Lian	Èrhíquánduìliàn	二十拳對練	二十拳对练
Patting Hand	Phah Siu	Pa Ciu	Pāishǒu	拍手	拍手
Intercepting Strike	Chiȧt Tùi	Ziat Dui	Jiéchuí	截搥	截捶

CHAPTER 18: SI MUN DA GAK LO

English	Táiyǔ (Taiwanese Hokkien)	Mǐnnányǔ (Southern Min)	Pīnyīn (Mandarin)	Traditional Chinese logograms	Simplified Chinese logograms
Four Gate Striking Corner (Si Mun Da Gak Lo)	Si Mn̂g Táⁿ Kak	Si Mun Da Gak	Sìméndájiǎo	四門打角	四门打角
Ascending Hook Strike	Siōng Kau Tûi	Siong Gao Dui	Shànggōuchuí	上鉤搥	上钩捶
Shoulder Bridge	Keng Kiô	Gian Giao	Jiānqiáo	肩橋	肩桥
Coiling Bridge	Tîⁿ Kiô	Di Giao	Chánqiáo	纏橋	缠桥
Head Bump	Thâu Chōng	Tiou Dong	Tóuzhuàng	頭撞	头撞
Willow Leaf Palm	Liú Iáp Chiúⁿ	Liu Iap Ziu	Liǔyèzhǎng	柳葉掌	柳叶掌

CHAPTER 21: DAI DOU

English	Táiyǔ (Taiwanese Hokkien)	Mǐnnányǔ (Southern Min)	Pīnyīn (Mandarin)	Traditional Chinese logograms	Simplified Chinese logograms
Big Knife	Tōa To	Dai Dou	Dàdāo	大刀	大刀
Chopping Knife	Phek To	Pi Dou	Pīdāo	劈刀	劈刀
Carry-on Back Knife	Āiⁿ To	Buê Dou	Bēidāo	揹刀	揹刀
Stabbing Knife	Chhì To	Ci Dou	Cìdāo	刺刀	刺刀
Lifting Knife	Thio To	Tiou Dou	Tiāodāo	挑刀	挑刀
Knife Blade, High Vertical Chop	To Phiàn Ko Tit Khám	Dou Pian Gou Dit Kam	Dāo piàngāozhíkǎn	刀片高直砍	刀片高直砍
Diagonal Chopping Knife	Kak Khám To	Gak Kam Dou	Jiǎokǎndāo	角砍刀	角砍刀
Knife Blade, Chopping Slant	To Phiàn Khám Chhiâ	Dou Pian Kam Cia	Dāopiànkǎnxié	刀片砍斜	刀片砍斜
Standing Pushing Knife	Lip Thui To	Lip Tui Dou	Lìtuīdāo	立推刀	立推刀
Horizontal Push Knife	Hôaiⁿ Thui To	Hing Tui Dou	Héngtuīdāo	橫推刀	横推刀
Shelf Knife	Kè To	Gê Dou	Jiàdāo	架刀	架刀

English	Táiyǔ (Taiwanese Hokkien)	Mǐnnányǔ (Southern Min)	Pīnyīn (Mandarin)	Traditional Chinese logograms	Simplified Chinese logograms
Shelf Push Knife	Kè Thui To	Gê Tui Dou	Jiàtuīdāo	架推刀	架推刀
Grasping Knife	Ak To	Ak Dou	Wòdāo	握刀	握刀
Covering Stance	Kài Pō͘	Gai Bo	Gàibù	蓋步	盖步
Covering Pommel (Head)	Kài Siú	Gai Siu	Gàishǒu	蓋首	盖首
Horse Stance	Bé Pō͘	Ma Bo	Mǎbù	馬步	马步
Lifting Knife	Thio To	Tiao Dou	Tiāodāo	挑刀	挑刀
Spread Knife	Boah To		Mǒdāo	抹刀	抹刀
Embracing Knife	Phō To	Pou Dou	Bàodāo	抱刀	抱刀
Entwine Back (Head) Knife	Tîⁿ Thâu To	Dian Tiou Dou	Chántóudāo	纏頭刀	缠头刀
Single Standing Stance	Ta̍k Lip Pō͘	Dak Lip Bo	Dúlìbù	獨立步	独立步
Level Chopping Knife	Si Phek To	Si Pi Dou	Sìpīdāo	平劈刀	平劈刀
Pattern Push Knife	Keh Thui To	Gê Tui Dou	Gétuīdāo	格推刀	格推刀
Raise Knife	Thio To	Tiao Dou	Tiāodāo	挑刀	挑刀
Single Butterfly Stance	Tan Tia̍p Pō͘	Dan Diap Bo	Dāndiébù	單蝶步	单蝶步
Double Bow Stance	Siang Ki-ong Pō͘	Sang Giong Bo	Shuānggōngbù	雙弓步	双弓步
Bring Knife	Tài To	Dai Dou	Dàidāo	帶刀	带刀
Turning, Jumping	Tńg, Tiô	Deng, Diao	Zhuàn, Tiào	轉, 跳	转, 跳

CHAPTER 22: DAI DOU DUI LIAN

English	Táiyǔ (Taiwanese Hokkien)	Mǐnnányǔ (Southern Min)	Pīnyīn (Mandarin)	Traditional Chinese logograms	Simplified Chinese logograms
Big Knife Partner Drill	Tōa To Tùi Liān	Dai Dou Dui Lian	Dàdāoduìliàn	大刀對練	大刀对练
Pattern Knife	Keh To	Gê Dou	Gétdāo	格刀	格刀
Hiding Knife	Chhàng To	Zong Dou	Cángdāo	藏刀	藏刀
Holding Knife	Phóng To	Pong	Pěngdāo	捧刀	捧刀
Intercept Knife	Chia̍t To	Ziat Dou	Jiédāo	截刀	截刀
Rolling	Kún	Gun	Gǔn	滾	滚

CHAPTER 23: NGO CIAK GUA

English	Táiyǔ (Taiwanese Hokkien)	Mǐnnányǔ (Southern Min)	Pīnyīn (Mandarin)	Traditional Chinese logograms	Simplified Chinese logograms
5 Foot Staff	Ngó͘ Chhē Kùn	Ngo Ciak Gua	Wǔchǐgùn	五尺棍	五尺棍
7 Foot Staff	Chhit Chhē Kùn	Cit Ciak Gua	Qīchǐgùn	七尺棍	七尺棍
Level Eye Brow Staff	Chiâu Bâi Kùn	Zê Mai Gua	Qíméigùn	齊眉棍	齐眉棍
Meteor Staff	Liû Chhiⁿ Kùn	Lau Xing Gua	Liúxīnggùn	流星棍	流星棍
Grasping Staff	Ak Kùn	Ak Gua	Wògùn	握棍	握棍
Double Hand, Upright Grasping Staff	Siang Siu Chiàⁿ Kùn	Sang Ciu Zia Gua	Shuāngshǒu-zhènggùn	雙手正	双手正
Pulling Staff	Lah Kùn	La Gua	Lāgùn	拉棍	拉棍
Slanting, Embracing Staff	Chhiâ Phō Kùn	Cia Pou Gua	Xiébàogùn	斜抱棍	斜抱棍
Chopping Staff	Phek Kùn	Pi Gua	Pīgùn	劈棍	劈棍
Stabbing Staff	Chhì Kùn	Ci Gua	Cìgùn	刺棍	刺棍
Diagonal Chopping Stick	Kak Khám Kùn	Gak Kam Gua	Jiǎokǎngùn	角砍棍	角砍棍
Line Staff	Keh Kùn	Gê Gua	Gétgùn	格棍	格棍
Shelf Staff	Kè Kùn	Gê Gua	Jiàgùn	架棍	架棍
Collapse Staff	Pang Kùn	Bing Gua	Bēnggùn	崩棍	崩棍
Opposing Roll Staff	Hóan Kún Kùn	Huan Gun Gua	Fǎngǔngùn	反滾棍	反滚棍
Opposing Grasp Stabbing Staff	Hóan Ak Chhì Kùn	Huan Ak Ci Gua	Fǎnwòcìgùn	反握刺棍	反握刺棍
Opposing Grasp Pull Staff	Hóan Ak Lah Kùn	Huan Ak La Gua	Fǎnwòlāgùn	反握拉棍	反握拉棍
Point Staff	Tiám Kùn	Diam Gua	Diǎngùn	點棍	点棍
Hanging-Up Staff	Kòa Kùn	Gua Gua	Guàgùn	掛棍	挂棍

CHAPTER 24: NGO CIAK GUA DUI LIAN

English	Táiyǔ (Taiwanese Hokkien)	Mǐnnányǔ (Southern Min)	Pīnyīn (Mandarin)	Traditional Chinese logograms	Simplified Chinese logograms
5 Foot Staff Partner Drill	Ngó͘ Chhē Kùn Tùi Liān	Ngo Ciak Gua Dui Lian	Wǔchǐgùn-duìliàn	五尺棍對練	五尺棍对练
Turn Staff	Póe Kùn	Bua Gua	bōgùn	撥	拨
Roll Staff	Kún Kùn	Gun Gua	Gǔngùn	滾棍	滚棍
Slanting Strike Staff	Chhiâ Táⁿ Kùn	Cia Da Gua	Xiédǎgùn	斜打棍	斜打棍
Pushing Staff	Thui Kùn	Tui Gua	Tuīgùn	推棍	推棍
Shelf Push Staff	Kè Thui Kùn	Gê Tui Gua	Jiàtuīgùn	架推棍	架推棍

ABOUT THE AUTHORS
SIGONG HENRY LO (LO, ZU-MING)
SIFU DANIEL KUN 鄞萬人
(YIN WANREN OR KUN BAN LIN)

HENRY LO

Henry Lo was born in 1961 and started training in Ngo Cho Kun in 1971. In 1995, after the passing of his father Grandmaster Dr. Lo King Hui, Henry became the Headmaster of Dr. Lo Yan Chui Memorial Institute of Kong Han Martial Art Club, Philippines. That same year he also won second place in full contact sparring at the International San Shou Tournament at Zhengzhou, China. Sifu Henry has won many awards and recognitions and is very active in leading Kong Han in several international and national tournaments and conventions. For Tambuli Media, Lo is co-author of the book Kong Han Ngo Cho Kun. A more detailed bio is found in Chapter 6.

DANIEL KUN

Born on March 4, 1958 at Manila City, Philippines, a third generation ethnic Filipino-Chinese; Hokkian name: Yin Wan Ren or Kun Ban Lin (鄞萬人); my father was Kun, Tien-Po (鄞天健) and my mother's name is Mary Tan (Tan, Kim-Chu) My grandparents left China for Manila, Philippines during the Chinese civil war of 1912.

As a kid, I was very timid; however, my athleticism allowed me to overcome my shyness and gained recognition from my peers. I was very active in playing basketball at 5'5" I could out jump players, who were as taller. I was very fast and known for being a spitfire.

I have always been interested in Kung-Fu, but I wasn't familiar with the process of enrolling into a Kung-Fu club. Back then to be accepted at a Kung-Fu club one has to be recommended by a school official or a club member I didn't know anyone; so one day, I approached my parents, because I knew they were active members of the local Filipino-Chinese community.

My father was not supportive of the idea of joining a Kung-Fu club, because Kung-Fu clubs back then were known to be either trouble makers or volunteer social community policing. He wanted me to concentrate on my studies; just like what every parent wanted their children to do. My mother was more understanding. So, one day she accompanied me to Chinatown; the first Kung-Fu club we approached was Beng Kiam Athletic Club the club located at Nueva Street they were closed for lunch and the care taker ask us to come back later. We proceeded to the next block and tried the Hong Sing Athletic Club; some instructors were there, but the office manager was not available. Then we proceeded to Kong Han Athletic club the office manager, Mr. Ong and two senior instructors were present: Teddy Chan and Nick Tan; one of the instructors knew my mother's family. Both of the instructors were courteous enough to vouch for me and my registration was accepted; I became a student of Kong Han Athletic club; I was 17 years old, and was filled with so much enthusiasm.

Training was three times a week for 2 hours from 5:00 pm-7:00 pm it was very rigorous and powerful; lot of cardio, strength exercises, forms, and drills. I never missed a single class; we were allowed and encourage to spend extra time at the club to practice during off hours and I took full advantage of it, especially, when I had free time. I would be at Kong Han practicing; going through all the homework and coaching tips from my instructors and from Dr. Lo, King-Hui. After a few weeks, I was considered an extraordinary athlete by my instructors and by Dr. Lo, King-Hui, himself. I was a quick learner, I was able to absorb Sam Chien, Tien Te Lin Chien, Di Sip Kun, Si Mun Pah Kat and Song Sui within 2 and half years. This normally took 5-7 years to accomplish. I personally attribute my rapid promotion and progression was due to the hard and diligent training that I undertook.

On Saturdays, I will join my other martial classmates on one on one training with Dr. Lo and listening to his lectures about Ngo Cho Kun. After training I will spend the weekdays focusing on what he had taught me, returning the following weekend to have him go through my materials again and again until he is satisfied that I have grasped everything. I made it a point to never miss any of those Saturday classes.

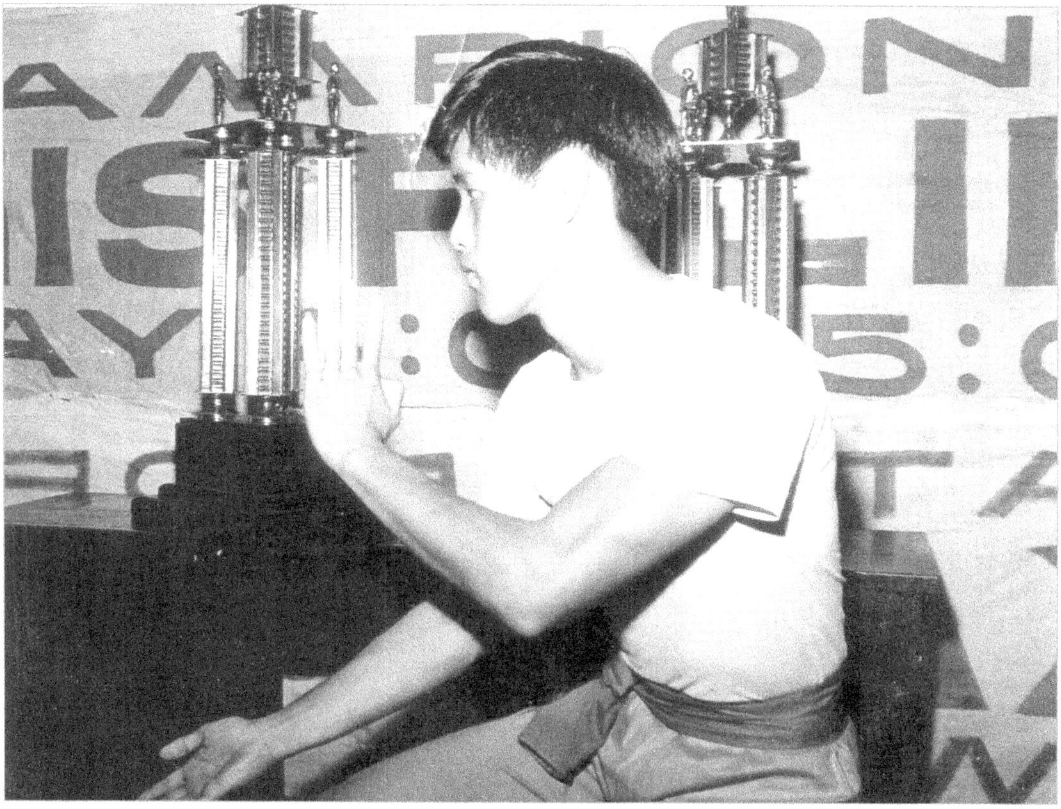

1977 advancing to the grand championship after successfully defending the ring for 7 consecutive weeks of wins.

The Author, on the left side in short hair 1977-78

Grand Championship 1978, the Author in the front row, second from the right.

In 1977, I felt that I am ready to compete on the national level of full-contact martial art fighting to put my skills and training to the test. Equip only with my Ngo Cho Kun training and with support from Dr. Lo, King-Hui and my fellow Kong Han classmates, relatives, and friends I train hard to improve my techniques; such as: the Di Sip Kun punching, the X punch, sweeping, and punch-kick combination. I was honored by taking direct lessons with Dr. Lo application through special lessons from my teacher, Dr. Lo/

I competed in my first full-contact national martial arts tournament in the Philippines, called "Karate Arnis Pilipino," I fought in the Jr. Lightweight division (120 lbs) and I won that division. After successfully defeating nine challengers from 1977-1978.

My success was a big surprise to many in the tournament, because I was only 19 years old. I was the youngest fighter in that tournament. I have no experience in any actual fighting on a national level; especially, compare to my opponents, who were all veteran fighters with many years of experience. Also, not many "Kung-Fu" fighters were successful. My achievement in that tournament brought great pride to Kong Han, to my family, friends, and to my entire neighborhood. What I realized later was that my success in the ring was greatly embraced by the community, because they relate it to the old Chinese martial art tradition of Léitái fighting.

Léitái was traditionally a challenge match that was fought on a raised platform. The fighter, who succeeds in defeating all challengers would be consider the Léitái King in that community. For a moment I was the king of my community, which was due to my Ngo Cho Kun...

In 1979, I was promoted to instructor level in charge of teaching new students; I concentrated my teaching in applying Ngo Cho Kun forms, contact sparring, set sparring drills and demo team. I was an active member and have participated in several public demonstrations and convention. During my coaching session with Dr. Lo, he would always remind me to be creative, be proactive to explore the many hidden techniques within Ngo Cho Kun forms.

Some of the techniques that he taught me were the: X punch drill, striking combinations, sweeping and proper execution of the kick-punch combination. Also, the intense execution of the forms in full fighting mode to be mentally, physically, and spiritually prepare myself. It proved to be helpful in my success in the ring.

One of my signature moves was the sweeping punch combo, kick-grabbing skill, and my orthodox, eccentric side kick; that for some reason my opponents had difficulty in checking.

In 1981, after six years with Kong Han, Dr. Lo initiated me and 17 other members as disciples: (Arranged according to age)

1. "Balbas",
2. Gum-po,
3. Tony "Talon",
4. Maximo Go,
5. Willy Ong,
6. Milo Ong,
7. Mariano,
8. Robert Liong,
9. Julian Ong (Tien King),
10. Jose " O-sai",
11. William,
12. Nick Tan "A-tiong",
13. Samuel Po "Suan-uy",
14. Johnson (Tien-un)
15. Arsenio "RC",

16. Emilio Tan,
17. Danny Kun "Ban-Lin" (the author),
18. Henry Lo "Zu-Ming" present Headmaster of Kong Han (son of Grandmaster Lo, King-Hui),

We would become sworn martial brothers and were initiated in a traditional martial "pai si-kiak pai" ceremony in front of the altar of Ngo Cho Kun and altar of Dr. Lo, Yan-Chiu, this type of ceremony is usually reserved only for the most deserving students, and our brotherhood would be baptized "Kong Han 18 Flying Dragons Martial Brothers or "光漢18飛龍結拜兄弟".

In 1984, In response to mainland China's invitation to assist in re-introducing Ngo Cho Kun in China, the Philippine Kong Han Athletic Club in 1984 send a 50 man delegation led by Grandmaster Dr. Lo, King-Hui in which I was a part we travel to different parts of China to Beijing, Fuzhou, Xiamen and to Quanzhou China the birth place of Ngo Cho Kun.

Eventually, Kong Han concentrated on coordinating with local Ngo Cho Kun

Masters and with other Ngo Cho Kun lineages and help in rebuilding the Quanzhou South Shaolin temple the hard work finally bared fruits that epitomized with the creation of the International South Shaolin Wuzuquan Federation and the full reconstruction of the South Shaolin Temple at Quanzhou, Fujian China.

In 1979, I finish my college degree at Adamson University, Manila City

Philippines, graduating with a Bachelor of Arts in Political Science, I also study 2 years of Law from 1980-1982 at the same university. At that same time, I continue to train to improve and advance myself in Ngo Cho Kun the more I train the more I realize the extensiveness of the Ngo Cho Kun. In 1986, I was chosen to be part of the Philippine National sparring team of the Philippines Wǔshù Federation to compete in the First International Sǎnshǒu Invitational in Shenzhen, China. I fought at the feather weight under 120 lbs division. There were originally four fighters in that division China, Philippine, Mexico and France both France and Mexico bowed out of the fight due to

Plague of recognition for being part of the 1st Philippine National San Shou team 1986

health reason so I and China advanced to the medal rounds the Chinese fighter was very good and powerful and I tasted my first ever lost to team China.

From 1987 to 1994 I will continue to take part with Kong Han in attending several Wǔ shù and traditional Kung-Fu events in promoting traditional martial art under the Kung-Fu style Ngo Cho Kun. In 1995, my family and I relocated to Vancouver, Canada. Without abandoning my roots and heritage I continue to research and train in Ngo Cho Kun and in 2002 after discussion with Headmaster Henry Lo, I have begun to introduce Ngo Cho Kun in Canada.

My team would be active in the local community by participating in local martial arts tournament such as the Tiger Balm International and the Can-Am West Coast Championship to fund raising in helping the Children's hospital, the Tsunami that hit Indonesia in 2004 and several performances at the Chinatown Night Market festival.

In 2005 I will travel to Ohio, United States to meet with Jeffrey Yang a long time member of Kong Han and together we introduce Kong Han Ngo Cho Kun in Canton, Ohio. In 2011 I will travel to Lillehammer, Norway and introduced Ngo Cho Kun to a small group led by Erlend Kristofferson I also travel to Tampa, Florida and introduced KHNCK to Nigel Poulton. In 2012 I travelled to Sao Paolo, Brazil and introduced KHNCK to Sifu Ademilson headmaster of Fei Long Kung Fu Academy he and Sifu Renata will become full representatives of Kong Han in Brazil

In 2007, I decided to start cataloguing everything I know about Ngo Cho Kun and its history. My first book "Kong Han Ngo Cho Kun Fundamentals Book I" covered the history of Ngo Cho; the Legacy of Kong Han; Concept of Ngo Cho Kun, Sam Chien form and how make it applicable in actual self-defense not just another choreographed martial art.

At present I am actively promoting Kong Han Ngo Cho Kun as a member of the

Wǔshù BC Federation of Canada, Kong Han Philippines Athletic Club and The International South Shaolin Wuzuquan Federation with frequent visits to Quanzhou China to take part in its convention and competition.

O Duan 8th certification from the International South Shaolin Wu Zu Quan Federation

On the 20th founding anniversary of the Southern Shaolin Wuzuquan International Federation celebration in February 10, 2010 at Quanzhou, China, I will be recognized and awarded the rank of 8th Duan by the Federation.

I continue to pursue my knowledge and skill on Ngo Cho Kun and it is my goal to pass on everything I know and have learned to deserving students I am satisfied to witness that Ngo Cho Kun has not yet died out in fact, there has been a slow and steady growth with a new generation of students displaying interest to learn, absorb and inherit Ngo Cho Kun with this I am confident that Ngo Cho Kun will continue on to the next generations to come.

Sifu Daniel Kun:

It is the goal of Kong Han Ngo Cho Kun Kung Fu Association to immigrate and integrate the tradition, heritage and culture of this great martial art to make it an integral part of Canada, United States, Central America, Europe and other parts of the world just like it became an integral part of the Philippine culture.

Web site: www.konghankungfu.com

Email address: dantankun@shaw.ca

Philippine Kong Han Athletic Club delegation to China 1984, Sifu Daniel Kun second from right.

With Master Dr. Lo King Hui 1990, Gary at left of picture and Sifu Daniel at right.

1993 for my outstanding dedication and efforts with Kong Han I was awarded with a special certificate of recognition from Kong Han by Grandmaster Chua Kian-Tiack.

2005 seminar at Canton, Ohio, USA by Sifu Daniel Kun

Sifu Daniel Kun with students at the 2006 Can-Am West Coast Martial Art San Shou Championship.

Kong Han Canada Sifu Daniel Kun second from left with Sifu Yao Hung of Quanzhou Ngo Cho Kun 2010.

Sifu Daniel Kun with students representing Kong Han Canada at the 20th anniversary celebration of the International South Shaolin Wu Zu Quan Federation, February 10-14, 2010.

Sifu Daniel Kun in Norway with students Erlend and Bryan 2011

Brazil Kong Han 2013

Sifu Daniel with students at the Tiger Balm International Martial Art tournament Vancouver Canada.

Home coming visit to Kong Han main Kwoon in Manila, Philippines with Grandmaster Henry Lo, Master Rene Lao and Master Julian Ong.

Vancouver Chinatown Chinese New Year Parade.

Kong Han Club Hymn

ACKNOWLEDGMENT AND REFERENCE MATERIAL

Grandmaster Henry Lo (Lu Zuming) Headmaster of Kong Han Athletic Club.

To Andy Chan and to my students Bryan, Joan, Abigail, Andre, Benetta, Victor, Devan, Scott, Laura and Thai for assisting.

Daniel Co, writer and editor of *Rapid Journal Martial Art* magazine, Phil. Book 14 year 2000 Vol. 4 no. 4 *The Legacy of Lo Yan Chu*

The Way of Ngo Cho Kun by Grandmaster Alexander Co

History of Shaolin Martial Arts, (History of Bai Yufeng) by Dr. Yang Jwing-Ming
http://ymaa.com/articles/history/history-chinese-martial-arts

Taiping Research Institute, *History of Tai Zu and Wuzuquan*
http://www.satirio.com/ma/home.html

Confucius Institute Online
http://www.chinese.cn/kungfu/en/article/201001/15/content_102356.htm

Grandmaster Salvatore Canzonieri 1996 article *Flowering of traditional Chinese Martial Arts (History of Bai Yufeng, Five Elemental Fist, Five Animal Fist and Northern Wuzuquan)*
http://www.blackdragon.itgo.com/Shaolin/Shaolin_History.htm

Master Alan Tinnion disciple of Grandmaster Chee Kim Thong, *History of Bai Yufeng-Wuzuquan* http://www.alantinnion.co.uk/core/ckt_lin_xian.html

Grandmaster Han, disciple of GM Chee Kim Thong, *History of Bai Yufeng-Wuzuquan* http://www.wuzuquan.com/history.asp

Sifu Laurent Tambayong of the Kwik-Ngo Cho Kun family-Indonesia-Chua Giok Beng-Ngo Cho Kun, "History of Lo Ban Teng"

Origin of Five Ancestors Fist from Xin An Village, Xiamen China http://fiveancestors.webs.com/originoffiveancestors.htm

Master Zhou Kun Ming of Quanzhou Fujian China South Shaolin Temple

Chinese Gentle Art Complete: The Bible of Ngo Cho Kun, by Yu, Chiok-Sam translated by Alexander L. Co (Tambuli Media 2014).